GUTTER GLITTER

GUTTER GLITTER

A gritty personal insight into opioid addiction, mental illness and survival against all odds

Kirsten Moore

GUTTER GLITTER

First published in July 2023
This edition June 2024

3 4 5 6 7 8 9 10

Copyright © Kirsten Moore

Kirsten Moore asserts the moral right to be identified as the author of this work and all associated products.

ISBN 978-0-6457326-1-0

All rights reserved. Except as permitted under the Australian Copyright Act 1968 (for example, a fair dealing for the purposes of study, research, criticism or review), no part of this publication may be reproduced, stored in a retrieval system, communicated, or transmitted in any form by any means, mechanical, electronic, photocopying, recording or otherwise, without the prior written permission of the author.

A catalogue record for this book is available from the National Library of Australia

For additional copies contact the author at
kirstenmoore.com.au
or inquire at your favourite bookshop.

Cover design by Hannah Nichols
hannihalation.myportfolio.com

Edited by A Way With Words
awaywithwords.net.au
Managing Editor: Phaedra Pym
Editor: Thymen Hoek

Produced for the author by Eric at exlibris.com.au

*Dedicated to the gentle and fragile-hearted.
I see you.*

Oh, and my cats, obviously.

Contents

Prologue	ix
He said you're really an ugly girl	1
In my head, the flesh seems thicker	13
Let go of that which keeps you ill	25
No one laughs at God in a hospital	31
This world ain't exactly what my heart expected	43
Come rescue me	55
Help I'm alive	65
Whenever you look at me, I wish I was her	77
I can't fit the feelings in	87
Bring me a higher love	99
Girl, where do you think you're goin'?	107
I'll kill her	117
A fucked-up holiday	129
There's a starman waiting in the sky	137
You shoulda seen the other guy	145
He swims in my eyes by the bed	155
My drug dealer was a doctor	159
High all the time	177
Help, I have done it again	187
I don't ever want to drink again … I just need a friend	193
I wanted them all	205
I gave you all my money	217

I'm ready to release	231
I haven't seen Barbados, so I must get out of this	237
Some things only God can forgive	251
I must go on standing	259
It's always darkest before the dawn	271
Acknowledgements	275

Prologue

On New Year's Eve 2016, I found myself standing on the balcony of a Sydney rehab facility, viewing the early fireworks show in broad daylight. We watched in feigned awe as tiny sparks shot up, barely visible behind distant trees. The 30 or so sad, angry inpatients who had crawled out of their hovels to join this rather pathetic viewing party were collectively silent for the first time since I'd arrived. We gazed at the freedom of the Roman candles as they tore across the sky, emitting the occasional 'ooh' and 'ahh'. I didn't dare look at the individual faces that surrounded me. I was afraid I would see in them everything that was surfacing within me: misplaced wonder mixed with a longing for the outside and a shame that grew deeper as sobriety strengthened.

All the planned programs for the day had concluded, and as it was a holiday, we had been given the night off from attending our 12-step meetings. So when the lacklustre spectacle concluded, I made my way downstairs to the art area, joining the others who were seeking a night of distraction from their usual raucous New Year's Eve plans. On the floor, a patient from Overeaters Anonymous attempted a puzzle that, ironically, looked like it had been chewed up and spat out, a schizophrenic girl made delightful cards to thank the nurses for putting up with our utter fuckery, and I coloured within the lines of a cartoon porpoise without so much as a millimetre's deviation. Secluded as we were, it was still possible to hear the occasional faint roar of the crowds outside and passers-by getting ready to welcome in the new year, drinks in hand. At one point, I looked down at my work to find a graveyard of broken crayons, shattered pencils and coloured textas that had been gnawed within an inch of their lives. My peaceful diversion clearly wasn't working, so I solemnly took myself to bed. It would be 'lights out' by ten, anyway. I lay awake on my rock-hard hospital mattress as the party raged on without me and wondered, *how the fuck did I get here?*

In 'da Hab', as the resident gambling addict called it, you were made to analyse your childhood a lot. I didn't fully comply with this because, as I saw it, my trauma didn't take off until I welcomed in my 20s. However, after publicly arguing with my group counsellor and being told to 'sit down and listen or get the hell out', I'd reluctantly decided to stay. I spent the rest of that session pouting and rolling my eyes like a petulant teenager.

He said you're really an ugly girl

Soundtrack: *Tori Amos – 'Precious Things'*

I am a millennial child of the 90s who grew up in a white, middle-class home in the safest suburb of Australia's 'most liveable city' (Melbourne). Ending up here was a considered choice by my parents, who migrated from England to Australia with my brother Ben and me when we were just 26 months and 10 months old, respectively. I was the youngest of the jetsetters, with my big bro by my side taking good care of me – a thankless task to which he would become accustomed as time went on.

My neighbourhood was right on the cusp of wine country and suburbia. We weren't in the outback, but it was bushy enough that when kids from other schools came to play school sports, they would ask us if we rode to school on kangaroos.

Despite growing up in the safest place on earth, wedged between a Christmas tree farm and a field of adorable alpacas, I lived in fear. Today it would be diagnosed as a severe case of GAD (Generalised Anxiety Disorder); however, as I had no formal diagnosis, I was left to assume that it was normal to live in a state of perpetual terror. I thought everyone felt that way, and the other children had just learned to hide it better. So that's what I did. I pretended my way through life. I performed 'okay'. *You are okay,* I would tell myself as my heart raced inside my chest. *You are okay,* as my stomach churned with raging wasps instead of peaceful butterflies. *You are okay,* as I lay awake at night, creating monsters and demons out of shadows in my room. *You are okay,* as I was seriously not okay.

From the age of 11, I was afraid of going to school, where I was teased about everything from my body size to my 'slutty walk'. The walk comment fascinates me now – I was even chastised by adults, who told me it was too seductive. Welcome to womanhood, where you're only allowed to be sexy when we tell you to, and the rest of the time, you're a whore! At 14, during my first foray into the world of amateur theatre, I was told in front of the entire cast of *The Sound of Music* that if I didn't correct my walk, I wouldn't be allowed to play 'Nun Number III'. At 14, I was publicly slut-shamed for my walk. When I think about it now, I'm sure I was channelling my insecurities into what I thought was a strong, confident stride in the hope it would make me feel more powerful. That and the fact I came from a dance background. So while everyone around me was trying to shrink themselves to fit in, I was puffing my chest out, loud and proud, as if to say, 'Make way, world, I've arrived!' The world would soon bite back.

There is a myriad of reasons I could hypothesise as to the cause of my anxiety: my dad working interstate with minimal contact for as long as I can remember; Ben and I being uprooted as infants and taken to a strange new land; Or Ben's severe asthma, which plagued my parents with worry for the first two years of his life and, understandably, drew attention away from me as a newborn. These were all destabilising events for a very young child, but it's hard to point the finger and say, *This. This is what caused my unrelenting terror.* Because I never actually felt 'traumatised'.

What I do remember is regularly watching horror flicks like *Scream, I Know What You Did Last Summer* and even *The Shining* at a friend's house in primary school, then lying awake for hours afterwards, petrified. And I remember the moment when I had watched one film too many; something in me just snapped. To this day, my family and I refer to *The Sixth Sense* as 'the film that shall not be named', because it was the straw that broke this camel's back. After seeing this film at the cinema when I was ten, I didn't sleep properly again for two years. I had to play the radio at full volume and make my room so bright it resembled a torture technique used by the Cartel. *Ahh, soothing.* Every time I closed my eyes, I could see Haley Joel Osment's creepy little face getting locked in a cupboard or Mischa Barton choking down poison soup. Nobody needs that much Haley Joel in their life. Nobody.

I had no idea it was unusual to feel like you could die at any moment.

Did you know guinea pigs are so sensitive that the slightest change in environment can shock them to death? *Yeah, dat me.* When I was at school, I would worry about having to go home, where sleep and nightmares were inevitable. Though school wasn't exactly a sanctuary either – the anxiety got in the way of my learning, and I was badly bullied. I was trapped in a constant cycle of fear that would last the entirety of my school career, but unlike that little guinea pig, I was never given the sweet relief of death.

The first time I became aware that I was lesser than the other girls was in kindergarten, at just four years old. I decided I must be the ugly kid during a game of kiss-chasey because no one wanted to play with me. Who knows what those kids were really thinking? Probably that girls had cooties, but I clearly recall feeling that their disgust was my fault. Confused, I looked at my blonde, sun-kissed friend who didn't have my little belly of puppy fat and figured that must be it. That's why they don't like me: I'm fat, and fat is wrong. It's an interesting memory because it is so vivid, yet I'm unclear how I learned – so young – that being fat was the worst thing a girl could be. My parents never spoke critically about their bodies in front of me or commented negatively about mine.

My first memory of being told I was fat wasn't until the ripe old age of seven, when a friend asked, with a smirk, 'Why are you fat?' *I dunno, bitch, why is your face so busted?* is what I should have said. But I just grimaced awkwardly and put down my ham and cheese sandwich.

As a teenager in high school, I worked in Before School Care. I was preparing the kindie kids their snack one morning when I observed an interaction between a little boy and girl. The little girl sat at the table, eating a slice of apple and rubbing her round belly. The little boy leaned over and started rubbing it, too. He was beaming. I watched nervously, readying myself for a speech on bodily autonomy, when he declared with utter appreciation, 'You have a bea-U-tiful belly!' The little girl laughed and proudly presented her belly to the room. Everybody delighted in her full belly as she giggled and smiled, ear to ear. I often think about that exchange and wonder how different my body image would be if someone had responded to my differences with curious amazement rather than disdain.

For me, the bullying was relentless. I was too embarrassed to tell my parents, so I bore the burden alone. Occasionally, I would tell Mum about a new fad diet I was trying out, but I felt I had failed unless I lost a dress size in a week. I enjoyed dance, long walks listening to my Discman and yoga but loathed team sports – the latter being unsurprising, given that every time I tried to join in at school, I was reprimanded for letting the team down. When teams were picked for a game during PE, groans and eye rolls would emanate from the side that acquired yours truly. At 33 years old, I still don't know how to catch a flying object because no one ever threw to me. Based entirely on how I looked, it was assumed I couldn't do sport. Thus, a self-fulfilling prophecy was born: you never get a chance to practise, so you never get any better, you continue to get teased, and, eventually, abandon sports altogether, hence, weight gain!

Every day, groups of pre-teen boys would remind me I was hideous, fat and talentless. I remember gazing at myself in the mirror at 12 years old, thinking, *I fucking hate you. You disgust me.* At 11, I was already experimenting with extreme dieting and frequently ruminating about my body. I was a little pudgy, sure, but I was also a normal, healthy, goddamned cutie pie. Yet, with nothing but their words, my classmates had turned my physical appearance into something monstrous, something worthy of their abuse. So began my unhealthy obsession with thinness. I stand with the long line of girls who were told they have such pretty faces, are surprisingly light on their feet and would be really pretty if… [insert generic weight loss suggestion]. These comments came from teachers, well meaning friends and occasionally their parents. In response, I was supposed to smile and be grateful. And, pathetically, I did, and I was.

The cruelty of the boys was nastier and undisguised. It wasn't that I was given swirlies with my head in the toilet bowl or had my lunch money stolen – in a way, that would have been preferable. At least it would have given me something concrete to report to my teachers. Instead, there were infinite subtle microaggressions that were easily missed unless you were the subject of them.

It was the sniggering when I ordered my lunch at the tuck shop. It was the exact same lunch as the girl next to me, but it was unacceptable for me because I was chubby. It was impossible to win. If I ordered a sausage roll and Twisties, I received judgemental jeers, suggesting, 'no wonder she's fat.' If I ordered a salad and Diet Coke, it was, 'yeah, right, as if you eat that.' They would whisper and stare on Swimming Day (the worst day of the fucking year) because my thighs touched and my belly stuck out.

Then, there was the boy I liked who, by some miracle, actually liked me back! He came right up to me in the first week of year seven and asked me for my phone number (or landline back in those days). Quite bold for a 12-year-old; shit, most men in their 30s are too afraid of rejection to pull that off! I was impressed. Shaking, I recited my phone number to him in disbelief. Part of me was sure this was a cruel prank, the rest of me bursting with excitement. I went home that afternoon, sick with nerves, waiting for the call to come. Finally, the phone rang.

'I'll get it!' I announced to the household a millisecond after the first ring. I'd never been so nervous.

'Heh-hello?' I said, quiet as a mouse, and suddenly realised I was too nervous to produce any sound.

'Hello, it's James. Is Kirsty there?' Everyone in 2001 was called James.

It's me. It's Kirsty, I replied, but only in my head. I was so overcome by the shock that he had actually called that I couldn't speak.

'Hello? Is anyone there?' he said again.

I was mortified. It took everything in me to squeak out the words 'It's ... me.'

'Oh hey!' he said, cool as anything. 'Sorry, I can't really hear you ... Can you speak up a bit?'

I'm trying! I thought. Why was it so loud in my head, but any attempt to speak resulted in me opening and closing my mouth silently in the kitchen like a guppy?

At that point, I must have blacked out because the rest of the conversation (if I can call it that) is a blur of me trying to breathe words into the phone loud enough for him to hear and him asking me to repeat myself. After a while, he gave up and said, 'Okay, well ... I'll see ya at school, Kirst.'

Oh my god, he called me Kirst!

I mouthed the words *Goodbye, James,* and he eventually hung up. I looked at the floor, waiting for it to open up and swallow me whole, but sadly it did not. I hit myself in the head with the receiver a few times and hung up.

'AHHH!' I screamed, now seemingly able to produce sound.

Despite this horrifying interaction, he still made an effort to gaze lovingly at me from across the classroom and talk to me at our lockers between classes. This lasted only a few bittersweet days before he began vehemently denying that he had ever liked me. It turns out he couldn't take the relentless ridicule thrown at him for having a crush on someone like me. *What was wrong with someone like me?* I know this because he told me himself, years later. We were at a house party when we were 16. He fell into my arms drunkenly and poured his heart out about how he wasn't strong enough to carry the burden of loving me. He couldn't take the bullying. I comforted him as he cried, because *of course* I did. I hated myself, but I still loved him.

Throughout high school, I became so desperate to lose weight that some days all I ingested was celery sticks and water flavoured with Berocca, yet I still had all eyes on me during Health class when the subject of obesity came up. It was constant and humiliating, and it bred paranoia. To this day, I hate my physical appearance and fear that weight gain will result in ridicule and assumptions of laziness. Uselessness. I fear it probably more than anything else in the world.

Though I wasn't innocent either; I felt so small and insignificant after years of incessant humiliation and name-calling that I took out my hurt on people who never deserved it. I could be intimidating and mean. Of course, I only ever picked on kids younger than me. What a big strong girl I was, bullying those who couldn't fight back. If I have contributed to anyone's lifelong insecurities or suffering with my cruelty, as my bullies have done for me, that will be the deepest shame of my life. To those people, I am *so* sorry. I know it is such a small, insignificant word. I know it means nothing if the damage is already done, and I know it's not enough. I just hope that the rest of your world was kinder to you than I was and that you flourished in spite of me.

In my 12 years of schooling, I only had one teacher who noticed what I was going through and made a conscious effort to protect me. Not by calling people out, which he knew would only make things worse, but by avoiding situations that would invite derision. Mr Howes taught PE and maths, my two most dismal subjects and, therefore, minefields for taunting. On this particular day, it was time to test our sit-up game. Now, as a teen, I had yet to discover the joys of cardio (JK, there are none), but I had dusted off Mum's old Jane Fonda *Bums, Tums & Thighs* VHS tape in an attempt to fit the mould. Naturally, it didn't change my body shape one iota because of my peasant genes (cheers, Ma 'n' Pa), but beneath 'all that jiggled', I was strong.

The test was to attempt 100 sit-ups in a row. I smashed it out of the park with ease, but as the class called out their scores – 47, 72, 81 – I was getting progressively more anxious about announcing my own. I knew that in admitting my perfect score to the class, I wouldn't be met with congratulatory responses but rather a barrage of disbelief from the boys, who considered themselves athletes yet had failed at the task. When it came to my name on the roll, Mr Howes looked at me and mouthed, 'One hundred?' I replied with a subtle nod, he marked it down, and we moved on. The class was none the wiser, and

I saved my dignity. It may sound small, but this one act of kindness made me feel seen. This teacher knew what I had been going through and understood that even a positive achievement could be twisted and used against me. The fact I had to hide my successes to protect the fragile egos of those little boys enrages me now, but at the time, I was just a timid little kid. So I would retreat into my wobbly shell and try to blink my tears away until I got home.

It would be remiss of me to lay all my self-loathing and body dysmorphia on the shoulders of a few 13-year-old dickheads. I also grew up at a time when print media was still highly prized, and *Dolly* magazine was allowed to routinely post articles about how the Olsen Twins stay 'Oh, so tiny!' Do you want to know how? Because I will never forget it. They claimed to put a little squirt of dishwashing soap on all their meals. That way, their food tasted so awful they could stomach no more than a few bites. Mother-of-fuck? That is a real article that was really allowed in a magazine designed for children. Of all the people who had to sign off on it prior to publication, how is it that none saw a problem there? This is what I came to believe was expected in order to achieve success in the entertainment industry. Something I wanted more than anything.

Every week during library reading time, I would slip my aspirational teen dream magazines underneath the bookshelves, sliding my celebrity bible out inch by inch as I read to avoid getting caught. I'd gaze in desperate admiration at Britney Spears' midriff and Kirsten Dunst's iconic *Bring It On* body. I wanted to be them so bad it was like a gnawing ache inside me. I would lie on the floor of the school library as I scoured these magazines for celebrity diet tricks. I found reading books impossible. It broke my brain to try and understand the works of Shakespeare, *Of Mice and Men* or *Eli*, but I could study a diet journal like nobody's business. I learned that carbs are the devil and to fear them at all costs. I discovered the importance of egg white omelettes and the benefits of replacing meals with water flavoured with maple syrup, lemon juice and cayenne pepper. Yum yum.

Nothing came easily to me at school. I was a below-average student with severe anxiety and mild learning difficulties. These days, they would likely diagnose me as having dyslexia and dyscalculia, perhaps even some of the ADD varieties. I would fixate on the things I liked, like music and drama, but couldn't, for the life of me, concentrate on anything I wasn't interested in – ie everything else. In certain subjects, like maths and history, I simply gave up. Having fallen so far behind, I was too overwhelmed to try and catch up. I'd watch students and teachers become frustrated with me because I held the class back with my incompetence. I lost count of the times I sat at the kitchen table, head in hands and bored to tears, as Dad tried to explain basic maths to me. I felt like an idiot.

Teachers must have thought I didn't try – but I did. I drove myself mad with studying, but nothing went in because I didn't understand the words on the page. My best option was rote learning, which was limited in its usefulness. Each time there was a test or quiz, I would read the questions over and over, trying to make sense of things. I would know all the individual words but was unable to put them together in a cohesive sentence in my brain. I liken it to learning a new language. When you're starting out, you learn a lot of vocabulary and are able to understand many individual words, but as soon as they are mashed together in a sentence, it's gobbledegook. Other times my brain would almost split in two, one half continuing to uselessly read the words while the other half sang Mandy Moore's *Candy* on repeat. I would become sick with anxiety as I felt the tick of the clock bearing down upon me. Oh, right, to anyone under 30, 90s Mandy Moore was a pop star before she decided to dye her hair brown and become a serious actress.

Perhaps in an attempt to limit my feelings of failure at an academic and sporting level, I developed an overriding obsession with the things I was naturally good at, like music and performance. More accurately, with fame. Lights, camera, action. *See me, hear me, love me!* Having received some encouragement through several years of choir, I added cello, dance lessons, drama classes and private singing tuition. My goal was to be a triple threat by the time I was 16, like Britney in the *Crossroads* era (she was brilliant, okay)! But as the only vocal coach in the school was classically trained, I was forced into a more Charlotte

Church-like bubble. Not great for my already dwindling popularity but fabulous for my vocal development.

When not anxiously shivering in the corner like a freezing chihuahua, I spent my youth pursuing my fame objective like a job. It was more important than education, more important than friendship, and certainly more important than my sanity. It was all I cared about – well, that and love. This is cute when you're five and tap dancing your way into your mother's heart; it becomes less adorable as youth recedes and your thirst for approval has become nauseatingly palpable. Still, I didn't care. I had my goal, and nothing was going to get in my way. You know that shit you see written on throw pillows at your aunt's house? 'Reach for the Sun, and you'll end up among the stars!' Well, *screw that*, I thought, *I am the Sun, and you will revolve around me!* I felt like I had a powerful secret. I had been blessed with a vision of my destiny, and if I could just work really hard and throw everything I had into my craft, I would achieve greatness.

Most of the time, however, while waiting for my sun to rise, I was burdened by crippling self-doubt and a constant sense of failure, vehemently confirmed by my classmates. In truth, I was pretty good. I had a nice enough voice to score places in a couple of teen vocal eisteddfods and continued to perform in amateur theatre with retired drama folk and young desperados just like me. But good wasn't good enough to be noticed, and as the years went by, the burden of failure grew. Eventually, I was forced to admit I was no longer enjoying myself. In fact, I was really struggling. I had turned something I enjoyed into a kind of evangelical commitment. I wasn't just under my own personal pressure to succeed, but I would be denying my God-given gifts if I decided I wanted to direct my attention elsewhere. Despite the taunting I received or the numerous soul-crushing disappointments I endured, I never gave myself a break. I didn't know how.

Now that I have been diagnosed with Bipolar II Disorder, these wild shifts in my sense of self and general inability to experience middle-ground emotions make much more sense. But when you are young, your feelings are gospel. All you can rely on to understand the world are your feelings, and I had a lot of them. It was humiliating to learn that what I had identified as guidance from above was nothing more than mental illness. I wasn't special. I wasn't chosen to achieve greatness by some higher power. I was sick, I was delusional, and everyone who had laughed at the stars in my eyes and put me down had been right.

You would think that being so harshly judged throughout my school career, largely by boys, would have led me to disregard the male species, but it didn't. In fact, it made me seek their approval with even more fervour and desperation. I had been so damaged by their daily comments about my appearance and abilities (or lack thereof) that I had no self-esteem left to bolster myself up. I gave them all my power and decided they must know best. If everyone is saying I'm wrong, it must be true. It was deeply confusing because I could seemingly do nothing right, and all I wanted was to get whatever 'it' was right. Even on the days I saw my reflection and was lucky enough to see myself for what I truly was – a Goddamned gift to the universe – by the end of the school day, having been chastised for everything from how my curls looked like pubic hair to wearing too much or too little make-up – and of course my general appearance – I resented myself again. I was never free of their abuse because even when they weren't around, their voices rang so loud in my head that I would end up berating myself as their stand-in.

I yo-yo dieted for years, eventually 'successfully' developing anorexia. Sadly, this actually helped with my popularity. *Ugh, society, be better.* I began to believe that I was absolutely worthless and that 'they' were the all-knowing deities of my adolescence. If I could just make 'them' love me, I would be okay. If 'they' loved me, I was lovable – but they didn't, so I wasn't. There were times I even relished the bullying; at least I was receiving some form of attention. For a moment, I was being noticed, and that was worth something. No … it was worth **everything**.

In my head, the flesh seems thicker

Soundtrack: *Silverchair – 'Ana's Song'*

My childhood anxiety evolved over time, adding severe muscle tension in my upper body. By the time I was 15, I was in chronic pain, suffering frequent headaches and throbbing backache. I'd assumed this had something to do with the 'hip' way I would sling my navy-blue Country Road bag over my shoulder, but looking back, it's clear where I held all my tension. At one point, my jaw froze from the strain, only allowing my mouth to open to half its usual capacity. This was less than ideal for an aspiring singing sensation but wonderful for my budding eating disorder.

I joined the local gym at 14 years of age in an attempt to sculpt my body into a standard of beauty that hopefully wouldn't be ridiculed. I hated the tedium of working out. I hated running nowhere on the treadmill. I hated swimming laps in bandaid-riddled pools. And I hated repetitively lifting weights while surrounded by grown men who would give me unsolicited tips on how to improve my bicep curl. *Yeah, bro, lift and repeat. I think I can handle it.* I enjoyed dance classes on Saturday mornings and yoga in the church hall with my mum. On summer nights, the beautiful instructor, who looked 25 in her 50s, would guide us into Savasana just as the Sun set. It was warm and nurturing, but therein lay the problem. It felt good. I was naturally bendy and graceful, so I was praised for my participation. It wasn't humiliating or gruelling like I'd learned exercise was supposed to be, so I decided it was ineffective.

Exercise and sports had always been a place of ridicule for me, first from classmates and then mirrored by the internal voice of my eating disorder. It had always been a punishment, never something that could be fun or rewarding. I despised it, but I went to the gym every day without fail. If I decided not to go because I was exhausted from malnutrition, I would flagellate myself until I felt so overwhelmed with guilt that going for a run outside was easier than doing nothing at all. Even if it was so hot that I would hallucinate or so freezing and wet that my clothes would soak through, I would whip myself like an injured horse and keep running until I collapsed at the finish line. I can't count the tears I have shed while on a treadmill or feeling the dead weight of my feet pound the pavement. *Please let me stop.*

'Ana' is the name creatively given to personify anorexia, given to her by terrifying online pro-eating disorder forums. Bulimia sweetly shortened to 'Mia'. What a cute way to refer to one of the deadliest diseases imaginable. I hoped that if I just did what 'she', Ana, wanted, then maybe she would let me rest. Maybe she would quieten down for just a moment – but she never did. I was never doing enough to please her. I was a constant disappointment, and she was right; I believed her every word. The saddest part is that *she* was me. My inner voice, mutated by the years of cruelty I had endured about my appearance, now played as a constant tape in my head, reminding me of my many failures.

By the time I was 17, she was so loud that she had seeped into all facets of my life. During classes, she would force me to count calories, work out when I was going to fit my exercise in, or simply remind me what a lazy slob I was. I struggled to hear my teachers speak over the volume of her taunts, praying that I wouldn't be asked any follow-up questions. My friends got tired of repeating themselves to me and bored with my constant refusal to come out with them. How could I schedule my acceptable foods around their choice of restaurant? Naturally, my family bore the brunt of it. Dad routinely did the grocery shopping, and if he dared to mistake *no*-fat yoghurt for the *low*-fat variety, he was chastised and ripped to shreds for sabotaging my goals. I loathed him at times for his careless mistakes. *'As an obese man, what could he know about health,'* Ana would cruelly gibe, *'He wants you to end up like him. He's going to make you obese, too.'*

Dad and I were unpacking groceries in the kitchen. I remember holding a tub of low-fat strawberry yoghurt in my hands and staring at it, considering all the power this little tub of goop held over me. I was trying so hard to override Ana by convincing her it wasn't so bad. One little tub wouldn't hurt me. But she was unrelenting and unforgiving. I held the yoghurt in my hands, unopened, and began to cry. I slid my back down the cupboards to the floor and sobbed. A yoghurt. A fucking yoghurt had complete control over me! Dad, unable to cope with the outward display of emotion, left the room. Once again, I was alone with Ana, just the way she liked it.

Mum dealt with my rude outbursts every day. She would say that she could tell by the way I got into the car how I was feeling. I was so tired by the end of the school day, juggling arguments with Ana with study and friends, that I had nothing left to give. 'How was school?' was the heaviest question in the world.

It was hell. It was hell on earth. I'm exhausted. I'm terrible at everything. I can't sing. I'm failing all my subjects because I can't think or see straight from malnutrition. I'm surviving on carrot sticks and celery. I force myself to go to the gym on zero fuel. Despite all of this, I'm still getting bullied for being fat, for having acne, for my curly hair, for being a bitch, for being a show-off, for trying too hard, for not trying enough, I hate every fucking inch of myself, and I want to cry all the time! 'Fine,' I'd reply.

One time in the kitchen, where Ana was the loudest, Mum was trying to have a conversation with me and I snapped back at her so aggressively that she physically took a step back in shock. She was afraid of me. We looked at each other for a moment before we both started to cry. 'How can you speak to me like that?' she asked.

I was so ashamed. I broke down and told her, 'Oh my god, I'm so sorry, Mum. It's so loud in here. I mean, that's what it sounds like in my head. It's so cruel. It's evil. *She's* evil. She hates me, and I can't make her stop!' Mum held me, and we cried together. Ana wasn't just ruining my life; she was hurting everyone around me as she did it.

This was a rare moment of communication between Mum and me, forced on us by circumstance. I never spoke about my bullying or body image with anyone in my family, partly due to shame and partly because there was nothing they could do. I didn't want my parents getting involved at school or talking to the other kids' parents. That would not only have been mortifying but would have likely made matters worse. So, I held it all inside until the shame literally began eating me alive, and it could no longer go unnoticed.

Despite the ripples of destruction I was causing, part of me was proud of my suffering. That's a symptom of eating disorders that I haven't experienced in other mental illnesses. The connection to the pain is its own kind of comfort. Suffering and illness are confirmation you are on the right track, so rather than wanting to heal and find a more peaceful existence, you actually want to get worse. You want to get sicker because sicker means thinner, and thinner is *everything*. Even as your hair thins and falls out in clumps in the shower. Even as you lose your period because your body needs to preserve energy for its most vital organs. Even as your blood moves so sluggishly that you are constantly shivering and you develop blisters on your fingers and toes because your heart doesn't have the strength to send fresh blood to your extremities. Even as your tissue paper skin bruises at the lightest touch. All of this is confirmation that you are winning – not that you are dying. In fact, if you look and feel like you are dying, that *is* winning.

Whenever my tummy grumbled, begging me to eat, I registered this as illness, cramps or a tummy bug. I had been starving my body for so long that something as human as hunger became unrecognisable. At night I would dream about gorging myself on food – my brain trying to break through my subconscious to get to me – but all it did was produce more guilt and anxiety. Even in my dreams, I would feel deep shame for eating foods that were not on my list of 'safe' options. In the dream world, I would be unable to stop myself from eating mounds of ice cream, sweets or just a decent meal, and I would wake in the morning in a panic for letting myself down. I'd berate myself for hours as I tried to forget the smell, taste and texture of the decadent foods of my dreams. That's how insidious this disease is. Even when given the opportunity of an *imaginary*, calorie-free feast for the senses, you still can't enjoy it. You still hate yourself for not being able to control your unconscious mind.

When I did eat, my stomach cramped and churned. I would lie in bed, grasping at my tummy in agony as I felt the movement of food scraping through my intestine. It's a scary thing, being aware of your internal organs. These bodily functions, as natural as a heartbeat, are supposed to happen without our awareness, but my poor digestive system was confused by what I was asking it to do – digest.

When I finally summoned the courage to confide in outsiders about my eating disorder, I was looked up and down like a piece of meat, assessed and judged for the body I loathed before being dismissed with, 'Well, you don't look *that* skinny. It's not like you're anorexic thin.'

There it was, confirmation that I had failed. Even anorexic wasn't anorexic enough. It was a prison. I was underweight, but I wasn't frightening to look at. I still had colour in my cheeks. I wasn't going to step out on *Dr Phil* and have his studio audience audibly gasp as my skeletal frame gingerly shuffled towards the stage, fragile as a paper doll. Yet my body was shutting down. I was dying.

All the while, I continued to be complimented on how great I looked. How much better I looked. I was *just* thin enough to be acceptable as a human, but not as someone desperately needing help. There I was, willing myself to be an inch from death, and I was being validated for it. And let me tell you, being validated for being thin just confirmed my deepest fears: you are less valuable in a bigger body, and there is fuck all you can do about it. What a fucking world.

People commonly forget that anorexia is, first and foremost, a mental illness and, therefore, possible at any size. It depends on how you feed, see and punish yourself. It is self-harm and nothing more than an agonisingly slow form of suicide. It is not to be taken lightly, brushed aside as teenage angst or excessive vanity. In fact, the opposite is true. It is motivated by deep self-loathing and severe anxiety – terror, really

– with mine being that if I didn't look perfect, I would never achieve success. And if I didn't achieve success, no one would know who I am. And if no one knows who I am, I will disappear into nothingness.

I was 17 the first time I contemplated suicide. I told my GP, with the calm of a psychopath, how I fantasised about getting hit by a bus. She decided to send me to a psychologist. My first session was spent crying hysterically, without breath, about the abandonment of my best friend since meeting her boyfriend. The psychologist asked me if I was in love with the friend because my reaction was so extreme.

'Huh? No,' I replied, confused. I wasn't. I genuinely missed my friend and found the pain of discovering I was replaceable excruciating. It was then I realised my emotional responses might not be normal. My whole life, I had been told by my classmates that I was 'too sensitive' and 'too emotional'. I was simultaneously too much and never enough. It was utterly exhausting, but it was all I knew.

I longed for boys to love me. I ached for friends who had moved away or changed schools. I would imagine them missing me as much as I missed them, crying as I listened to sad songs in bed. Years would go by as my heart bled for boys who never knew my name and friends who had long since moved on. I thought it was normal. I thought we all walked around with deep sadness in our hearts. Watching the psychologist's shock as she witnessed my heart breaking in front of her made me realise just how intense I was. No one would ever lament or ache for me the way I did for them. No one would ever love me the way I loved them. That felt incredibly lonely.

By my second visit, she had identified my anorexia. She directed me to a dietician and a second psychologist who specialised in eating disorders. I didn't like the new psychologist much. She looked a bit like Angelica's Cynthia doll in *Rugrats,* with her straw-like hair and long gangly limbs. She was so skinny it was distracting, and I spent most of each session wondering if she got into this profession because of her own eating disorder. But the dietitian was fantastic. Denise was in her mid-30s and attractive in a mousey kind of way. Her smile lines were deep, and she was tanned from the Sun; she obviously enjoyed a life of laughter and the outdoors. Most importantly, she had a perfectly normal body. She told me she tried to maintain a body that was fit and healthy but not underweight, so as to avoid troubling her patients. *Thank you!* The fact she had even thought about that made me trust her. She knew how we thought, and she promised me there was a way out.

Over the weeks and months that I saw her, she challenged me to confront the rules I had put in place to keep myself safe from Ana's wrath. She made me aware that the perceived control I gained from following all my rigid rules was a completely false sense of security. I may have meticulously weighed myself, portioned a sparse amount of food, and sustained a completely joyless life while maintaining the 'ideal' physique, but Ana was in control, not me. I was under her thumb. Something as simple as eating a tiny bowl of pasta with my family, reducing my exercise by one day a week or adding a small snack would have her degrading and humiliating me for the rest of the day.

One of the most impactful recovery exercises Denise taught me was to work on thanking the parts of my body I had regularly abused. Going from telling my stomach I hated it and wishing I could hack it off with a butcher's knife to placing my hands on my belly and physically connecting with it was horrible at first. I was revolted, feeling the squishy folds of my stomach beneath my hands, but after a few minutes, I started to feel really sad. All my body ever tried to do was its best, and I repaid it with scathing abuse. I wept as I mentally apologised for the bullying I had internalised and inflicted on it, echoing words of hatred onto this body that is my home. There are no quick fixes in recovery, but regularly practising gratitude might be the closest thing. It feels icky to thank a part of yourself you have loathed for so long; it takes patience and tenacity. But so does maintaining an eating disorder. I wondered what would happen if I put as much effort, focus and energy into rebuilding myself rather than tearing myself down.

There are things you forget when you have been manipulating your eating for such a long time. You forget what a regular portion of food looks like. You forget what hunger feels like. You forget that most people aren't attached to specific types of milk or use particular plates and tiny spoons to make their meals last longer. You forget that most people aren't panicking about food 24/7 or looking for a mirror or window to 'check' they haven't ballooned to the size of a whale in the hour since they last checked. You forget what you thought about before. Your mind is so loud and so full that when plans change or you have to adjust your schedule in any way, you become completely overwhelmed and cannot cope.

There is no concession made for basal metabolic rate and the fact that even if a human is comatose, their body still requires a minimum of 600 calories per day just to keep their basic bodily functions ticking over. There is no space for exercise-induced increased metabolism. There is absolutely no thought given to the simple pleasure of enjoying food for its taste or soul nourishment. Enjoying food is for weak people who don't care about their 'health'. It's for unsuccessful losers who are destined to fail because they don't have any willpower. Who needs to enjoy food? Who needs to enjoy life? 'Nothing tastes as good as skinny feels', right, Kate Moss? The struggle was important. The struggle meant you were working hard, and if you were working hard, you were *successful*. If you were successful, you weren't the giant fucking failure you felt like inside.

By the time I got help, I had been 'playing' with fad diets and eating disorders for seven years. Knowing the calorie content of a green apple or Weight Watchers points for a hard-boiled egg was second nature. I was so tired of living in fear of doing the wrong thing by Ana. I was tired of being sick, cold and exhausted all the fucking time. I was tired of fighting with Mum and judging Dad for not being as 'health-conscious' as I wanted him to be, and I was just really fucking bored with myself. I'd lost most of my friends to this bullshit disease because I was no fun to be around. I was doing poorly at school and worse at the music career I needed to make all of this worthwhile. The only place I was excelling was attention from boys because, suddenly, I was hot enough for them not to be embarrassed being seen with me. But that just made me hate them. I was fucking over it all, but I was stuck and didn't know how to get out.

The only way to escape was to look Ana dead in the eye and bear her taunts: I would never be lovable, I would never achieve my goals and

I would just get fatter and fatter for the rest of my life if I didn't do exactly as she said. She would try to manipulate me, telling me she was the only one who was on my side, but ultimately it was an abusive, co-dependent relationship, and it was killing me. Had she only been hurting me, I probably would've kept listening to her, but hurting my mum and weakening my body so much that I no longer had the strength to sing made the price of thinness too high.

I had wanted to be thin to avoid ridicule but even more to conform to an appearance that I had seen celebrated in Hollywood. Fame looked a certain way, and it wasn't the chubby, frizzy-haired little weirdo that stared back at me in the mirror. However, fame also required talent, sustainable energy and work ethic, and all I wanted was to Bruce Bogtrotter my face into an entire mud cake and take a nap for a year.

By the time I was in year 12, my anxiety had risen to Vesuvius levels, and I was on the verge of eruption. I was gearing up for one of my biannual nervous breakdowns, which generally resulted in a rebirth from the ashes, but this time it was different. Perhaps because I'd been running on empty for so long due to the anorexia, or maybe my nervous system thought this would be a more productive use of my adrenaline, but this was the first time I stepped outside myself. I watched myself act in a way that seemed totally insane, and yet I was unable to do anything about it.

I'd been struggling with geography and had been warned I was likely to fail the final exams if I didn't try harder. I didn't know how I could possibly do any more. I was exhausted all of the time. When I wasn't at school, I was studying, sleeping or working out. I was constantly overwhelmed and had nothing left to give. So, like any rationally thinking teenager does, I took my gold and silver Posca pens and wrote an entire year's worth of geography notes all over my deep-blue bedroom walls. It was as if I was building a giant cheat sheet, willing the information to enter my consciousness while channelling *A Beautiful Mind*.

I wrote for hours until the entire room was covered, wall to wall, with facts about Australia's Great Artesian Basin and issues with methane-producing cows. In the back of my mind, I hoped that when my parents came home and witnessed this scene, they would scoop me up and take me to the nearest hospital to be institutionalised. I wasn't okay. But because my parents are either totally awesome or totally oblivious (likely both), they just stood in the doorway in awe of their brilliantly creative daughter. *Huh?! I've just openly vandalised your home, and you love it?*

I should've expected it, really – I came home once sporting a new eyebrow ring and instead of shock and appal, Mum simply commented on how beautiful it was. Dad never noticed it. This time, Mum – the artistic hippy soul and drama teacher – loved how the colours shimmered brightly against the blue background. Dad, the historian and mathematician who got his first PhD by 21, enjoyed learning all he could about the current state of global warming and what this meant for coral bleaching in the Great Barrier Reef. *Well, fuck*, I thought, *I've starved myself to the bone, shown you bold as a gold Posca that I'm unhinged, and you still can't hear my cries for help. I guess I'm all alone.*

Dad referred to my current state of psychosis as a 'phase'. Having never had a teenage daughter before, I guess he had heard of our changeable emotional states and presumed this was normal. *Bitches be cray! Am-I-right?* And Mum was in denial. Even when I told her that the psychologist had diagnosed me as anorexic, she shook her head in disbelief, 'I don't think so. I see you eat.' And she did, but she didn't see the mental energy that went into preparing that plate of grilled salmon and steamed broccoli. The mathematics involved in determining the quantity of protein, the allowed foods, the elimination of carbs, my resistance to her cooking, my disordered eating disguised as pescetarianism and various intolerances. She didn't see the mental gymnastics because I didn't want her to. I hid it because I didn't want to stop, but when the psychologist named my illness, I felt a wave of relief come over me that I hadn't anticipated. Someone had finally seen how sick I was, and now that they knew, they couldn't possibly let me live like this any longer.

I saw Denise for two years, from the age of 19. She taught me so much in that time, but one thing she did that I found surprisingly effective was tell me there would always be someone thinner than me. She wasn't saying I wasn't thin. She actually made a point of validating my progress and confirming that I was extremely underweight. She acknowledged the tenacity, self-control and hard work it had taken to get to this point and gave me the permission I needed to stop. What she was doing was telling me that there would always be someone willing to die for this disease. Death is the highest achievement an anorexic can reach, and if that's what it took to be the best, to be the thinnest, did I really want to win?

Eventually, I felt strong enough to invite Mum along to one of my dietetic appointments, and that's when it clicked for her. Hearing about the intensity of my food and body anxieties from a professional and learning how much I truly loathed myself was very confronting for her. But she sat, cried and listened, and ever since, she has been my biggest supporter and challenger against my disease. She desperately wanted to help, but like any addiction, the person with the illness is the only one who can do the work. You can't force-feed anyone. You can't trick them by preparing special healthy meals for the whole family. Trust and believe they are already paranoid that you inject their apples with lard and fill the skim milk bottle with full cream under the cloak of darkness. It sounds irrational because it is, but that is the extent of our fear. All you can do is love someone so much that they feel safe enough to begin to heal. It will suck. You will feel helpless. They will lash out and accuse you of insane shit like being jealous and not wanting them to succeed. Do it anyway. Love them anyway.

Let go of that which keeps you ill

Soundtrack: *Kirsten Moore – 'She's Okay'*

After secondary school, I went on to study classical voice at the Melba Conservatorium of Music. I had a decent voice, but my perfectionism suffocated the freedom of my creativity. Everything I produced sounded like it was missing something. It was hard to identify because, technically, I could sing a near-perfect Schubert. But I knew what it was; it was missing a heartbeat.

I hate the identifier 'perfectionist'. Generally speaking, it's just code for anxiety driven by worthlessness. You're constantly striving for an unreachable goal because you don't feel your best will ever be good enough. Classical music requires a level of precision, but once the piece is learned, you're expected to add your own expression. Your *soul*. That's what makes you an artist and not a carbon copy. But I couldn't do it. I was wound so tight I couldn't let go and be free. I was rigid with my eating, obsessive with my exercise and every facet of my life needed to be planned down to the minute. Letting go even a little could unravel my entire life, which was far too risky. Therefore, there was no room for anything but rigidity in my music.

These days you don't need a talent to be a celebrity. You can shake your tits on TikTok and become an overnight sensation. Ah, what I wouldn't have given to be a teen in today's world. *Kidding!* For most of my life, I pretended I wanted to sing because I felt it was my destiny to share my story with large crowds of adoring fans. To heal them with my voice and hold them with my words. But if I am honest, what I truly desired was fame. My voice was just the vehicle that was most likely to get me there. I wanted it so badly that it ruled my life. It was the reason I wanted to be skinny: to emulate the minuscule frame of Christina Aguilera belting out 'Lady Marmalade' in the noughties like it *ain't no thang* in a wig that was twice the size of her vanishing waist. Of course, now she admits to having had the pressure of the industry breathing down her neck to maintain her underweight image and that she 'hated being skinny'. But sadly for myself, and I'm sure millions of other young girls, the damage was done.

By the time she was telling us that 'You are beautiful no matter what they say; words can't bring you down', I not only hated my body, but I was losing hope that my voice would ever be enough to bring me the star power I so achingly craved. I had become so jaded that even when I won singing eisteddfods and garnered roles in amateur theatre productions, I would berate myself for the ways my performance hadn't met my impossible standards. I'd spend days and weeks mulling over what I should have done better. Not even winning could make me happy anymore.

When I was a small child, I loved singing. At five years old, I would sing in the school choir and puff out my chest with pride as I sang as loud as I could to the audience of bored parents and my obnoxiously snoring dad. Teachers and parents would praise me for my enthusiasm and for the pure joy you could see bursting free of my heart as I sang. Not a care in the world, I soaked up the warm lights on my face, the audience's mediocre applause raucous in my ears. I'd chuckle overtly with my best friend on stage as we sang funny-sounding Christmas carols. *Good King Wenceslas? Wenceless last ...?* I'm still not sure. And who names their child Engelbert Humperdinck? C'mon, someone was having a laugh. Over time, my love of the stage developed into another unhealthy obsession driven by the need for acceptance. When others achieved successes, great or small, I would seethe with jealousy, seeing it as diminishing my own. This would go on for years before I realised that the dream I coveted so desperately no longer gave me pleasure or served me in any way.

During my tertiary music studies, my health should have been improving. I was eating better and fighting back against my anorexic inner voice. Instead, I was getting weaker and more exhausted by the day. It got so bad that even breathing was a struggle. I was at Melba to sing bold, sexy Italian opera, and yet I barely had the capacity to sing a nursery rhyme. My muscles were weak, and my voice was breathy and dry.

As a way to cope with my failing operatic voice and unwillingness to give up on my destiny, I began to write my own music. I was inspired by artists of my generation, like Jewel, Regina Spektor, Kate Miller-Heidke, Alanis Morissette and Tori Amos. Women whose music spoke to the heart in ways the factory-produced pop icons I grew up worshipping had not. These women had unusual voices that couldn't be boxed into a single category, and rather than singing about 'putting their hands up in *da clurb*' or 'shaking dat ass', they wrote about heartache, longing, rage and the darkness within themselves and others. Their music showed me what music should be: a safe place to put your deepest hurts and insecurities down on a page. A place to unburden yourself, and if you're lucky, you might even connect with someone who has felt the same. Pop stars taught me that if I could just be pretty enough, skinny enough and cool enough, I could make it. But these talented artists showed me that maybe I could be more than that.

Every day, I would catch the train from bushy, quiet Eltham, where I lived with my family, to North Richmond for uni. North Richmond opened my eyes to just how sheltered I was growing up. For the first time in my life, I witnessed true desperation in those streets. I regularly saw muggings. Syringes littered the pavement that guided my path to the Conservatorium, and often I would see people passed out in their cars with needles still hanging out of their arms. My eyes were opened to the true dangers of the world, but the school itself was wonderful. I was surrounded by other students passionate about music and performance. People who wanted to make a career out of music and believed it was possible despite, I'm sure, being repeatedly told it wasn't. True artists with real talent resided in those walls.

On the train in, I would write lyrics and inspiration in my leather-bound notebook that screamed 'deep and moody'. I wrote with the intent of creating the most achingly beautiful piece that would touch the hearts of millions and shoot me to superstardom. I imagined dismissing my fame when bombarded by paparazzi. 'Please, for the love of God, just let me *live!*' I would plead with the hordes of crowds desperate to get a glimpse of me in my oversized sunglasses and dollar-store wig. I imagined that when I died – way before my time, as any starlet worth her weight should – they would find my stash of journals and marvel at the extraordinary mind behind the craft. 'An Artist and a Genius, Gone too Soon', the tabloids would read. In reality, I churned out more clichéd bullshit than an after-school special, with only a sprinkle of insightful gems. It was that monkey and a typewriter kind of thing. If I wrote enough, something decent was eventually bound to fall out.

At uni, we studied our craft, took drama lessons, learned music theory and practised romance languages so we wouldn't butcher Delibes' *Flower Duet*. I appreciated Melba for the size of the school. It was small, so students from different year levels and varying instruments got to know each other well. We formed strong friendships and connections that, to this day, include some of my favourite people, all of whom went on to have various careers in music. One guitarist, in particular, Rhys, would become an important player in my journey to musical freedom.

Looking back, I wish I had been healthier and able to enjoy it more. I was consumed with anxiety and would flit from my classes to the gym, to therapy, to part-time work and to band rehearsals with Rhys, who I'd roped into playing my tunes with the promise of world domination. As a way to explain my weakening voice, my high school music teacher would tell me I'd been nothing more than 'a big fish in a small pond', and now I was experiencing my abilities in the real world up against the best of the best. *Um, rude!* I really felt like something was physically wrong, but having no better explanation, I accepted that I must have been imagining any talent, and this was the brutal truth. My dreams, like my voice, were trash.

Despite this crushing revelation, Rhys and I kept plugging away. We wrote a lot together over the next two years. He would play catchy pop hooks on guitar, and I would sing over them with my lyrics. It was the first time I had ever put my poetry to music, and I loved it. I was feeling betrayed by my ailing body and dwindling singing abilities, but with Rhys, we made the rules. We didn't have to conform to the confines of classical music or sell out and adapt to a particular pop mould. We were in charge and could make the music work for us. No right, no wrong.

Rhys and I were often reprimanded for making acoustic-pop at a highbrow classical college. We didn't care; we knew we were good. He was inspired by the glam rock of the 80s crossed with Ashlee Simpson, and I by tearful female poets crossed with Ashlee Simpson. Somehow it worked. We made music together for two years, gigging semi-regularly around Melbourne and recording some of our own demo CDs. It was exciting. We shared a drive and passion for performance and the music industry, but over time my health worsened. My chest got tighter, my breath weaker, and I had acquired unrelenting back pain that squeezed like a boa constrictor around my ribs. It was getting harder and harder to ignore.

To earn money while at uni, I taught Body Balance, a yoga-inspired fitness class. This kept me consistently learning new yoga postures and demonstrating as I taught. As a result, my back pain and tight chest were dismissed as stubborn, strained muscles. For months, I saw physiotherapists, osteopaths, expert singing teachers and Alexander Technique specialists who told me how young and healthy I was and how I really should be getting better. My lack of improvement was an insult to their practice. Maybe I was wrong? Maybe the pain wasn't so bad? I just had to push through and suck it up! Is everyone this tired? Does everyone always feel like this and just go about their lives ignoring the pain?

I continued to teach yoga even though I would cry myself to sleep every night, surrounded by ice packs to dull the burning in my spine. I kept performing at uni, even though I was humiliated by my ever-weakening voice and disappointing performances. And I kept writing music and rehearsing with Rhys, even as I watched my dreams rapidly slip away. I had been so used to pushing myself through any circumstance that I didn't consider taking time out. The show must go on! If you make a mistake on stage, you sing through it and *never* let it show. If you have been crying backstage minutes before you go on, you slap some Vaseline on your teeth and smile so bright that no one notices your red, tired eyes. Even if you lose your voice right before you are meant to sing in front of thousands of your peers for House Music at Hamer Hall (true story), you get up on that stage and you razzle-fucking-dazzle 'em because that's your job. You are the entertainer, or you're nothing. So, when I had to get on that carpeted, sweat-soaked stage ten times a week and teach yoga with a spine full of fire, I did it. I would frantically call Mum in tears minutes before class for a pep talk, but then I would slap on that million-dollar grin and take centre stage. I lived like this for six months before I got any answers. Razzle. Fucking. Dazzle.

No one laughs at God in a hospital

Soundtrack: *Regina Spektor – 'Laughing With'*

For as long as I can remember, I have loved obsessively. I believed that fate would play a role in finding my soul mate. I believed that you fight tooth and nail for love, to the point of insanity, even humiliation if it's called for. To me, that was the height of romance. After all, it was written in the stars, and who am I to deny the stars? Our calling as *Romeo-and-Juliet*-style lovers was just a pebble thrown at my window, a boom box serenading me with our song or a pre-planned dual suicide away. *Sexy.* I was in constant agony – whether in a relationship or not – because my vision of love was completely unattainable. And, like my eating disorder, suffering was key to it.

I wasn't looking for a relationship when I met Simon. I was 20, single and out in the big wide world for the very first time. I was content creating stories in my mind about imagined love affairs as I sipped my coffee and gazed out the train window on the way to uni – as if someone was capturing all of this for their indie cinematic masterpiece. I was busy working hard to ignore my illness so I could get back on track with taking over the world. But, despite me, I fell in love. It was the first time in my life that love had ever crept up on me. It was butterflies, not lightning bolts. At first, I didn't trust it. I was used to love rushing in like a wave and crashing into me, knocking me off my feet with its intensity, but with Simon, it was different.

I fell in love with him gently, purposefully. I loved *him*, not some warped delusion I had created within the messiness of my mind. I loved the freckles on his arms, the crook of his nose, his tired eyes in the morning and the way he learned to cook just to impress me. I loved how he kissed me like it was the most important thing in the world and how we would fall asleep with our bodies wrapped around each other as if we were scared we would be torn away from each other in the night.

I remember constantly wanting to be closer to him, *needing* to be closer. Our bodies intertwined, skin to skin, so close I could feel his heartbeat. We were completely open to each other with full vulnerability, utterly absorbed in our love, and still I thought how sad it was that this was as close as we would ever be. I could feel the love bursting from every cell of my body, but it wasn't enough because we were still individual entities. I lamented the fact we weren't puddles of water that could just melt into one another and become inextricably merged forever. My heart was simultaneously as full as it had ever been and devastatingly pained. I had heard people say that 'love hurts', but I always assumed that referred to the end of its cycle. For me, the emotion itself was so overwhelming that I didn't know where to put it all, and as much as I loved him, my heart struggled to contain all of my love peacefully. I felt like one of those Play-Doh toys where you fill some kind of garlic-press-like contraption with Play-Doh, squish down on it, and it overflows, squirting out of every hole. Love was bursting out of me, and it was too much.

We learned that his mother had terminal brain cancer three months into our budding romance. Within a few short months, it would take her life. As he told me the devastating news, I wondered if I would be strong enough to handle something of this magnitude. I'd never faced death before, and I was already so fragile. Would I be able to support him through this? Could I watch someone I loved die? I didn't know, and I'd be lying if I said I wasn't terrified.

I came to love his mother, Sue, though I hadn't known her long. Sue was a beautiful woman with a giant heart in a tiny frame. Many times, over the course of her illness, I would leave her house where I would be visiting Simon and spend half an hour crying in my car before I was able to drive home. I had no concept of what cancer would look like before I witnessed it. I knew it ate away at the sufferer's body, but I wasn't prepared for it to take over every aspect of their life. I watched it grow, rapidly taking over not just its host but seeping into the lives of anyone who got close enough.

Now I know cancer intimately. I've seen its insidious nature and undignified cruelty. In Sue, I witnessed chemo so severe that she would be sick for days, bones so brittle her spine would crack while she was seated on a comfy old sofa. I saw calls for help go unanswered, her children far too emotionally exhausted that they would turn up the music in their ears, searching for a pause button on reality. And I've seen personalities forever altered, as large amounts of brain tissue had to be surgically removed. I can't imagine the agony of having to relearn who your own mother is.

The moment that shocked me into adulthood was visiting her in palliative care in her final days. She waited until all of her children had left the room, then took my hand, weakly, saying, 'Hopefully tomorrow…' She wasn't sad nor hopeful; she was matter-of-fact. I felt all the air in my lungs desert me, but she didn't seem afraid. I didn't know what to say, so I said nothing. I just held her hand and hoped my presence was enough. Then she asked me to please take care of her son and love him in her absence. If there is any beauty that can be taken from this tragic moment, it is how much I loved him. I could promise her – hand on heart – that I would love him forever. That's a promise that, a decade on, I have not broken. Did I take care of him? That's debatable. But love him, I have.

In 2009, after seven months of suffering, Sue passed away. Simon, unable to cope, detached himself from life and went deep down inside, somewhere quiet, somewhere safe. He was impenetrable. It was like playing peek-a-boo with a child, where they cover their eyes, thinking you can't see them anymore. *If I can't see you, you can't see me.* If he only shut down long enough, the world would be back to normal when he ventured out again. He was so good at playing the part of a happy-go-lucky Aussie bloke that most people didn't even notice any changes. They didn't need to. He continued to fill his role in their lives, and they didn't witness his grief; all was well. Only he couldn't hide it from me.

Simon was a beautiful person, but he always carried an emptiness after his mum passed. I never saw him complete again. Part of him died with his mum, and it was an absolutely incredible part. It was the part that wasn't afraid to love or be loved. I miss that person every single day.

I was 20 years old and entirely overwhelmed. Both my own grief and watching Simon's withdrawal seriously tested my eating disorder recovery. Part of my therapy was to challenge the food and exercise restrictions I had put in place, but issues still needed addressing. One obsession was my strict consumption of a specific type of soy milk. This milk was very popular and widely distributed; however, it was also poisonous.

In 2009, Maurice Blackburn launched a 50-million-dollar class action lawsuit against the milk company, which they won. The original recipe contained a type of seaweed powder called kombu, which provided 50 times the daily limit of iodine in a single cup. Iodine at these levels is highly toxic and majorly disrupts the thyroid gland, which regulates hormones and controls metabolism.

Over 600 people, myself included, became very unwell for years before anybody noticed. Many claimants went on serious medications, spent money on specialists, and some even had surgery to remove their thyroid. Mothers who were breastfeeding their babies had unwittingly made their children sick. I drank the toxic elixir for two years before realising that this soy milk was harming my health. It was difficult to spot because many of the symptoms of anorexia correspond with thyroid disorders. Symptoms include fatigue, hair loss, weight loss, weakness, period loss, bowel and bladder problems, heart palpitations, sleep disturbances, eye dryness, depression and anxiety. That's the short list of issues I personally endured. Others had different symptoms. In short, if you fuck with the thyroid, you fuck with the *whole fam*. Every bodily system was affected.

I was extremely unwell, but at the same time, I was totally wired. You know when you are so overtired that your body kicks into overdrive and you go all silly on adrenaline? It was like that, but *all* the time. It was exhausting. I would wake up in the middle of the night and have this overpowering urge to run. I could barely keep my eyes open, but I needed to put my excess adrenaline somewhere. My brain was fatigued beyond function; I couldn't tackle anything useful like university homework, so I'd bake. At three in the morning, I'd be on the kitchen floor surrounded by the recipes of Nigella Lawson and Maggie Beer, deciding what to create.

I stopped drinking the milk when it was recalled in 2009, and many of my thyroid symptoms naturally resolved. Many, but not all – my energy, breathing and back pain never returned to normal. Finally, my doctor ordered some scans of my spine. At the hospital, in my starched white gown, I waited to be called for my first CT scan. I waited a long time, becoming more and more restless with each passing moment. I thought about Sue and how many times she must have experienced these moments of anxious waiting. Waiting for appointments with specialists, waiting for scans, waiting for results, and waiting for doctors to sit you down with bad news and bated breath. In her case, waiting for the inevitable.

Finally, it was my turn. There were a lot of people in the harshly lit room. I lay down on the hard, plastic trolly, and it pressed painfully against my spine. A pretty blonde lab technician stood over me, gently pushing the IV of contrast into the cannula in my arm. I was surprised that she was the first to explain to me that the dye, currently being pumped into my vein, had side effects, most notably that I would feel like I'd pissed myself. *Lab tech. says what?* As the bed was mechanically driving into the centre of the giant, doughnut-shaped scanner, I lay there panicking about the warm liquid sensation in my pants. I was mortified. I couldn't look around because my head was secured in place by a plastic neck brace, but I was certain everyone around me was stifling their giggles as wee trickled down the sides of the bed. I felt my face flush with embarrassment. When the scan was complete, the bed reversed out of the doughnut cam. I opened my mouth, ready to apologise but realised I was completely dry. I hadn't wet myself! I maintained my dignity in front of a group of stupidly attractive, highly intelligent doctors. At least until I stood up and my gown fell open at the back, revealing my laundry-day underwear … cool. Cool. Cool.

A few days later, I received a call from my doctor, who asked that I come in for the test results. I've learned it is never good news when the doctor asks you to come in rather than let the receptionist give you the results over the phone. When I arrived at the doctor's office, I was already feeling off-kilter. Dad came with me, which was highly unusual. Not once had my father accompanied me to a doctor's visit. It reminded me of the *one* time he picked my brother and me up from school; by the time he found us, it was practically nightfall. He was flustered and grumpy as he told us he had struggled to find the entrance to the school. A school that my mother taught at and that both my brother and I attended for *14 years*. This was not his domain. I can only imagine I dragged him along because I could tell it was serious, and I wouldn't be able to withstand Mum sniffling obnoxiously beside me. Turns out, it wouldn't have mattered; it was uncomfortable anyway.

I had seen this doctor since I was a little kid, yet I'd never seen him look quite so serious. I could tell by his face that it was bad news. Suddenly, I became very aware of my own face. *What does a face do at rest?* I pursed my lips and flared my nostrils in an attempt to act natural. It did not work. I decided that whatever he told us, I was not going to cry. It would be too painful waiting for the socially awkward men in the room to figure out when and how to pass the tissues or place a comforting hand on my shoulder. I couldn't look at Dad in case he, too, was panicking about what face to wear, an even greater task for a man on the spectrum. So, I took a deep breath and steeled myself. I barely heard a word the doctor said, as I was so focused on my strong and stoic performance. *C'mon, flare your nostrils some more. That will help.* Words I do remember are *cancer, spine, eaten* and *jelly*. The last one, tragically, is not a menu item.

The pain in my spine was caused by something called a Giant Cell Tumour. A 'grey area' in the cancer world because although technically benign, it is treated as a malignant tumour. This is due to the rapid pace at which it grows, the high rate of recurrence and, in my case, the way it had eaten into my vertebra, wrapping dangerously around my spinal cord and encroaching upon my lungs. *Ohhh, so that's why I can't sing, or, like, breathe 'n' walk at the same time, but mostly sing.* As he spoke, I didn't have an out-of-body experience. It was more like a deep *inner* body experience. I slipped deep down inside my body like I was hiding beneath the soft squishy layers of my skin and muscles. I felt like the tiny alien from *Men in Black,* living within the head of his human-shaped robot. I was present, but I was out of harm's way. Maybe that's where Simon went after his mother died, a kind of *sunken* place. I even heard myself ask a few measured questions as if this was just any ordinary consult on any ordinary day.

On the drive home, all I could think about was how I was going to break the news to Simon. We had laid his mother to rest just months ago, and I was about to ask him to go through 'it' all over again. I felt sick. *Really* sick. Like I'm going to be *sick* sick! 'Dad, pull over!' He swerved to the side of the road. I stuck my head out the door and dry-heaved. Nothing came up, but then, after one too many false starts, something happened. Something felt like it crunched in my back and pain shot through my spine. It was that intense – the targeted pulling you feel when you get a stitch, but on steroids. I couldn't sit up, lie back, or move at all without making it worse. Within seconds, my clothes were soaked with sweat and I felt like I was going to pass out, vomit and split in two, all at the same time. Eventually, the pain subsided. I've never been more relieved in my life. Later, when I mentioned this to a doctor, I was informed that as the tumour grew, it would increasingly put pressure on my spine. As it did so, small pieces of bone would periodically crumble away. What I felt must have been one *hefty* chunk of my crumbling spine.

Overnight, I became 'the sick girl'. People around you change when you're sick. One thing they love to do is tell you how inspirational you've suddenly become. *Bitch, I've been inspiring the masses since I was in nappies and you're just now noticing?* As a creative and arguably interesting woman, it's frustrating when something you have zero control over becomes the most fascinating thing about you. If I'm going to be attracting attention, it better be for my witty intellect and stunningly good looks. Sure, it's always nice to be described as inspirational, but it's a strange compliment to receive for being sick. If it was for my writing or my voice, or someone took one of my fitness classes and suddenly burst through this basic evolutionary plane into enlightenment, then, by all means, feel encouraged to feed my fragile ego, but I literally did nothing. In fact, I did less than nothing; *I malfunctioned*. They call cancer cells 'mutated cells'. I mutated. I became a mutant. *Actually, that does sound pretty cool.* Truth be told, some people deserve the title of inspirational. Me? I did not. I didn't suffer in silence or pretend I was grateful for this challenge the universe gifted me. *Gag.* No. I was in pain, exhausted, grumpy and panicking because I was already way behind in my plan for world domination.

I was told the tumour was the consistency of jelly, which put me in a very dangerous position. As my orthopaedic surgeon so delicately put it, 'Imagine your spine like a carrot. If something were to cause a severe enough jolt, like you have a fall or get into a car accident, your spine could quite easily snap in two as there's nothing [but jelly mush] holding it together in the middle.'

Excuse me while I vomit in my mouth. You know when you've forgotten a cucumber in the vegetable crisper and months on, it resembles a slimy, floppy dildo? Yeah, that was my spine. Well, technically, *part* of my spine, vertebra T6, for any anatomy nerds out there. For the rest of us mere mortals, that's basically at the bra line. Where once nice, sturdy bone connected my spine's upper and lower portions now sat a ball of jelly. Soft, squishy, useless jelly. Naturally, my surgeon couldn't in all good conscience have someone walking around with a jellied eel for a spine, so as soon as I got the news that the tumour existed, I was sent to Epworth Hospital and scheduled for surgery. My quickly assembled team of doctors was going to rush me into ten hours of surgery by morning. *Help.*

Thankfully, that evening while I was in the hospital, my dad received a call from another member of my ever-growing medical entourage. They were worried about the surgery. *Lol. Same, dude.* Apparently, because of the consistency of the tumour, it was more than likely that no matter how well the surgery was performed, even a single cell left behind would result in recurrence. If that happened, any subsequent surgery would be impossible due to the metal rods and scar tissue in my back. Their only option then would be radiation; however, this was not advisable as radiation would cause the tumour to further mutate and become malignant. *'kay.* This was when I was told that if I did not have the tumour removed, it would continue to grow, put pressure on my spinal cord and eventually paralyse me. *I see.* However, the surgery itself could also result in paralysis. *Well, fuck me, I guess.*

Don't worry, guys. This is all great for building my harrowing, phoenix-from-the-ashes story! It was not until way later that I lost all faith in existence itself.

The next morning, I was released from the hospital to meet with my medical team. We talked again about my options, eventually deciding that my best chance of success would be to join a drug trial at the old Peter MacCallum Cancer Clinic. I essentially had to interview to get into the trial *(no joke, I was given prompts)*, but, fortunately, I got the role and was allowed to take part in what would end up being an 18-month clinical trial for a drug called Denosumab. Originally designed for osteoporosis patients, it was now being tested for treating alternative conditions. The idea was that the drug would calcify my tumour, making it firm and easier to remove than in its jellied form. Easier to remove meant less chance of cells being left behind, meaning a major decrease in my chance of recurrence. These appointments were long, tedious and both emotionally and physically painful. I'm grateful for the trial, but going to a cancer clinic is dehumanising and demoralising. There is nowhere I have felt less like a person and more like a patient (and not even an important one). You're seen as a dying patient whose clock is ticking. Your very existence is irritating. I was 21 with a bone tumour that could paralyse but not kill me; therefore, I was one of the lucky ones. This place was grim.

I didn't have intravenous chemotherapy. My treatment was a special concoction that was only prepared once I'd arrived at the clinic and had my preparatory bloods taken, followed by a quick chat with the duty oncologist and trial practitioner. It sounds special and important, but this just meant I was usually waiting four to five hours in three different waiting rooms, only to be finally stabbed in the belly by an exhausted nurse. It was simple. It was sad.

I was told there were no side effects to the medication. I later found out this actually meant there were no known side effects because it was still an early clinical trial. It would be several years before I stopped receiving letters about newly discovered issues caused by the drug. Here's a cute example: they found that if you received dental work while the drug remained in your system, your jaw bone was unlikely to heal and would subsequently rot away. *Mmm, jaw rot.* Or, how I was pre-emptively put on the contraceptive pill because if I was to get knocked up during the trial accidentally, my baby would develop without bones. Just a big ol' bag of flesh and organs, slopping around like human soup. Human. Baby. Soup.

Sometimes, when doctors have to tell you something they know is really disturbing, their faces contort into this odd little smirk. It's as if they are about to punch you in the arm and say, 'Ahhhhh, gotcha! Human soup? I can't believe you fell for that! Wouldn't that be crazy?' Only the punch line never comes. I suspect it's because they have no idea how you are going to react and are bracing themselves. Often, I would try to make a light-hearted joke in order to ease the tension. I regret this now because, in trying to make the doctors more at ease, I neglected to feel the gravity of a lot of hardcore traumatising shit. For example, MY UNBORN FOETUS COMING OUT AS A BAG OF *SPAGHETTI FUCKING BOLOGNESE!*

I was also told quite flippantly that it was unknown if there would be any long-term effect on my fertility. To this day, I haven't received a letter about this, so chances are I'm in the clear. I often think about how this was delivered to me as if it was no big deal. I've noticed this trend over the years. When something is unthinkable, it's played down so much that you end up questioning your own feelings about it. Like how we treat children – if they fall and you react by making a fuss, they pick up on your energy and start crying and freaking out. But if you remain calm, they brush themselves off and carry on. I don't think we ever really grow out of that, but as you get older, it feels less helpful and more like gaslighting.

What if I am infertile? I'm fairly certain I don't want children, but I didn't know that at the time, and I reserve the right to change my mind as often as I change my underwear. I had the opportunity to freeze my eggs then and there, while they were still young, perky and full of life. Yet no one wanted to talk about it. Not my doctors, not my boyfriend, not my parents. *Soz if my cancer eggs made you all uncomfortable!* When I look back at that time, I can't help but feel young, irrelevant and voiceless during one of the most pivotal moments of my life.

This world ain't exactly what my heart expected

Soundtrack: *Rudimental ft. Emeli Sandé – 'Free'*

Two weeks before my diagnosis in September of 2010, I had signed up for a 12-month yoga teacher training course to deepen my knowledge from fitness instructor to bona fide 'namaste yogi'. It was part-time, but there was a lot of homework, which gave me a sense of purpose beyond my mind-numbing survival mission. I was no longer allowed to physically practise yoga or even exercise at all, bar gentle walking. It was considered too dangerous. Carrot spine equals snap crackle 'n' pop – you remember. So, I joined a lunchtime meditation group where I found myself surrounded by squishy, 70-year-old women who smelled like sandalwood and draped themselves in layers of linen. They loved me because I was young and fragile; they wanted to mother me. I let them because I needed all the nurturing I could get.

The first time the meditation teacher/psychic healer hugged me, she pulled away, wincing with pain and grasping at her left side – a place of much-referred pain for me. I hadn't told her about my illness, but she knew. She looked at me with shock and sadness for the pain I was carrying. She held me close, keeping me safe in her arms, and I believed that healing was possible.

While most of my healing took place in sterile, fluorescently lit doctors' offices and hospital beds, it was comforting to be in a space filled with the warmth of scented candles, essential oils, crystals and chai tea. It was a time of blissful ignorance and possibly misguided faith that I might be able to assist in my own healing. It felt nice to have faith in something. It provided a sense of control, which is often taken away during times of serious illness. You can't choose who your doctors are, what medication you take or where you go for your appointments. It's like someone constantly waggling a finger in your face and scolding you, 'Your health comes first!' And I suppose it should, but it just gets so *tedious*. When your life is on hold and your treatment plan is entirely in other people's hands, little things like putting rose quartz under your pillow and drinking green smoothies become incredibly important.

I wasn't the only one seeking comfort in alternative arenas. In times of desperation, it's quite common to throw everything at the wall and see what sticks. Long before GOOP advised us that shoving a jade egg up our vajayjay or activating our almonds would change our lives, health-seekers were coming together in rural Australia to drink beetroot juice and practise laughter therapy as a way to heal their terminal cancer and multiple sclerosis. I, 22 and desperate to avoid spinal surgery, was one such hopeful participant of the Gawler Foundation.

The two-week retreat was intense. It wasn't at all what I expected. I had envisaged lying around, popping acai berries and basting ourselves in a slurry of activated charcoal while someone who smells like 'nag champa' rain-danced around us as we rested in Shavasana – literally 'corpse pose' (which was slightly sinister, in hindsight). In actuality, we were made to confront all the ways our current lifestyles were killing us. A short list of things we learned to be afraid of: radio waves, Wi-Fi, Big Pharma, negative thoughts, horror movies, the news, chronic stress, chemical additives in our food, cleaning products, beauty products, seafood, the dairy, meat and wheat industries, sugar, alcohol, caffeine, anything not certified organic (and even if it is, be wary because someone somewhere may have sprayed a pesticide nearby once), and anything that the Amish community would likely frown upon. In essence, unless we grew or produced it ourselves, assume it was poisonous.

I believe the founders of this educational health retreat meant well, but the hardcore rules and restrictions only amped up our stress levels, one of the largest indicators of disease production and progression. Enter my 'health paralysis', a disease I just invented. It is similar in presentation to anorexia in that one has major anxiety around food and struggles to eat, not due to fear of weight gain but fear of getting the rules wrong and eating something that may accidentally kill you. *Gah!*

The retreat day started at six am. *Gross.* We were awoken to participate in two hours of guided meditation. I would lie in the meditation nook, trying to sleep without snoring too loudly and fantasising about my first cup of dandelion 'coffee'. One perk of having a spinal tumour was that I was allowed to lie down and didn't have to sit up like the rest of the chumps! My stomach would grumble and groan along with the thoughts floating through my 'monkey mind'. I like meditation and find it useful in this high-flying rat race of a world we have been flung into without our consent. However, I was still in my early 20s and valued sleep and *real* coffee (that didn't taste like an old lady's armpit) over rising at the crack of dawn to just lie back down again on a hardwood floor.

We practised three two-hour meditations every day. These often consisted of guided visualisations where we imagined our cancers shrinking, shrivelling, dying and being pecked at by birds before our bodies were reborn like the Terminator reforming his face after it's been blown to oblivion. It was boring and repetitive, but I did my best because it was supposed to be good for me. Between these sessions, we would have lectures on various topics ranging from *What would you do if you had three months to live?* (a reality for many people in there) to *Juices for boosting antioxidants!* The lectures were regularly interrupted by a dishevelled kitchenhand wheeling in organic, cold-pressed vegetable juices for us to drink. The goal was seven per day: 50/50 lemon and water in the morning, and celery and cucumber, pure carrot, or beetroot and parsley throughout the day. Did I mention I have an irrational phobia of beetroot? No one knows where this came from, but suffice it to say, this did not help my stress levels.

At night, if we had been good little cancer kids, we were allowed one green juice with half an apple squeezed in for sweetness. *Oh boy!* Do you know what happens if you drink this much beetroot juice? Your shit turns pink and you convince yourself your cancer has progressed to the bowel because now you're shitting blood. If you're really lucky, you might even call your mother in distress to tell her about your issue, only to have her remind you what happened that year she ordered a Batman birthday cake for your brother and all the kindy kids shat blue dye for a week.

Another enlightening workshop was *How to perform an at-home coffee enema.* If you've never made yourself a nice big pot of coffee, grabbed a pillow and some lube and taken to the bathroom floor to slowly filter tepid coffee up your own arsehole, you haven't lived. Coffee consumption via mouth was a no-go, but coffee by way of anal ingestion was highly encouraged. I'm talking three times daily. As dedicated as I was, this was a practice difficult to look forward to, and I decided to 'pull the plug' early on, so to speak.

Once a day, we could make contact with home, but as mobile phones were another thing that could kill us, these conversations were limited. This meant that when I finally got to talk to Mum or Simon, the ten-minute conversations were emotional. I would hold together all the pressure of living with a tribe of people facing their mortality until I got on the phone and could just cry. I was 22, and most of the people around me were going to die. People whose children's names I was learning. People who had amazing careers and big dreams. One man had been an unstoppable, wild rock star in the 80s, and now he was just an old man in a leather jacket, quickly deteriorating from cancer just like the rest of us. Simon didn't understand why it was so difficult, and I couldn't understand how he couldn't. So, these short phone calls often resulted in arguments left unresolved.

In the midst of all of this depressing lunacy, I met Sam. Sam, who brought three pairs of sparkly slippers to alternate over the short stay. Sam, who brought her iPad to watch downloaded episodes of *Long Island Medium* before bed. Sam, the most generous, ridiculously funny, incredibly brave, magnetic and vivacious girl I've ever had the honour of knowing. Sam, my best friend.

She arrived at our dorm with her mum and a massive suitcase. She was wearing a tracksuit, but it didn't look like the faded, dishevelled one I had been wearing for eight years. It was colourful, fresh and adorned with sequins. She wasn't wearing a stitch of make-up, but her Mediterranean skin glowed, making her chocolate-brown eyes sparkle. She was petite in stature but took up space unapologetically. Looking at her made me inadvertently lift my chest and tuck my shoulders back a little, trying to emulate her confidence. Her short dark hair was pulled back from her face by a headscarf, which I would later learn covered an impressive scar on her skull. She set her things down on the bed opposite mine.

'Welcome to our humble abode,' I said, trying to sound casual and immediately regretting it.

'Hey, I'm Sam. I tried to get one of the private rooms, but we booked too late.'

I instantly worried that she didn't like the room and felt responsible for her having a pleasant stay. 'Oh yeah, that sucks,' I mumbled. 'Um, anyway, I'm Kirsty.'

'Cool. Help yourself to a nut. I have heaps.'

'A nut?'

'Yeah, here. Take 'em anytime. I've got a stash.' She opened her suitcase like a dealer opening their trench coat, but instead of drugs or weapons, she revealed a dozen large zip-lock bags filled with different kinds of nuts and sugar-free treats. She literally brought a forbidden commissary.

Damn, girl, I think I love you. I smiled and gingerly took a brazil nut.

We were the two youngest people attending Camp Cancer by at least 20 years, and as such, we clung to each other for dear life. To this day, she is the coolest person I've ever known. Like, annoyingly cool. It was always effortless for her. She walked around as if she was an ordinary person, when in reality, she was anything but. When Sam entered a room, it was as though you had been graced by a celebrity. You were special just by being in her vicinity. Even with a terminal brain tumour, she was sunshine personified, and she had chosen *me* to be her friend. Being seen by Sam, realising she really wanted to know me, is probably the most important I've felt in my entire life.

Sam and I shared a cabin with three other unwell women, all desperate for a Hail Mary. It should have been tragic – one was a mother of three small children and had an aggressive stomach tumour – but it wasn't so bad. Because next to my little trundle bed was Sam. Each day during our lunch break, we would walk around the gorgeous Yarra Valley property covered in dry grass and kangaroos basking in the summer sun. The giant muscly marsupials concerned me, but not Sam. She walked past them with unwavering confidence, singing *Hot Child in the 'Country'*.

During one of our walks, we took a break to rest by a gentle stream. Sam sat on a small wooden bench a few feet away while I took my shoes off and slid my feet into the cool running water. For the first time at the retreat, I felt settled and content. *Maybe everything would be alright after all.* I leaned back on my hands and gazed through the trees. I closed my eyes and listened to the rustle of leaves as the wind delicately brushed passed them. Suddenly, I felt something skim past my foot, jolting me to the here and now. I quickly yanked my foot out. I leaned in towards the riverbed, and out of the dark water, a bulbous yellow head, full of layers of sharp gnashing teeth, was staring back at me.

'AhHhHh!!! What fresh hell?' I screamed, as I fell backwards, panting in horror. 'I can't even relax by a goddamned babbling brook without something trying to kill me! What the actual fucking fuck?'

That is when I heard Sam's signature cackle for the very first time. She was falling over herself with laughter while I tried to process the trauma of being face-to-face with a hideous, slithering water mutant, most likely a moray fucking eel. *Nope!* Nah-ah. No thank you!. I stared at her in shock for a moment and then burst into a fit of laughter with her, something that would become a regular occurrence in our friendship.

That night, over unseasoned lentil 'meatloaf' and pear juice laced with slippery elm powder (to keep us regular), Sam had a grand old time recounting the story to the rest of the exhausted recruits. I sat there picking at my lentils and rolling my eyes, but I was happy because the group members were laughing and distracted. A moment of peace away from their pain, fear and grief.

Inmates at the cancer retreat came from all over Australia, yet, by some gift of fate, Sam lived only ten minutes from my family home. We became fast friends and, once back at home, would catch up several times a week for lunch dates and debrief the week's symptoms, our meditation groups or where we could buy the best quality organic products. We worked very hard to maintain the eating habits we had learned at the Gawler Foundation in an attempt to preserve our lives. It was tough for me to focus so heavily on my diet as it brought back some of my old obsessions, but Sam was more relaxed. She did her best to follow the guidelines but wouldn't panic if, for example, she slipped up by eating pre-shelled nuts instead of those she had cracked herself – a rule employed to ensure freshness and avoid rancidity. I honestly have no idea if that is even a thing, but I followed the rules like gospel. I was desperate to avoid being 'honoured' by one of the regular group emails indicating another life lost from our group. An entire life boiled down to a generic email about our two weeks together. Faces I can hardly picture anymore and names that are long gone.

There were times when we felt betrayed by our bodies and were overwhelmed with anger and fear. All my friends were graduating from university and starting their first 'grown-up' jobs. Their biggest concerns were where to meet for Saturday night drinks and whether their new colleagues would like them. Then there was me: unable to work, isolated, bored to insanity, in extreme pain and pumped with experimental poison. At 26, Sam was a few years older than me, but she felt just as stunted. This is when we really leaned on each other. We were two young, fierce, fabulous gals who still looked 'normal' at this stage. We could function relatively independently, and our main disability was everyone else's inability to understand what we were going through.

From the beginning, I knew I was on borrowed time with Sam. She had the same brain tumour as Simon's mum: glioblastoma. It was terminal – most people receive a prognosis of 6 to 12 months.

I knew how this story ended and it scared the shit out of me. But I loved her so much that I decided whatever time I got to have with her was a gift. So, every week we would get together and vent about the shit-storm that was our lives. We would complain about our socially inept doctors, the weird side effects of our medications, our social isolation, our idiotic boyfriends who were trying so hard and failing so spectacularly, and our friends and their comparatively trivial problems. Note: everything pales to insignificance in comparison to brain and spinal rot. *We win! Suck it!* Together, we found some relief. I can't imagine going through this experience without her.

Sam knew her worth and was utterly comfortable with who she was. As someone who had spent my entire life hung up on the opinions of others, her self-confidence was both alarming and inspiring. Flipping through a magazine and intermittently puffing on a joint, she told me her boyfriend Aiden was good friends with one of the *Australia's Next Top Model* winners.

'Oh my god. How do you feel about that?' I asked, while my stomach did backflips on her behalf.

'I think it's awesome! That's my favourite show, and Aiden said he's going to introduce me to her! I love her fashion so much. She's who I wanted to win.'

'Wait, so you're not jealous or insecure?'

'No, why would I be?'

'I dunno, just 'cause she's a supermodel?'

She threw her head back and laughed. The thought hadn't even crossed her mind. 'No way! Aiden can't get enough of me! They're just friends,' she said, dismissively. 'I can't wait to meet her. She's so cool.'

'Okay, well, now *I'm* getting jealous.' I pretended to pout, but I was actually starting to get jealous of the elusive beauty queen.

'Aww, poor Shmoomy,' she teased. 'You know you're always my favourite.' This made me feel better – because I am a toddler.

I know I would not have been okay in that situation. I would have spent the entire time comparing every inch of myself to the flawlessness of the model and assuming everyone else was doing the same. It would have ruled my thoughts to the point where I couldn't be present for a single second. Sam didn't give a shit about that stuff. We went on her dad's boat once, and the mental pep talk I had to give myself to put on a bikini – despite being tanned, shaved from head to toe and snatched as fuck from the Gawler Foundation diet – was next level. She rocked out in her tiny two-piece, and her mum jokingly said, 'Your broccoli's showing,' in reference to her little trail of untamed bikini hair. If it were me, I would have been mortified and crawled into a tub of hot wax, never to be seen again with a single hair on my body 'til the end of days, but Sam didn't give a fuck. She laughed, shook her plump butt at her mum and jumped off the boat into the ocean. When she came up for air, she held two shells against her boobs and pretended to be a mermaid. Fuck, I love that girl.

She radiated excitement and pursued it as if it were her life's purpose. She was loud, brash and the most wonderfully silly person I've ever known. She didn't carry the burden of striving for happiness; she was driven by *fun*. I've learned there is a difference. In theory, her secret weapon was simple: she made people happy. In practice, that's a remarkable talent.

Sam made my dumbest ideas feel important. If it mattered to me, it mattered to her. The more outlandish the idea, the better! She introduced me to the South African hip-hop duo *Die Antwoord*. In recent years they have become problematic, but it was still okay to enjoy them at the time. One day I opened Facebook to find Sam had tagged me in a music video by the band *I Fink U Freeky (and I like you a lot)*. The black and white clip focused on images of a creepy young woman's face. Her eyes were black, her hair ragged, and she crawled with rats while disembodied hands caressed her body. Throughout the video, a series of unusual-looking people dance around, smiling and embracing their inner freak show. It's oddly uplifting, disturbing and fucking batshit. Sam's caption to me accompanying the video? 'You should make stuff like this!'

This would be the most ridiculous concept to anyone who didn't know me. That I, the girl who makes acoustic folk-pop and largely clichéd music videos about sad, misunderstood, pretty white girls, could venture into the realm of the surreal. But Sam knew me and my inner weirdness. She knew the parts of me that made me dark were both important to understanding me and fascinating and exciting if you let them in. She knew I held back in my art but could be brave, bold and shocking. Not just that I was capable of it but that it was the only way I would ever be satisfied with my work. In short, she saw *me*; unlike most people, that didn't scare her. It's what she loved about me.

When I felt like I wasn't enough, she would look me dead in the eye and say, 'Do you think I would be friends with someone boring?' And that was all it took. If the most interesting person I've ever met thinks I'm enough, I must be pretty awesome. I think about that a lot – if I don't at least try to love myself, I am insulting the choices of others who already do.

Whenever anyone talks about cancer, it's usually about the fight or battle ahead. I hate that – it implies that all it takes to heal is grit and determination. It's slightly more nuanced than that. You're not trying to get an 'A' in English Lit., you're trying to reverse your body's attempt at killing you. I'm telling you now, if all it took was grit, Sam would've had me beat a hundred times over. Nobody worked as hard as she did to survive. Nobody loved life as much as she did. While I was lying in bed awaiting my demise like a sickly Victorian lady, she was hungry for every experience she could sink her teeth into. I don't know where her energy and excitement for life came from, but I loved being around it. I hoped some of her lust for life would someday spill over onto me.

I'm sure she was terrified, but she appeared fearless. Losing part of her brain meant she lost the peripheral vision on her left side. I could be walking right next to her, and she would stop and call out, 'Shmoo! Where'dya go?' To which I would reply that I was right next to her, making her jump out of her skin.

After a while, her brain started to fill in the missing gaps in her vision, I suppose with things it expected to see. She told me once that she saw a young boy running around her in circles, playing a game with her. 'Um ... that sounds fucking traumatising. Are you okay?'

'I'm fine! I like it. I think it's funny,' she replied, as if it was totally normal to hallucinate a small ghost child.

I was tempted to tell her to sage herself, but with the amount of weed she was smoking, I'd be surprised if a bad spirit could get anywhere near her. *She be irie.*

Sam had five brain surgeries over four years and spent a year as her own nurse, attached to an IV bag that constantly dripped experimental chemo into her veins. Her skull disintegrated into what the doctors would describe as a 'honeycomb' from infection, yet she was still charming and beautiful enough to uplift everyone around her. Sam was unstoppable. She advocated for herself on the phone to uninterested receptionists and took charge of her healing. On the other hand, I spent most of my time in the foetal position, whinging and watching *Celebrity Rehab with Dr Drew* for days on end. To each their own!

I tend toward pessimism and often find life to be cruel and meaningless. At any one time, a hundred things are trying to kill us (see previous shortlist), but unless you want to spend the rest of your life living in a bubble, there isn't much we can do about it. In a sense, this is quite freeing. There is absolutely no use in berating ourselves for developing cancer or any other illness. If you want to blame something, blame the illness. Be like Sam and wear a t-shirt that reads 'F#@K CANCER!' Wear that shit every day until you direct that anger, hurt and fear away from your precious self and direct it to what really deserves it. Because you are a revolutionary human made from fucking stardust, and cancer is a mutant death cell.

Girl. Bye.

Come rescue me

Soundtrack: *Sia – 'I'm in Here'*

Another six months was added to my chemotherapy treatment, meaning I would be on the drug trial for a total of two years. That may not sound like a big deal given the circumstances, but at the time, it was devastating. I already felt like I had wasted so much of my life in hospital waiting rooms or recovering in bed. Life was a series of appointments screaming, '*Hurry up and wait!*' Sometimes, the boredom alone would have me in tears.

Boredom is a curious thing. It can be valuable in igniting ideas and inspiration that wouldn't otherwise have time to germinate, but it can also drive you completely mad if you are prevented from actioning those ideas. I think about giant sea beasts in captivity, swimming 'round and 'round in circles in their desperate attempt to break up the mind-numbing monotony that is their lives, their enclosures only marginally larger than their enormous frames. The only variety in their days is the faces that come to gawk and stare at them, flaunting their freedom. I think about prisoners locked in solitary confinement and know without a shadow of a doubt I wouldn't last a day before I was banging my head against the concrete wall as a way to escape both the confines of the room and the chaos of my mind. Hospital waiting rooms became prisons to me. Left to stare at blank walls, forced to suppress my growing anxiety with quiet politeness and the urge to continuously ask, 'Do they know I'm still waiting? Have they forgotten about me?'

I was eventually scheduled for surgery. The night before the long-awaited event, I was placed in a four-bed hospital ward with three other patients. It was eerily quiet, aside from the occasional wounded moan that made the subsequent silence even more disturbing. I had been given Valium to calm my nerves and help me sleep, but it hadn't worked the way I'd hoped. Instead of drifting into a relaxed slumber, I felt as though I was peering through the eyes of someone else's limp body. Like I had *Freaky Friday*'d with a corpse. The physical symptoms of anxiety had subsided – my heart no longer raced and my body felt heavy – but I was still hyper-aware that the countdown was on for what would be an interminable recovery. I was starting to regret asking so many detailed questions about the procedure. My mind raced with images of bone saws, metal screws and medieval devices. I lay in bed thinking *I want my mummy*.

Sleep evaded me, so I spent the night staring at the ceiling. Light slowly began to peek through the curtains around 6 am, and I knew my family and Simon would soon arrive to see me off.

They walked in with smiles and dry eyes, which I found odd, given that I could be dead within hours. Perhaps Mum took them aside for a quick pep talk before entering, just like she did for my brother and me when we were young and visiting our grandpa for the first time post-stroke. 'Now kids, Grandpa might look different and you might feel sad, but if you feel like crying, just leave the room for a moment and take a few breaths to calm down. We don't want him to worry about us today.'

> I remember panicking because it sounded like there was an appropriate reaction to this situation, but I had no idea what it was. Questions swarmed my nine-year-old mind. *Was I heartless if I didn't need to cry? Was I bad if I accidentally did cry?* I even asked Mum when I was allowed to be happy again, to which she chuckled and assured me it was okay to be happy – but I wasn't convinced. As I stressed about the minutiae of human interaction, Ben played his Gameboy, unperturbed by the concepts of life, illness and the inevitability of death.

As it happened, I needn't have worried. Grandpa had a plan of his own. We walked in to see my frail Estonian grandpa looking pale and withered. His mouth was open and his eyes softly closed. The room was so still that I stifled my breath so as not to break the silence. We had flown to Canada to see him, but we were too late. He must have passed away while we were en route. I could feel my eyes like two dried prunes in my head. *Why aren't I crying?* I clamped down on the inside of my mouth in a final attempt to express emotion when Grandpa suddenly let out a dramatic gasp as if waking from the dead.

Mum screamed and subsequently chastised him for faking his own death in front of her two babies who were facing mortality for the first time. Shocked, Ben and I looked at each other and laughed nervously. We had not been adequately prepped for this.

Hospitals are strange places. Behind every door is a scene worthy of a *Grey's Anatomy* plot. But, although declarations of love are made and heartfelt tears are shed, it's never really like the movies, which, for someone like me who has lived their life believing they are cast in their very own version of *The Truman Show*, is endlessly disappointing. Your family are still your family. They won't magically morph into an attractive cast of sad faces with perfect hair and over-bright veneers. They aren't going to have a neat script or stage directions depicting the ideal balance of worry and stoicism. No. Mum will be the first to break, crying a lot and making everyone uncomfortable with her outward display of emotion. Ben will provide the dry-witted comedic relief. Simon will say nothing I need to hear, and I will go into surgery, spitefully hoping to die so he feels guilty for eternity that he didn't propose to me on my deathbed. Dad will pull out a giant hanky and sneeze at the top of his lungs, waking up all the other patients in the room, and I will play martyr, pretending I'm not utterly scared to death. I'll dramatically brush away a single tear as I sigh weakly and say, 'I'm fine, really, don't worry about me.' Cough, cough.

Despite his uselessness in situations that require emotional support, I wished Simon could have stayed with me. Through the sterile hospital environment and stench of alcoholic hand wash, he smelled safe. His smell was comforting, like a child's blanket. With just a hug, I could burrow into the nape of his neck and breathe in love, protection and warmth. He smelled like home, and that's exactly where I wanted to be.

I was wheeled into a private pre-surgery waiting room, and Mum followed. She kept me distracted with some anxious chatter, which I greatly appreciated. Soon I was wrapped up in a body-length, inflatable plastic sheet called the *Bair Hugger*. This thing was fucking awesome! Essentially, it's a blanket-shaped balloon pumped with warm air used to raise your body temperature before lying naked in a cold operating suite for hours. Imagine hugging one of those giant inflatable wiggly-armed men you see out the front of car dealerships, except this dude cuddles you back, and he's *smokin' hawt*... well, adequately warm. Honestly, he sounds like the ideal boyfriend. *Am I right, ladies?*

People hurried excitedly around me. Each new face added yet another cannula to my pin-cushion arms. This was no easy feat, as I had been 'nil by mouth' for 24 hours and my veins had become dehydrated and slippery. By the fourth failed attempt at inserting my anaesthetic IV, the anaesthetist gave up and decided to knock me out with gas. As I counted down from three and took a deep breath of happiness, I wondered why he hadn't done that earlier. Gently the sides of my mouth lifted, and it was lights out. *Here we go.*

From this point on, things devolve into a bit of a blur. This is due in part to the IV of morphine being mercifully pumped into my veins, as well as the way my body decided to cope with the torturous level of pain it was enduring by repeatedly falling unconscious. It was early the next morning when I started to come to in the ICU. A nurse tried to perform my 'obs' without waking me but was unsuccessful. It was dark and I could tell I was no longer in the operating suite, but beyond that, it was a mystery. I couldn't see anything useful to get my bearings, and all I could hear was the incessant beeping of hospital machinery, randomly interspersed with guttural screeches and desperate groans. I was scared. I felt displaced in space and time, both in the room around me and in my own body, which was screaming with pain.

I had made a friend at Peter Mac from my time spent waiting around. Jack was around my age, with an identical tumour but only a little further down his spine. He'd finished his treatment a few months before mine and had already been through the surgery. He told me the first thing to do when you wake up is wiggle your toes. 'If the surgery has paralysed you, they won't move; if you can move your feet, you're in the clear.' I hesitated as the gravity of this notion suddenly hit me like a ton of bricks. Then I took a shallow breath, gazed up to the ceiling in the blue light of dawn, and wiggled. I was so weak it took every ounce of strength I had to make those piggies move, but move they did. I was okay. *Praise fucking be!* I was okay.

As quickly as the relief had come, it deserted me. As I gained a little more consciousness, I began clawing at my throat in a blind panic. *I'm choking! Oh fuck, this hurts. Oh fuck, fucking hell, fuck me, this hurts.* I was in pain everywhere. All different kinds of pain. *Everywhere.* The overwhelming sensation was that I was suffocating.

I looked toward the nurse with wide, terrified eyes, which screamed, '*Help me!*' It didn't help that each arm had been filled with three or four cannulas, so moving was awkward and uncomfortable. I needed to get my hands toward my throat to mime that I was choking, but the plastic tubes pumping various things in and out of my body stabbed at the inside of my arms when I tried to bend my elbows. I felt like a Halloween mummy, grunting loudly, arms outstretched and flailing uselessly. I must have been quite the sight, but she just smiled softly and told me that my anaesthetic ran out earlier than anticipated and I shouldn't be awake yet. *Oh, okay, cool. No probs. Except actually, HUGE PROBS! BECAUSE FUCKING OUCH!*

I couldn't speak because I still had the breathing tube down my throat from the surgery. While under anaesthetic, it propels air into the lungs as they can't breathe on their own. Once conscious, however, the brain wants to control your breathing again. So, essentially, my lungs were now being controlled by two opposing wills that were not cooperating with each other, and I had a nurse who refused to punch me in the face until I passed out. It was horrendous. I had no idea humans could experience that level of pain without falling into unconscious shock. The amount of pain we can endure and still be alive is inconceivable. *It's actually rude.*

Imagine, if you will, a freshly caught fish. You catch it and plonk it down on the pier as it flops and writhes around, gasping hopelessly for oxygen. It is so desperate that it flings its little body from side to side, searching for water to help it catch a breath. Its gills open and close frantically, but nothing gets in. It becomes increasingly desperate, taking quick, shallow, empty breaths, but it's unsuccessful. Nothing else matters. It's fighting for its life. Everything fades to black, and then … well, you know what happens next. *That's* how it feels to be conscious with a breathing tube down your throat: like a hopelessly desperate dying fish.

At that moment, I regretted having the surgery (as if I had a choice) and wished with every fibre of my being that I would just die. *Please let me die.* I couldn't let myself cry because if I cried, my breathing would be further fractured, and I would likely lose the small amount of air I was able to draw in. Instead, my eyes welled up to the brim before the tears slid out. The nurse stood by, quietly wiping away my pathetic tears and telling me everything would be okay. I didn't believe her. She told me the doctor would come down in about two hours and remove my breathing tube, but, for now, I was still too weak to breathe on my own. This was torture – two more hours of suffocating, spluttering and praying for death. *Please, I'm begging you, let me die…*

I had lost ten per cent of my blood, leaving my blood pressure dangerously low. I was kept on the breathing tube for what ended up being four more hours. I called upon every bloody bullshite meditation/calming/relaxation tool I had ever learned in my years of yoga training and psychotherapy, but all I could do was watch the clock taunt me as seconds ticked by like hours. Occasionally I was blessed with unconsciousness, likely from the blinding pain or lack of oxygen that comes from breathing like a fish outta water. Either way, it was a small mercy. Each time I came to, desperately hoping that the clock would tell me an hour had passed, I'd find it had been only minutes. This happened regularly until, *finally*, I was told it was time to remove the tube. It had taken all my will to resist yanking it out myself, à la Kourtney Kardashian pulling her own baby from her very loins (season four KUWTK finale for anyone keen to fill in the blanks – I do not recommend it).

The nurse slid the foot-long plastic tubing from my throat, and I was filled with relief. I was encouraged to breathe deeply to prevent fluid from settling in my lungs, so I eagerly took my first deep breath. However, rather than being flooded with oxygenated relief, I was met with a sharp, stabbing pain in my sides, forcing me to return to my horrible-but-safe shallow fish breath. Nothing had changed.

'Nothing has changed!' I barked, in a panic, at the heavily pregnant nurse stationed at my bedside. Well, not *nothing* – now I can speak. Now I can choke out, *'I'm dying,'* and *'why is a woman whose waters are about to burst my primary carer? GO HOME!'* If this were a film, one of her patients would have to die to make way for her unborn son. I listened intently for the most severe of the death rattles ringing through the ICU. Solemnly, I bid farewell to my fallen comrade and let pathetic tears slide down my pale cheeks, which the nurse dutifully dabbed away.

It turned out that the breathing tube was only a minor part of the problem affecting my breath. I had tubes and wires coming out of every orifice, and because I clearly didn't have enough holes already, they decided to create some more. Namely, a drainage tube wedged between my left lung and ribs was designed to reduce fluid build-up. My lung was partially deflated during the surgery, as this was the best way to get to the tumour. This meant that as I breathed in, my lungs would push against my ribcage and crush against the drainage tube. It was reminiscent of the sharp pain of a stitch in your side – if stitches were caused by being repeatedly stabbed by a steak knife.

I was handed a folded-up towel to press against my ribs for supportive pressure as I breathed or – God forbid – coughed, sneezed, cried or vomited. It would be two days before the drainage tube was removed. This meant two more days of breathing with that horrible death rattle I had only ever heard once before, in Simon's mum, just days before she died. This association left me to assume I was dying and that everyone – doctors and family alike – had decided it was best not to tell me. It was inevitable, after all. *Let her live out her final days in blissful ignorance.* But I didn't die. I lay there waiting. Two more days of trying not to cry through the most all-consuming pain I've ever endured. Two more days of living on the verge of death. *Please, for the love of God, just let me die.*

That was the day I gave up striving for everything I believed I was *owed* just for purely existing. That was the moment I relinquished all control and the hope that we could create the life we desire by simply working hard and being 'good'. I had grown up monitoring every morsel of food I ate and every anxious word I said. Every single move I made was born out of an idealised future, planned years in advance. I worked hard at school, never smoked cigarettes or took drugs, and I had big dreams and ambitions driven by this convoluted idea of destiny. Yet here I was.

I had been good to the point of turning myself inside out, as I starved myself in an attempt to achieve a standard of beauty that didn't even interest me. Yet nothing I wanted or desired was manifesting itself through my blood, sweat and tears. My dream to be a singing sensation was on hold because, as it happens, it's quite difficult to sing opera with a tumour pushing on your lungs. My yoga career was suspended indefinitely, as it's unwise to bend yourself into a pretzel when your spine is the consistency of baby food. The man I loved was pulling away because my cancer reminded him of his mother's death. And now all I wanted to do was cry, and I couldn't even do that for fear of passing out from the pain! *Well, fuck that.* I was mad.

That day, anger awakened in me the likes of which I had never felt before. And rather than diminish over time, it grew each time my power was taken from me. Each time my loved ones turned away in fear. Each time I lost yet another part of who I thought I was, or saw who I wanted to be slipping further away. It grew until it became the raging, uncontrollable fury that would carry me for years to come. Unafraid and unburdened, hunting down anyone who dared get in my way.

That was the day I unconsciously decided to give the middle finger to life and become *The Anti-Kirst* (Kirsten actually means Christ, so it's terribly clever, you guys). It turns out that the opposite of the permanently anxious, rigid, *good girl* version of me is a looselymoraled, highly corruptible, wildly volatile *bad girl* ... and she's fucking terrifying. In the words of Tay Tay, *'The old me can't come to the phone right now. Why? Oh, cause she's dead.'*

Help I'm alive

Soundtrack: *Metric – 'Help I'm Alive'*

If you were to look at an x-ray of my spine today, you would see the length of my thoracic spine fused together with titanium rods and screws. As my surgeon so colourfully described, there is a kind of makeshift vertebra in the middle of my back built from 'medical chicken wire'. During the surgery, this contraption was filled with powdered bone taken and ground down from one of my healthy ribs. Over time, this bone dust will 'remodel' into new solid bone. Funny, I always imagined that getting my ribs removed would finally see me slipping into a Kardashian waist trainer. Sadly, it was not to be. Having a spinal fusion isn't like having a normal spine. It doesn't move, and that's the goal. It's as though the fused areas are one long, unbending trunk. If it moves, it breaks, and if it breaks, *I* break.

After the nightmare of waking up with the breathing tube down my throat, things slowly started to improve. By day three, I was moved into a private room and out of the madness of intensive care. Finally, I would be relieved of the drainage tube between my ribs and lung, and although it was still painful to breathe, I no longer felt like I was suffocating. I was still nil by mouth, meaning I wasn't allowed to eat or drink anything for five more days to prevent fluid from entering my lungs. I was so sick I wouldn't feel like eating properly again for months, but the lack of water was tough. I wasn't even allowed ice chips to suck on. When I was really lucky, my nurse would lean over and dab a small water-soaked cotton bud onto my dry, chapped lips.

I was pathetically grateful and lapped up those cool droplets of water like a human succulent. I began begging every nurse that entered my room to give me even the tiniest sip of water, but all my efforts were denied.

The first time I was allowed my very own cup of ice was incredible. I must have looked ecstatic because the nurse looked at me with a slightly sorry grin as she handed me the tiny cup of frozen delight. One by one, I placed single cubes into my mouth, savouring each morsel. I would let it melt on my tongue, enjoying the cold liquid for a moment before feeling it drizzle down my throat with utter satisfaction. *Ah, sweet relief.*

I lay in bed, realising that I had lost all control over my bodily functions, my autonomy and even something as simple as having a sip of water. Had I wanted to break the rules and get my own ice chips, I physically couldn't. I couldn't roll over without the assistance of four nurses. Hell, I couldn't bend my *knees* on my own. I lay flat on my back, 24 hours a day, wearing some highly fashionable leg cuffs that rhythmically inflated and deflated to aid blood flow on my lifeless behalf.

We don't realise how much incidental movement we do until it's taken away. A simple scratch of the cheek meant sorting my way through a collection of twisted wires and tubes, working out how much energy was required to lift my arm, bending it without disturbing any insertion points, and then trying to quickly get the sweet spot before getting told off for moving. The strangest part was falling asleep because there was no process involved. There was no shuffling about or preparing the cold side of the pillow, no rolling from one side to the other to find my comfy spot. All I did when it was 'lights out' was close my eyes. That's it. Like a light switch, I was on one minute and off the next. Except I wasn't because we aren't robots who power down as soon as we close our eyelids. It's not like putting a blanket over a birdcage to confuse their tiny bird brains into thinking it is nighttime. *I'm not a bird. I'm a human woman!*

I knew it would be a long and difficult road to recovery, but there were so many unexpected things that I couldn't have prepared for, which tested my basic human instincts. Breathing comfortably was out. Drinking water? Out. Crying? Out. My pee was already draining into a catheter, so that was sorted, but when it came time to poop ... I mean, there was just so much wrong with it. *Please note: shit's about to get real.* When you can't use your usual poopin' muscles because they are attached to your out-of-order back, you kinda just hope your shit slides out of your body like an accidental fart. Something which it isn't wont to do on a good day, let alone when you are packed to the gills with constipating opioids. Aside from that, I was lying down. Those of you who have ever tried to push a brick out of your arse with zero muscle contraction, lying flat on your back, while a bed pan digs into your shattered spine, know what I'm talkin' 'bout. That may be a rather niche demographic, but for those of you out there, I see you, I acknowledge you – you're valid.

Being washed was difficult. Not because I'm overflowing with dignity; I could probably do with a healthy helping of modesty. More so, because my body was so unrecognisable that I felt obligated to apologise for it. Here's something you don't learn watching *Grey's* – apparently, when your body goes through extreme physical trauma, fluid moves toward the skin's surface as a protective mechanism, creating full-body swelling. I went to sleep looking like a svelte EmRata *(she wishes)* and woke up a human pufferfish. This was confronting. Not only because of the exceptional discomfort of skin stretched to capacity or my hands looking like someone blew up a pair of rubber gloves but also because I was deeply ashamed of my body.

Let's attempt to make some sense of this utter head fuckery, shall we? Firstly, I am but a girl raised in an image-focused world. Additionally, I had gone into surgery underweight due to the major food restrictions I had been implementing. So, when I woke up looking moonfaced and six months pregnant, it was an additional and unexpected shock.

I used to think that overcoming something as supposedly life-altering as cancer guarantees a personal evolution. As it turns out, it's not always that simple. I was in a hospital with brilliant nurses, who I was required to trust with everything from feeding me to wiping my butt, and I was worried that they thought I was fat. Even in my morphine-fuelled paranoia, I could step outside myself and see how ridiculous that was, but *fuck me,* old habits die hard. *Ugh, I annoy myself.*

I was so disappointed in myself for caring that my body had blown up like Violet in *Charlie and the Chocolate Factory* instead of directing my energy into my healing. This anxiety was completely unnecessary and unhelpful but not uncommon. I had seen it before in both Sam and Sue when they were sick. These incredibly brave, wonderful women who were dying furthered their own suffering by torturing themselves over the weight gained from certain medications. It hurt my heart to watch, yet here I was, doing the same thing.

My depression and crushing fear had evolved into a newfound fury, but ultimately I was just at the other end of the spectrum. I was still ruled by emotions and deeply hurting, but this time I wore rage as armour. Still, somewhere locked deep in my solar plexus, impenetrable to change, was the me who carried scars from being bullied about my weight in the third grade. The me who excitedly absorbed thousands of images of airbrushed celebs every time a new issue of *Girlfriend* mag hit my doorstep as a teenager. The me who now contends with Instagram influencers selling me Flat Tummy Tea on a daily basis and desperately wants to try it even though it goes against everything I believe. All three of us, Sam, Sue and myself, were ashamed of the weight we gained while we were fighting for our lives. That's not an individual problem; that's a societal problem, and it's really fucking tragic.

As I was lying in my hospital bed, stressing that I looked like a shiny overgrown baby, my nurses were more concerned with how to turn, wash and moisturise me. I had to be rotated and marinated like a pig on a spit a couple of times a day to avoid bed sores and encourage blood circulation. The problem with my spine being in two parts was that it was far too vulnerable to risk any twisting. It would take three or four nurses to turn me safely. There would be someone on each shoulder, at least one person on my legs and hips, and, on a lucky day, I would even have someone manning my head and neck. This was all to roll me onto my side for a maximum of 20 seconds – because that's how long I could hold my breath – so they could scrub me, lather me up with moisturiser, and then quickly lie me back down. Look, I love attention more than Ariana loves a high pony, but I did *not* look forward to these turns. I couldn't breathe on my side, as the pressure of the bed against my fractured rib was too much for my lungs to expand against. I would have to take a big breath right before they rolled me and hope I had enough air in my lungs to last the distance. Once, I was left on my side for too long and started to splutter for air. I was just about to pass out when the team of nurses returned me to my back.

Each time I had to give over another part of myself to be washed or wiped by a stranger, I would think, '*This is just a moment in time. You will be back.*' I gave myself permission to accept the process because the only other option was to ride it out in complete and utter humiliation. I couldn't change what was happening. I couldn't suddenly jump up and brush my own teeth or take a shower on my own. This was my life for now, and it royally sucked. But it wasn't forever.

My nurses were wonderful. They were kind, gentle and sensitive in delicate situations. The doctors, not so much. Extremely talented and proficient in their fields, they often lacked commensurate patience and compassion. I had a horrible experience in ICU, when the nurses designated to my bedside could not access a vein to insert one of my cannulas. The nurses had tried numerous times in each of my elbows, and just as I overheard them talking about shoving it in between my toes (in homage to Amy Winehouse – RIP), a doctor came over in a huff. We were clearly wasting his precious time. I was high as a fucking kite and only 24 hours out of surgery at that stage, but even I could tell this guy was being a jerk.

He was acting as if it was my fault for not having plump juicy veins while also implying the nurses were incompetent for not being able to access them. Angry at being called to perform such a 'menial' task, he started stabbing at my wrist with the thick needle. I don't know how many times he tried before he decided this was getting cruel and went to get some numbing cream so he might continue the assault. I do know that a decade on, I still have five small scars on my left wrist from this incident. For comparison, I had dozens of cannulas in each elbow and wrist over the two weeks I was in the hospital and hundreds of blood tests taken from the same elbow over my two years of chemo. This was all done without a single scar in any other area than where this man butchered me. I couldn't cry or tell him to get fucked without worsening my own discomfort, but there was no preventing the silent tears that rolled down my cheeks. The nurses felt my pain and comforted me gently, but they had no power in this situation either. He probably thought I wouldn't remember how he treated me because of the state I was in, but this was one of the most traumatic parts of the whole procedure. I felt like an annoying, irrelevant pin cushion.

Sitting with intense discomfort and allowing things to happen has been both hideous and life-changing. It's as though, by sheer force of will, we as humans can still access a tiny corner of ourselves within a glimmer of stillness. It's not peace or calm, but it's quiet, and that's enough. Even when everything else inside you wants to scream, cry and die, there is this part deep down, like *really* fucking deep down sometimes, that just wants to survive. It must be the animal in us, an innate survival instinct. It took the greatest pain and humiliation I have ever had to access my stillness, my spark, *my will to live*, but I got there. I am not special by any means. I did not access this place out of strength, tenacity or positivity (LOL)! Quite the opposite. I found it because I had no other option. Stillness found *me*. If I, the girl who was born existentially depressed, could find it, then there is no doubt in my mind that everyone else can, too.

After a week in the hospital, my condition was still extremely delicate when my primary surgeon came in to check on me and deliver some news. I had only relearned how to sit up two days earlier and wasn't yet walking or standing on my own. The doctor entered my room, where Mum was sitting by my bedside. He grinned at me nervously, which led me to press my personal morphine button repeatedly in preparation for the bad news. *It's spread. I knew it. I'm done for.* He told me the medical team had been analysing the section of my spine they had removed. I could tell he was dancing around something and wished he'd just spit it out, but I bit my tongue as he had recently saved my life. 'Okay?' I prompted hesitantly. I wanted to sleep. The morphine was taking hold.

He stood wringing his hands with his back to the wall, as far away from me as he could physically get in the tiny hospital room. He stammered anxiously over his next words, 'So, err, you see, when we examined the, ah, vertebra *clears throat* we found...it's funny, really! We found it no longer contains the, err, tumour we cut you open to retrieve.' He grimaced as he raced through the final few words, forcing himself to say them.

I felt Mum stiffen next to me as she looked at me for a reaction. I did *not* agree this was funny. I stared silently at the doctor, oscillating between blind rage and devastation. I was angry with my body for being so incapacitated, preventing me from shaking that awkward grimace right off his face. *How? What?* I fell deep down inside myself, mentally hiding in my corporeal safety blanket. *Ahh, shock, my old friend, you have returned.* I could feel the throbbing of my heartbeat between my ears as my blood pressure rose, accompanied by a deep internal heat radiating from my core. My skin prickled. I stared unblinking for what felt like forever, but realistically must have been a few seconds. When I finally blinked again, my eyelids scraped like sandpaper over my eyeballs. My vision was blurry from the high-dose opioids, but I was determined to focus on the man before me – this took concentration. Despite being a weak, immobile young woman, I must have worn my fury on my face because I'd never seen a fully grown, highly accomplished man so uncomfortable in my life.

There I was, lying in front of him in agony so severe I slipped in and out of consciousness, and he was telling me it was *avoidable?* 'You will feel like you've been hit by a train.' Those were his words of wisdom to prepare me for surgery. Not a bus, a *train*. He knew exactly what this would feel like, and yet... *Why?*

As I stared him down, I imagined all the ways I could destroy him once I was able-bodied. *Maybe I'll impale him with a spear. No, that's silly. Where would I even get a spear? An axe? Do I have the upper body strength for an axe? I can train. Ooh, train! I'll hit him with a train!* This helped a little. Meanwhile, a nurse came in to check if I was still peeing blood, informed me that I was, and left again. I swallowed to lubricate my dry, sawdust throat and asked in feigned calm, 'So...why did you do the surgery?'

He chuckled nervously and replied, 'I thought you'd ask that.' *No shit.* As he outlined what he suspected had happened, the throbbing between my ears proceeded to get louder and louder until it was like someone was thumping a bass drum inside my skull. *Don't cry. Don't cry. Don't you dare fucking cry.*

The doctor hypothesised that the denosumab treatment had been so successful in converting my jelly-like tumour into bone that it had not only calcified the outer crust but the entire tumour. He further clarified that had the tumour been somewhere less dangerous, such as a little toe, he would have considered postponing the surgery and taking me off the chemo to test whether or not the tumour would revert back to its previous consistency. However, due to the tumour's proximity to my spinal cord and the risk of paralysis, this was not a chance my medical team were willing to take. Despite my anger and confusion, I did understand their reasoning, but truth be told, I think I would have been happier never knowing. Or at least waiting until after I had healed so the team could face my full wrath! The timing was *not* ideal.

After two weeks in the hospital, my surgeons and physiotherapists were convinced I would be able to manage at home without them, and I was allowed to leave. I didn't feel ready. I could walk a few feet by myself but still required full-time care from Mum, who had taken time off work to look after me. Just to drive me home from the hospital, Mum had to push the passenger's seat all the way back so I was as horizontal as possible, cover it in piles of blankets and supportive pillows, and make sure I timed my medication perfectly so that it was hitting my bloodstream as we were taking off. Even so, I was shaking and sweating with pain by the end of the 40-minute drive from the Epworth.

Mum and Ben assisted me inside, guiding me to the lounge room. Dad had moved my bed there so that I wouldn't be hidden away in my bedroom and I could get a good view of the lorikeets and rosellas outside. It helped to hear the hustle and bustle of life around me, despite being unable to join it. We quickly discovered that I would need assistance to sit up or get out of bed, so the mic stand mocking me from the corner of the room suddenly had a job to do again. I would roll carefully onto my left side, take hold of the mic stand in both hands and use my arm strength to lift me to a seated position rather than utilising my abdominal muscles. This saved me from a lot of pain.

I would end up being almost completely bed-bound for three months and severely incapacitated for six. It was tough. Without distractions, all you do is sit in your pain, wallow in your loneliness and hope the next dose of OxyContin isn't too far away.

Although the internet was well and truly established by this time, Netflix was not yet a thing. It's true – I was forced to watch – *voice quivers* – free-to-air TV! I know, disgusting. I can still recite the TV guide from that period. The morning was filled with crappy shows where Karl Stefanovic would fail to make his chauvinism come across as charming. Midday saw *Dr Phil* grace my screen (the clear highlight), followed by *Ready Steady Cook,* back when George Calombaris still had hair and lacked the kind of money that breeds greed. Finally, the honourable *Judge Judith Sheindlin* would take us into the after-school program, at which stage Mum and I would settle in for a marathon of whatever reality show we were currently bingeing to pass the time. *Laguna Beach, The Hills, The Real Housewives* and *Celebrity Rehab* were big on our download list.

This spawned my reality TV addiction, unrivalled by any of my peers. When you've watched nine hours straight of Heidi Montag transforming into a bot, Janice Dickenson's rock hard tits on *Celebrity Rehab*, or can remember Vicki Gunvulson's original face and you still want more, you know you have entered the land of garbage humans. And if that's you, *welcome;* you are my beautiful garbage people! Between episodes, Mum would help shuffle me to the toilet, try to get me to eat something, and take notes on which meds I had taken and which were still to come. She was my carer, and she was brilliant.

Dad, not so much.

When I was in the hospital, he was great. He would come in and read to me from his stash of history books, his booming voice bouncing off the walls as I dipped in and out of sleep. But as soon as I was home, I saw him less and less. Mum was never more than a few metres away from my bedside at any given time. She often snuggled in next to me as we watched TV together. My clearest memory of Dad is him popping his head around door frames to ask how I am before continuing with his day. There had always been a massive disparity between Mum and Dad's attention around the home, but I guess I hadn't realised how much that translated to our relationships with them as well.

Some days, he wouldn't so much as say hello. I'd hear him come home from work and start pottering around the kitchen as he waited for the kettle to boil. I'd wait, hopeful that when he was done, he would take 30 seconds to see how I was. But as I heard his footsteps trail off into another room and the TV turn on, I would lie in bed, lifeless, heartbroken and invisible. As a small child, I never once felt forgotten or unloved when Dad would be interstate for months or years. This was different. This was a choice.

When I was in the hospital, being wheeled from ICU with a dozen wires, tubes and plugs coming out of my swollen, clammy body, a little boy whispered to his mother, 'scary...' The mum was horrified, but I actually found it pretty funny. The kid wasn't wrong; I looked like Frankenstein's monster. I believe my dad felt like that little boy staring down the barrel of mortality; for him, it was too much to bear.

I understood it, but that doesn't make it acceptable. Guess what? I was also scared; Mum was also scared; we *all* were. Fear doesn't mean you don't do something. Fear just shows you when you have to be brave. You don't turn away from someone who needs you – someone you love – just because it feels uncomfortable to look at them. That's not how love works. I didn't feel the anger and abandonment for me alone; I felt it for Mum too. Why does the entire world need to rest on her shoulders? *You're right there. Carry something!*

My dad was a kind but tortured soul. An over-thinker in a way that made him brilliant beyond compare but constantly heavy-hearted. His incredible mind took him to great places in his career, but sometimes I think he would have loved to drift in blissful ignorance, just for a moment. We are similar in that way – not in the intellectual capacity or illustrious career highlights, but in how we are both inescapably burdened.

When it came to my illness, I suspect Dad was overwhelmed to the point of shutting down. He was an academic, a historian, a physicist and an astronomer. He practised maths for fun and was incomplete without at least two calculators on his person at any given time. I'm not saying he was a robot, but I was once awoken by his sleep-talking to find him confidently reciting binary code, 'Zero one one zero one zero zero zero, zero one one zero one zero zero one, zero zero zero zero one zero one zero.' He was a problem solver, yet here I was: the ultimate problem. A problem whose answer was a big fat 'wait 'n' see.' We had to hope, and hope, by its very nature, lacks a solid answer.

Whenever you look at me, I wish I was her

Soundtrack: *Adele – 'Cold Shoulder'*

By the time I had the surgery, Simon and I had been together for two and a half years. I was deeply in love with him. Lovely, gentle, predictable, safe Simon. We had already been through so much together within such a short time. With hindsight, it's clear why I became so dangerously co-dependent, but at the time, we were just trying to survive as best we could. Co-dependency feels right when you're young. It's powerful and intense, like the love you see play out on the silver screen. It's what you imagine love is meant to feel like, in that it is never peaceful. For better or worse, you sit right at the pinnacle of your emotions, meaning things can change rapidly and frequently. I don't ever remember learning about 'peaceful love' when I was young. Love was always sold as passionate, earth-shatteringly intense and addictive.

I surprised myself with how much I loved Simon, especially as we had nothing in common. While he was watching AFL, I would hide in another room, illegally streaming reality shows from the US. I found listening to the dulcet screeches of Tamra Judge and Vicki Gunvulson soothing, and he anxiously rooted for whoever his favourite sports team was. *I really should know that.* It's simple, really; we fell in love because we were young, open-hearted and insanely attracted to one another. Friends would often remark how different we were, labelling me as the artistic wild child and him as the quiet and sensible IT nerd, but isn't that the basis for every great sitcom ever made? We were the ultimate *Odd Couple*. I can't list the reasons I fell for him; it wasn't like that. I wish I could because I'm sure it would help me make sense of everything, but for me, it was completely emotional. Being with him felt like my heart was home. Is that love? I had never felt anything like it before. It knocked me off my feet and changed my whole world.

I believed he was *the one*. My very own Ryan Gosling was right before me, and all my wallowing and crying along to Jewel songs had finally paid off. Simon was my first big love. I was still young and naive enough to throw myself entirely into our relationship without an ounce of fear. Once I fell in love, I could hardly remember life before him. It seemed dull and lifeless. That's the saddest thing about first loves – the word *first*. The implication being that there will be others. That somehow this feeling will come to a close, and all you have built and given your heart to so freely will end. Because once you come to realise it was only a *first*, you can never fall the same way again. You can never be delightfully naive or free with your heart, and to me, that's the saddest thing in the world.

During my home recovery, Simon would visit me every other day. The word visit doesn't really do him justice – he took care of me. He took the burden off Mum for a while by getting me medicine and ice packs for the pain. He'd take me for short walks around the garden, which is important in the prevention of scar tissue. And he'd lay beside me as we watched terrible daytime TV. He was doing all the right things on paper, but in reality, he was disengaged. In many ways, my disappointment was entirely of my own making. I blame '90s heartthrobs Freddy Prince Junior and Shane West for many of my idealistic dreams. If all it took to turn the ugly duckling into a clumsy yet beguiling beauty was a little lip smacker and a push-up bra, my story would've taken quite a different turn

I had learned from watching Nicholas Sparks' film adaptations that the 'sick girl' is actually a starring role. Once again, my suffering would all be worth it because true love was awaiting me on the other side. In my fantasy, I would lay draped weakly over a chaise longue, one hand to my forehead, the other falling by the wayside, as he – the infamous faceless 'he' – held my hand and read to me from one of my favourite books. Whilst on the verge of death, he would ask for my hand in marriage, and as a single tear ran lamely down my cheek, I would choke out, 'Yes.'

Now, having lived a rather different experience, I am quite sure old Nicky Sparks has never, not once, not *ever*, been around a sick young woman. Because in reality, it looks more like this: there I would lay slumped, clammy and pale with a greenish tinge, in my bed, damp with sweat from the OxyContin and morphine seeping from my pores. My cold hands filled with drips and needles that he is too afraid to disturb, so they go un-held for weeks. I notice but say nothing, planting the first seed of resentment that my fairy tale has been dismissed. Rather than ask for my hand in marriage, he asks me if we really must watch another episode of *Ready Steady Cook,* to which my reply is a forceful 'Yes', as tears of frustration fall from my face, now red with fury.

Physically, Simon was with me, but mentally he was miles away. I became obsessed with the idea that he was seeing someone else. If he was even slightly late to see me, I'd have already gone over every possible explanation in my mind ten times over. I would cycle through worry that he had been in an accident, to rage that he was cheating, and eventually come around to hope that he might be out buying me 'get well soon' flowers. By the time he would arrive, I had been on such an emotional rollercoaster that discovering he was late *just because* would throw me into a tailspin. *How dare you not be dead!* The high-dose painkillers I was ingesting on a daily basis were making me paranoid. I could no longer trust my own judgement, so instead of listening to my gut, I ignored red flags.

The medication and lack of proper sleep took hold, driving me to the point of insanity. Late one night, I awoke in a cold sweat, convinced a serial killer had snuck into the house and was butchering my family one by one. *Normal.* The house was dead silent, but that's because he was a very stealthy murderer, I rationalised. I hurried to strap on my back brace and slid into my fluffy slippers, ready to save the day. The next thing I know, I'm standing in the kitchen in the dark, wielding a butcher's knife. I shuffled into my brother's room. In his slumber, he heard the bedroom door slide open to see my head peeking through the crack, not dissimilar to Jack Nicholson in *The Shining*.

'Kirst?' he asked groggily.

'Err, nothing,' I announced, knife hidden behind my back. For the time being, I was satisfied that he was alive, although still concerned someone might be lurking in the shadows.

Then I made my way down to the other end of the house to check on my parents. Their obnoxious snores alerted me to their well-being. Relieved, I returned to the kitchen and carefully replaced the knife in the cutlery drawer. I made my way back to my room, unclasped my back brace and eased myself into bed. Everything hurt. Shuffling from one side of the house to the other was easily the most activity I had done in months. As the adrenaline subsided, the pain came flooding back, and with it came the realisation that I had finally lost my mind. That, and I was totally and utterly helpless. Had there actually been an intruder, there was nothing I could have done about it. I imagine they would have taken one look at the crippled girl in her PJs and laughed. But hey, a girl's gotta try!

When I wasn't rescuing my family from potential axe murderers, I would occasionally have visitors. Once you've been housebound for a long time, people tend to get bored, or simply forget about you once they have made their obligatory appearance. A lot of people dropped off during this time, but not Sam. Twice a week, for the duration of my recovery, she would stop by with wonderfully mind-numbing magazines and soup from our favourite café. She would read me this week's scandalous highlights, from K-Stew cheating on R-Pats to Amanda Bynes' latest DUI.

Sam was on chemo and recovering from surgery herself, yet she never forgot about me. She never put me in the 'too hard' basket and looked away. She would have done that for anyone. She was thoughtful and generous, unlike anyone I have known.

During one of my daily walks around the garden, I was confronted by a red fox. I stood frozen in my pink dressing gown and matching slippers as it stared me dead in the eye. *Fuckity fuck.* I knew the foxes of this area. These weren't the run-of-the-mill 'hunt in the dead of night for rodents' type of fellas. These were bold, 'come out in the broad light of day to eat our entire hen house' motherfuckers! My heart was pounding. If this thing charged at me, there was nothing I could do. I couldn't run. I could barely *walk*.

We stared at each other with wide eyes, each debating who would make the first move. *Right*, I thought, *let's do this.* I was closest to the basement door, but I didn't know if it was unlocked. The alternative was to make my way to the back door, up a flight of stairs. I decided to risk the basement. As quickly as a woman with a fractured spine and sheep's wool slippers can move, I shuffled in tiny little footsteps toward the door. The fox jolted as if it was about to make a leaping jump. *Welp, this is how I die,* I resigned. I can see the headlines now. *Girl Survives Spinal Resection, Only to be Mauled by Rabid Fox.* Just as I pulled the door open, I saw the beast scurry to freedom. I would live to see another day. When I made it inside, I recounted the horrifying story of life and death to my loving family, who naturally found this hilarious … because they are all sociopaths.

Life was hard. I had limited bodily agency, was paranoid, and I sensed Simon pulling further away with each passing day. So, when I suspected him of having an affair because he was smirking into his phone more than usual, I didn't know whether to trust my instincts or if I was rapidly unravelling. I've since learned that two things can be true.

There was a new girl at his work who quickly became the highlight of his days. At first, he avoided talking to me about her or made sure not to mention her gender, but over time he couldn't help himself. He would come over and excitedly tell me how they had made their mundane retail jobs more fun by mucking around throughout the day. *Pfft, see if I care.* I knew I was useless right now. I couldn't go out on romantic dinners or join parties with his friends. I couldn't wildly fuck him the way an energetic 23-year-old should. When we did attempt to have sex, not only was it fuelled by my intense fear of losing him, but I would have to wear my *sexiest* back brace. Like a bulletproof vest, it provided an all too real barrier between us. Then he would have to perch atop of me delicately, like a daddy-long-legs, limbs outstretched and balancing on a knife's edge so as not to crush my frail bones. *Hot.*

I had no filter of niceties due to my pain, and often I was demanding and short with those around me. If I needed medication, I needed it *now* because I knew what it felt like to go without it. If I needed to sleep, that took priority because it was the few hours in the day when my body wasn't in constant, throbbing agony. I needed him so much. I needed him for comfort, and I needed him to walk me to the toilet. He was my love and my carer, which was increasingly hard to navigate. I was frustrated, and he was bored.

On top of that, he was still freshly grieving his mother. I knew he needed to find joy where he could, and I wasn't the best source of that right now, but the more he smiled into the dim light of that phone screen, and the less he did with me, the more intense my fear grew. I felt it eat away at my gut, churning and twisting like a poison gradually taking hold. That little voice from the depths of my mind that had quietened down in recent years was back, and she was vicious. *He's found someone else. She's prettier. She's fun. She's healthy. You are a symbol of pain, grief and death. A reminder that his mother is never coming back and everything he loves will die. You are poison. <u>You</u> are the cancer.*

Whether a symptom of my paranoia or confirmation that I was right all along, I later found out that the infamous workplace 'she' was more than a friendly colleague. One day while he was smiling into his phone, I caught a glimpse of their correspondence: 'I want you.' It was simple, short, and enough for my heart to drop into my stomach. I lay in bed, heaving with tears. Tears that tore at my healing wounds and heart. He admitted that they had been flirting, secretly sexting and coffee-dating after work for months throughout my recovery. He would be late to see me because he was with her, having fun. *Fun.* Something I was unable to provide. I don't know if anything physical ever happened between them, and I don't need to because he had been infallible prior to this. He had been *mine.*

Mum was in my ear telling me, 'Ah, it's just a bit of a flirt. Let it go!' And I wanted to. Perhaps if I had been healthy, it would have been different, but I couldn't. He had shone a light on the deepest of my insecurities, and there was nothing I could do about it. I couldn't be better. I couldn't do more. I was as vulnerable as a person could be. I was isolated from everything that resembled the life I knew and completely entrusted my heart and my life to this man. He had my health in his hands, and I trusted he would protect me until I could be *me* again. He failed at the first hurdle. I wish I had paid more attention to that instead of following my dumbass heart.

> I spend a lot of time thinking about love. Does everyone feel it uniquely, or is there an underlining sameness that connects us all? Can true love last a lifetime, or is it futile? If given enough time, will we tire of the one that once stole our hearts? Even Jay Z cheated on Beyonce. Fucking *Beyonce!* Brad left Jen for his 'soul mate' Angelina, had 40 children and, even then, got bored and moved on to a woman half his age. Is love so special because it is destined to die? Are we just torturing ourselves for something fleeting, and if so, is it worth it? I'm genuinely asking. *Someone, please help!*
>
> I wonder about the interconnectedness of trust and love and how delicately they intertwine. They are so intrinsically linked that one cannot thrive without the other. I've always felt connected to animals. It has never made sense to me that just because we are humans with opposable thumbs and big brains (that are predominantly a pain in the arse), we get to rule over all other beings. I also take issue with the five-day workweek, but that's for another soapbox on another day.
>
> In 2001, I was so excited in year seven science class when we got to perform social experiments on baby chicks. I thought that meant we got to play with them and watch them grow. In fact, it meant separating one out from the rest of the brood and observing his decaying mental health. *I mean, wtf?* I was further disturbed when I heard what happened to the chicks post abandonment torture. Some of the older kids liked to tease us that they gassed the chickens once we were done with them. So, there I was, 12 years old, learning about the tragedies of the Holocaust in history class, and suddenly I was being trained to torture and kill innocent, adorable babies in science? Appalled, I stormed up to my teacher and demanded to take my chick home. I will *not* be 12-year-old Hitler!

Sure enough, at the end of the experiment, I was allowed to take two little chicks home, much to the dismay of my mother, who would become their primary carer. They were fricken adorable. Stinky, annoying and grumpy, but adorable. The only problem was they weren't chickens. They were roosters, and they were nuts. I adopted several more chicks over the years, all of which I inexplicably named Henry, until Henry the 14th decided he hated Ben and would attack him at every opportunity. I don't know if you've ever seen a fully-grown rooster attack a weedy teenage boy, but it is as hilarious as it is terrifying.

That same year, they aired an episode of *Survivor* in which the cast slaughtered a pig. As a family, we used to gather around and watch the tube of an evening (what a weird time). We'd enjoyed another fantastic episode of *Sliders,* with a young and devastatingly handsome Jerry O'Connell, followed by *Survivor.* They teased the pig's death for weeks leading up to it as if it was the event of the century. It felt voyeuristic and gross to me to celebrate ritualistic murder on prime time, but I was just a kid and hadn't yet realised that adults don't have a clue what they are doing. I trusted that they wouldn't do anything that would cause harm; it was just for ratings. *Ha! What an innocent idiot.* I looked away as it happened, but I heard the pained, terrified squeals. I saw the contestants celebrate, covered in blood and cheering each other on for their victory. I watched my brother and his friend revel in the 'entertainment', and I just remember feeling sad and hopeless. *How is this fun?* I wondered. That night I became vegetarian.

'Ha, you just ate lasagne for dinner!' Ben joked.

'Yeah, well, starting tomorrow then, duh.'

'Okay,' he said, rolling his eyes. 'I bet you don't last a week.'

'Just watch me,' I replied, with all the venom of a pre-teen girl.

I thank Ben every day for saying that. Had he not challenged me with failure, I wouldn't have been able to draw on the amount of spiteful energy it took to be veggie for the next 20 years (on and off, but he doesn't need to know that).

These days, I put that energy toward fostering felines. They often come to me timid, frightened or unwell because they have lived in unhealthy environments or shelters for too long, but they inevitably improve, given some TLC. I had one shy boy, Mimo, who was so terrified when he arrived that he hid under my bed for three weeks straight. I would have to take him food, leave the room, and hope that his bowl would be empty when I came back. I had to be fully guided by him. He never made a peep, so I would listen intently for the slightest of purrs to know if I was on the right track. New voices around the house sent him deeper into hiding, but he was slowly getting used to mine. So I started to announce myself as I entered the room. I never broke my patterns because this was a cat that needed stability to feel safe. I didn't do anything special. I just gave him a safe place to catch his breath, get used to his surroundings and show him I wasn't a threat.

He slowly started to come out from under the bed to explore the great unknown (*so brave*). He developed a deep trust in both myself and my other foster cat, the latter of which he would allow to clean the muck off his face when he was done enthusiastically hoovering up his food. He started coming to me to tell me, now using his voice rather obnoxiously, when he needed something (*snacks, always snacks*). He learned he could trust me, and in turn, for him giving me his trust, I never did anything to challenge that. I took care of his fragile heart because that's what I promised to do when I let him in.

Simon choosing to give his attention to another woman when I needed him most was a betrayal. It would be like walking up to my blissfully sleeping cat, who has just gifted me his trust and then booting him across the room. That cat may stick around because he knows I am his source of food, water, shelter and general survival, but he will never ever expose the most vulnerable parts of himself to me again. He will never trust me the same way as if I had never hurt him.

Like a stray cat, I stuck around, and my wounds were patched up over time. But I never fully trusted him again. My heart would never feel safe again. I didn't even realise how damaging that can be long term. Like tiny little cuts and bruises lining your heart every time your loved one is late, they go out without you or withhold emotion. You are forever questioning, *Is it happening again? Is he choosing her?*

I can't fit the feelings in

Soundtrack: *Fiona Apple – 'Every Single Night'*

My attachment to Simon grew with my paranoia. In turn, he withdrew, unable to cope with my neediness. This happened so slowly over the next two years that I barely saw it coming. It wasn't until 2014, after having lived together for about a year in our shoebox apartment in Fairfield, that the cracks we had been patching over became impossible to ignore.

I was at a place in my healing where I was relatively self-sufficient, except for the pain when I did too much, which was often. I had been stuck in my body for so long that I dove back into life, desperate to make up for lost time. After graduating from yoga teacher training, I began a Bachelor of Health Science with the goal of becoming a naturopath. By the end of the first year, I was struggling with my own hypocrisy. I was learning about herbs and spices that could supposedly cure all manner of ailments when I had just finished an experimental drug trial. I was ingesting a range of pharmaceuticals, and when I asked [my medical team] if drinking chlorophyll would aid my healing, I was met with, 'Look, it's not going to make a difference, but if you like the taste, go ahead.' *Nobody drinks chlorophyll for the taste, Sandra!* There go the natural benefits of the placebo effect.

Before the tumour, I would have fit perfectly with this crowd; I *was* this crowd. I had stacks of books outlining the healing powers of yoga, meditation and food as medicine. I made my own chai tea on the stovetop, had perfected 'bliss' protein balls and soaked my oats overnight for an 'activated' brekkie. Pete Evans would have been proud! More importantly, I believed in it. But now I didn't know what I believed. I certainly didn't think I would never have gotten sick if I had only munched on some kale chips. Or that all it would take to cure my deeply ingrained mental health issues was to increase my omega–3s. However, I also wasn't convinced it wouldn't. I'd had my world shaken, and things that felt so clear-cut before now came with more questions than answers. I decided to continue with the study but transferred to a Nutrition degree. It was a shorter course, meaning I could reduce my classes and focus on food as medicine. By now, I had a relatively healthy relationship with eating and my love of cooking had continued to grow, so it made sense.

In 2010, I entered a magazine cooking competition. I did so well that I was sent to Sydney to compete in a cook-off between bouts of chemo. I was so excited that I accidentally/on purpose failed to mention my health issues, just in case they asked me to leave the competition (for safety reasons). I smiled extra brightly to hide my sunken eyes, which must have paid off because I won! Seemingly, the judges enjoyed my prosciutto-wrapped chicken on a bed of parsnip mash. I got my face in *Good Taste* magazine (the Christmas special, if ya' don't mind), scored my first and only trophy (a gold-plated whisk that proudly sits atop my mantle), and to top it off, they threw me a cool ten grand. Yup. In the words of Chrissie Swan when she tasted my cooking on the morning show, *The Circle*, 'Thank you, chicken thigh!'

I had wanted to spend the money on recording my first EP, which would, of course, propel me into superstardom, but I never got the opportunity because I'd been incapacitated for so long and the pressure on my lungs from the tumour made my voice embarrassingly weak. Four years later, the timing was finally right. I joined a heavy metal band as the lead singer – a kind of *Evanescence* meets *Slayer* vibe. A hardcore wall of sound that was layered with my floaty vocals. I wasn't particularly suited to the style, but my bandmates were great, and we had fun. We wrote and recorded a handful of songs and even filmed our first music video, which gave me the confidence to take my solo music to the next level and finally record my solo EP. I worked with a producer to turn the songs I had written with Rhys into complete studio recordings. I filmed two more music videos, organising every detail myself, from cast and crew to make-up and set design. It was intense. My weekends were taken up with rehearsals, studio sessions, planning meetings and filming, which sounds fun and glamorous but, in reality, is really fucking exhausting. I began to realise I had enjoyed the idea of being a pop star more than the actual journey to become one. *Shocker.*

Nonetheless, I ploughed ahead, also planning an album launch for the new record: the 18th of November at the Wesley Anne in Northcote would see me debut my work. I had been working on some of these songs for as long as five years, and they were deeply personal to me. I assembled another band, this one made up of old school friends who had been exquisite musicians but now worked corporate jobs because #adulting. They brought my songs to life in a way that made me feel like a real musician. Their talent would be enough to override all my fraudulent smoke and mirrors. I had watched live music at the Wesley Anne for years, and now a poster of my face hung on the wall. It was thrilling.

I also bounced back to Body Balance and began to teach yoga as soon as my body would allow. I needed the money now that I was living out of home, so I pushed myself to go back to work before I was ready. Luckily, I had worked out the perfect ratio of opioids to active cognitive function, meaning I could mask my pain enough to teach without slurring my words. *Life hacks of an addict.*

Why didn't I wait until I was fully healed? Why is teaching a yoga class to ten geriatrics in a gym so important? The truth is, it isn't. They could've replaced me in a heartbeat, and the world would have kept turning, but to me, it symbolised that I was getting my life back. I was making money, not much, but it was my own money. I could make it because I was able-bodied. It wasn't given to me because I fit into a box on a form that said I was temporarily disabled. I could walk. Not only walk but bend and stretch and move in an accurate enough depiction of what my students should aim for. My body had a use; *I* had a use. So, if I had to be a little high to get myself to that sweatbox of a room where I was underappreciated and underpaid, I was going to do it. Only I wasn't just a little high; I was fucking flying. The dose I was on would leave the average person damn near comatose, but I had been on extreme doses for so long that I thought I was perfectly fine. I could drive to work, educate people about yogic philosophy and perform a headstand if need be. I was a high-functioning addict, but I was also in legitimate pain, so it was completely justified... *Right?*

As I finished a class and the painkillers wore off, I would feel everything. Exercise creates micro-tears in the muscles, which, in repairing, come back bigger and stronger. It was as though I could feel this process occurring in every cell. My broken muscles and scar tissue were forced to move against their will and beyond their current capabilities. Ripping and tearing, hot and throbbing. Once home, I would cover myself head to toe in ice packs, trying to dull the screaming deep within my bones. As I collapsed in bed, I'd try to recall anything from the class I had taught only moments ago. Often, I'd come up blank. Not a downward dog. Not a happy baby pose. Nothing. That was the opioids. They didn't just numb your body; they blissfully numbed your entire being – body, mind and spirit. I've lost entire days to those things. Weeks, probably. Even now, I'll occasionally feel the familiarity of a memory I can't quite latch onto, like waking from a dream and desperately trying to catch it before it slips from my mind. The difference between these elusive memories and a dream is the accompanying shame and guilt that inevitably follows. I've done something shameful, I can sense that, but all I've got to show for it are mismatched flashes in my brain, and truth be told, most of the time I don't want to unlock them.

Around the same time, I had an issue with crashing cars. I don't mean a little bingle here or a scratch there. I totalled three cars in five years! That's not normal. Naturally, I assumed I was a really terrible driver, but in hindsight, I was high as fuck. There was an incident where I could see the accident coming, playing out before me as if I was watching it in slow motion. I knew I should do something, but my body and brain didn't connect in time, leaving me to cruise into the shiny new Lexus in front of me. CLANG! Like Daria lamely reaching for the basketball in gym class, I watched it happen and internally shrugged. *Whoops.*

By November 2014, I was frantic all the time, but frantic was good. Frantic meant I was achieving things. Somehow, in my rush to conquer the world, I ended up booking my album launch during exam week at uni. *No worries, I got dis!* I thought as I pushed down my growing anxiety with a couple of painkillers. Simon and I had also created two websites: a personal one for my music and another for yoga and wellbeing called NiceAsana – pronounced Arse-ana. Asana is the Sanskrit word for yoga postures. It's very witty and hilarious (once explained). This website would include healing recipes, regular blog posts, and videos depicting the benefits of yoga asana and pranayama (breath work).

I organised a recipe photoshoot for the website with my friend Kamelya (Kami) as the photographer, who had been the director of photography on my solo music videos. We'd connected over a love of food, creativity and sarcasm. I had prepared all the recipes, including the pièce de résistance, my blueberry and lavender vegan 'cheese' cake. Look, it was a confusing time for everyone; *Masterchef* was using lavender as a herb, and cashews became a 'cheese'. No one knew what was going on. The food was looking good, and I could see everything coming together. *Make way Martha Stewart, there's a new bitch in town!*

We worked a long day but I was happy with the end result and, strangely, by the time I got home, I wasn't tired. Having CFS (Chronic Fatigue Syndrome) since my anorexia, this was impossibly rare. Suspiciously rare. *Did Kami secretly spike my food with ginseng or caffeine? Are those antioxidant-rich blueberries working their magic?* I reasoned it must be the adrenaline one has after a productive day's work and moved on. I anticipated my energy crash to hit as I drove home, but it never did. When I got in, I began excitedly chatting with Simon, telling him in explicit detail what Kami and I had been working on. I must have been rambling because when I stopped talking, he asked, 'Have you taken something? You seem … *on*.'

'Huh? What? No. What? What do you mean? I'm fine. I'm *great!* I'm just excited about how the images turned out. The food was so good, and Kami, man, she's so talented. Oh! You have to try my salmon. It's to DIE for. I'll make it tonight. Or tomorrow? When do you want it? What was I saying? Salmon!'

Simon looked at me, bewildered, but said nothing.

'Okay, I'm going for a run! Let me know about dins!' I said, blasting finger guns at him.

I'd decided to go for a run because, by evening, I was still wired. Please note: I do not run. I hate 'to run'. I'm from a family of round, squishy people. Our bodies do not move that way. We are less effortless-gazelle and more slinky-giving-up-halfway-down-the-steps. But on this day, I ran and did not stop. I felt like I was flying, as though running was easy. RUNNING HAS NEVER BEEN EASY, PEOPLE! I ran full pelt for half an hour before I arrived at the local river. I looked out at the glistening water (or sludge), through the iridescent green trees (brown and sunburnt), and up at the pink-orange setting Sun (woop-di-fucking-do). I began to weep tears of joy over the beauty of nature. Me, crying real human tears over a sunset! No shade if that's your thing, but I have never been that person. I'm 'a glass-half-empty kinda gal'. I'm 'life is meaningless and we're all going to die'. I don't wake up grateful for another day before sniffing a flower and gazing gratefully at the morning dew. I'm 'mother fucker' over 'mother nature' every day of the week. It was at this point I started to realise something was up. *Can you get high without knowing it? Did I stand near someone smoking pot? Do we have a gas leak?* I didn't want to question it too much, afraid I might scare the feeling away with over-analysis.

I looked around on what was, realistically, a grey, dreary day and was utterly overwhelmed with gratitude for life itself. *Isn't existence wonderful?* The birds were singing, the air was soft and comforting, and all around me was a collection of the most vivid, kaleidoscopic colours I had ever seen. It was like discovering a flavour you had never tasted before. It was impossibly moving. It was as if I was seeing the world for what it really was for the first time, and it was fucking mesmerising! Belinda Carlisle was right; heaven really is a place on earth. Tears continued to stream down my smiling face as I ran home,

Party in the USA bopping between my ears. It wouldn't have felt out of place to fling myself joyously around a lamppost. I was just waiting for the moment when a delicate little bluebird would perch itself atop my finger and join me in song. Life was picturesque.

I didn't sleep a wink that night. I lay in bed smiling to myself, staring at the ceiling, with ideas and inspiration circling my mind. My heart felt so full and warm. I would remain in this euphoric state for a whole month; it was bliss. It's the happiest, most content, connected, loved, energetic and powerful I have ever felt. It was like cocaine, ecstasy, falling in love and molten chocolate, all wrapped up together in one beautiful, orgasmic moment. I had been miserable and burdened my entire life, and now I was being let into the secrets of the universe that had been lying dormant in my mind all these years. What a gift it was to finally be able to see the truth! The world's true beauty was mine, and I couldn't wait to share it. *Who needs drugs when life is this spectacular?* That was a thought I genuinely had … right before the crash. These days I spend my life trying to forget how blissful a manic episode can feel because chasing that illusion means running head-first into death.

A few weeks later, after landing in my worst depression to date, I was diagnosed with Bipolar Spectrum Disorder.

'What you are describing is a manic episode. I'm going to place you on mood stabilisers for your bipolar,' my psychiatrist growled as he looked down at the papers in his lap rather than up at me.

'My what?' I had never warmed to this guy. Where my psychologists over the years had all nurtured me to a certain degree, this doctor was clinical and direct in a way I found rude.

'You have Major Depressive Disorder and now you are describing experiencing a strong manic episode, so I would suggest you have bipolar. You also have a family history of it, yes?'

'Well, my dad's undiagnosed, but yeah. He has epilepsy, so the medication he took for that kinda helped his bipolar episodes.'

'Ah yes, it is the same medication. Different doses, but yes, it would help a little.'

'Mmm. So which one do I have? Aren't there two types?'

'These days, we think of bipolar more on a spectrum, but if I had to put a label on it, I would suggest you have Bipolar II with hypomanic episodes, or less severe mania and more instances of depression.'

'Fantastic…'

I was jealous of all the people who got to experience full-blown mania. It must be next-level magical.

I wanted nothing more than to feel that euphoric high again. What you don't see in films about manic pixie dream girls is the much more common and seriously debilitating plummet into depression. Even when you do reach the highest highs of mania, post-manic depression is horrific, dangerous and inescapable. After all, what goes up must come down, thus is the psychiatric law of gravity. You go from an unimaginable state of elated euphoria to passionately hating yourself and everyone around you. Your energy, once unstoppable, is now depleted to immobile exhaustion. Your skin, which felt like it cloaked your bones in a warm hug, now stings and prickles at the slightest touch. Your body aches inside and out, and life feels meaningless once again.

> Over the years, Dad and I would very occasionally find ourselves in the kitchen at the same time and try to chat the way we thought a father and daughter should. We tried awkwardly to follow basic tropes we had seen in films and stumbled our way through stunted conversations. Within minutes, we would end up in tears talking about life and death, heartbreak and mental illness. This was more comfortable for us. Dad had many quirks, but to this day, he is the only person I have ever met who knew exactly what it was like to live inside my mind.
>
> By 2014, Dad had been in the UAE for almost a year, attempting to salvage a failing oil and gas company. After I was diagnosed with Bipolar II, he started calling me once a week. He would walk me through his experience living with mental illness and what he had found worked for him. He told me about the importance of routine, regular bedtimes and minimising workload. He calmly listened as I told

him how much I was drinking and how badly I wanted to die. If he was afraid for me, he never let it show, but I knew he must be by the sheer consistency of his communication. We had never spoken this often or as openly in my entire life. He never judged me; he just listened and understood.

Sometimes he would regale me with stories of his own impulsivity, such as how he would agree to take on piles of work when manic, only to crash and burn as the depression set in. Overspending was never my thing – I leaned much more on substance abuse to make me feel better – but Dad, being straight-edge, had his own ways of acting out. For example, he bought an abandoned coconut plantation in Fiji with dreams of building a mansion. **Normal.** He didn't ask Mum or discuss this with anyone; he just went for it when a 'good deal' came up. 'It's going to have six bedrooms, so when you get married and have children, you can all come and stay for as long as you want.'

A lot of 'Okay, Dad'-ing went on in our family during that period, as we all quietly wondered when lucidity would return.

The way he talked about his plans for the land was both insane and incredibly sweet. He was like a child imagining a perfect universe around him. 'Sounds wonderful, Dad. I can't wait,' I'd reply, genuinely excited to see how this played out.

It was pretty outlandish, but Dad had always dreamed of retiring to Fiji. His parents had lived there for a while when he was young, and although Dad attended boarding school in Scotland, his holidays were spent with his family in Fiji. He fondly remembered those times as the happiest of his life.

To pay for this staggering investment, he took a position in Ras al-Khaimah in the UAE. It was a highly stressful job, the pressure was insurmountable and the culture was bullying. But within two years, Fiji would be paid off and Dad would be free to live out his dream. That was his plan, anyway.

I've noticed that every day I spent manic, I tended to have three times that in depression. This meant that following my month-long energy-filled love-fest, I sunk into major depression and severe exhaustion for three months. It *suuucked*. I'd just gotten out of bed post-surgery, and now I was dragging my arse back in. Over the years, I developed a habit of joking about my fatigue because I'm embarrassed by how much sleep I need. In a world where we glorify busyness and 'the grind', admitting you need to rest is akin to giving up. I've been trying to get the nickname 'Sleeping Beauty' to catch on because it makes CFS sound like a delicate sighing damsel rather than a pale vitamin D-deficient vampire who hasn't showered in a week. Alas, it has yet to take off.

For months I slept, lamented the energy I'd previously been lapping up, and cried tears of frustration as I turned down plans and watched my work pile up. I took to laying naked on the small square of overgrown grass in the backyard to soak up as much sunshine as possible, hoping this might restore my depleted body. I basically became a kind of cold-blooded lizard woman, only scurrying inside at sundown.

I began seeing a psychiatrist who placed me on mood stabilisers to remarkable effect. I had spent 24 years feeling as though my head was a computer with 16 tabs open, but with the new medication on board, I could slow down time to a pace I could keep up with. Like Superman, I could change my internal orbit to a tempo that worked for me. I could focus during lectures and, for the first time, could listen to and absorb what my teachers were saying. I had spent my entire schooling believing I was dumb because it took me longer to learn basic skills and I found it hard to retain information, but I was starting to realise that perhaps I wasn't stupid. Maybe I had been managing too many tabs all this time and couldn't filter through the noise.

It had always been exhausting and loud inside my head, but I had no idea how intense it was until it stopped and the world went quiet. So quiet. Dare I say, peaceful? I was finally living in real time with the rest of the world, no longer worried about the future or wallowing in the past. I could stop running and just *be*.

With the distraction of my anxious striving now gone, I discovered that what was left was a very sad little girl who didn't know how to be still. I saw a healer once who said when she looked into my mind, she saw a girl. This young girl was dancing uncontrollably around a mirror. She danced 'round and 'round in circles, so fast that she created smoke under her busy feet. She spun and twirled in exaggerated colours, all to distract the world from seeing (her perception) that she had nothing of worth to offer. *Razzle fucking dazzle.* After the session, the healer encouraged me to spend some time sitting on the beach and watching the ocean. As I walked to my car, I could smell the ocean and hear waves crashing. I thought about following the path down to the beach for a moment, then got in my car and drove home. I was far too busy to stop.

My rapid transition from the erratic lightness of mania into the despair of depression was too much for Simon, so he checked out. I don't blame him, really. Once again, I was sick and incapacitated, but now I was also an emotional black hole desperate to be saved. He began to resent me. It was as if I was holding up a mirror to his inability to heal me. I would spend hours each night sobbing in our bedroom, desperate for him to hold me and tell me it would be okay, that I would be okay, but he didn't. He sat in the lounge room playing video games with his friends through a headset and let me cry until I passed out from exhaustion – like a baby he was sleep-training. I've never felt so lonely as I did in that bed, waiting for the man I loved to notice me. That's when I, in turn, began to resent him.

The problem I found with having such an extended period of life-changing euphoria is that nothing could compare. Even once I moved out of the intense depression that followed, I was still only back to baseline and, having seen and felt all the infinite joy of the universe, baseline itself was depressing. The palette of brand-new colours disappeared and in their place were lifeless, dull variants of grey. The smile was wiped from my face as quickly as it had come, and I felt angry and bored by the reality of life. *Why should I live in this shitty reality when all the pleasures of the universe lie dormant somewhere in my brain?* Happiness felt so close, yet I could not unlock it. It's the most medically-tangible mental illness has ever felt. Nothing had physically changed around me, but at the same time, I was changed forever within the confines of my tiny mind. It was like I had been watching life in HD and, suddenly, woke up to grainy static intercepted with jarring glimpses of *Friends* episodes from the '90s. *Me to brain: 'Could you be any more disappointing?'*

Up to this point, I had been able to manage my opioid dependence to a degree, but this experience rapidly propelled me into severe addiction. The pills would never achieve the ecstasy my brain had splashed out all on her lonesome, but it helped to feel as though I had some semblance of control over how I experienced the world again. I didn't know if I would ever have a manic episode again, but at least I could buy myself this small glimpse of chemical happiness once in a while.

Bring me a higher love

Soundtrack: *James Vincent McMorrow – 'Higher Love'*
(originally written by Steve Winwood & Will Jennings)

My father struggled to show affection, not because he was incapable of love but because he was raised in a harsh Scottish boarding school along Loch Ness and not in the warmth of a loving home. When home, over the summer, his mother lacked maternal instincts. She was strictly Irish Catholic and never missed a day of church in her life. She was so (let's call it) 'patriotic' that my father always stocked both Irish and English breakfast tea to avoid offending her with the latter. She was also riddled with anxiety. I never saw her at peace a day in her life. She was agoraphobic and never left the house without my grandpa to clutch onto. I never heard her speak more than a few words; she would always turn to my grandpa to speak on her behalf. I assume she spoke more when I was younger and she was sharper, but I have no memory of that. My memory of her is her constant anxious jittering, her permanently furrowed brow and her looking to Grandpa as she froze like a deer in headlights when asked, 'How are you?' *Primary school Kirsty can relate!*

My paternal grandfather is a jovial, wild and extraordinary man. A policeman, a judge and even an African shaman, who not once but twice burnt off his eyebrows performing 'healing' fire-breathing techniques. I suppose some would call him a show pony. As enormous as his heart was, it wasn't enough to counter the isolation of the Catholic boarding school that shaped my father.

Dad was remarkably intelligent and undeniably strange, making him a target for bullies. These days he would be diagnosed with Asperger's syndrome, but growing up, he was seen as a brilliant but unusual outsider. Because of this, examples of love and affection would have been rare and probably unwelcome. Not having these qualities displayed to him meant it was near impossible for him to emulate these emotions. Nevertheless, I never felt unloved by him. He was unconventional in his approach, but once every six months or so, like clockwork, he would tell me he loved me. It wouldn't have surprised me if he had it set as a biannual reminder in his diary. *Acknowledge love of Kirsty (daughter)*. He was so awkward about it that it was charming.

At the most arbitrary times, he would come to me and say, very matter-of-factly, 'You know, I love ya, Kirst?'

Bemused, I would reply, 'Yeah, Dad. Love you, too,' and that would be it until next time. The rarity of it didn't upset me. These moments were special; they were ours. I think it's when actions change that it hurts, like Dad pulling away after my spinal surgery. It hurt like hell, but over time, he proved he could be there for me in other ways. When you get used to a certain level of affection and it diminishes as a punishment, that's when you really feel the damage neglect can have.

That's what happened with Simon. He began to withhold affection. Too exhausted to dress, I lived in my PJs, but on the odd occasion I felt well enough to slap on a face and squeeze into my little black dress, I would go sight unseen, like an old dusty armchair in the corner of the room, used only as a placeholder for dirty clothes and shopping bags. I was no competition for the exciting world of Twitter and football scores that lived within his phone. *I'm right here. Can't you see me?* I started to doubt my very existence.

I've always been a big believer in asking for what you want. Mum's voice rang in my head, 'You can't expect people to be mind-readers.' So, I began to ask him if he thought I looked nice when I made an effort to pop on my Sunday best. But he couldn't have been less interested. The man who used to think I was the sexiest, most captivating woman in the world couldn't look up from his phone to tell me I scrubbed up alright.

The more I demanded attention, the more he withheld it. I began to feel insane or wrong for needing my partner to be attracted to me or even like me. I could feel his resentment quickly growing into pure loathing. I felt repulsive to him, and over time, I started to believe I was unlovable. If he couldn't love me, if he actually couldn't even stand me, then it must be my fault. *I'm too needy, I'm always sick, I'm not pretty enough, I'm boring, I'm annoying, I'm tired and I'm too fucking sad to love.*

Just like that, I was back in my school days – ugly, pathetic, worthless and clawing at the heels of a boy for validation. I watched the man I loved fall a little more out of love with me every day, and it was gut-wrenching, but I stayed because I was scared. Scared of being alone. Scared no one else would want me. Scared of how I would survive without him. Scared of him being happier with someone else, someone healthy. Just *really* scared. So, despite how much it hurt to be the shit on the sole of his shoe, at least I was still there, and that felt safer than not being there at all.

When love is withheld, it emphasises the moments where you do receive affection tenfold. When you haven't been held for a year, a warm hand or a kind word can bandage your tired heart a little longer. Reward centres in your brain are reawakened, and suddenly you have no idea why you were so miserable. Love is essentially one giant game of *Candy Crush*. If 'Deliciousss!' makes your heart skip a beat, then 'SuGaR CrUsH!' gives you full-blown arrhythmia. It's a narcissist's playbook, but Simon wasn't a narcissist; he, too, was just really scared.

Trust me when I say I have wracked my brain to find any other way we could have ended than how we did, but whatever way I look at it, I keep getting the same result. Allergic to being the 'bad guy', Simon would never have left me without good reason, and as unhappy as I was, I would never have left him of my own accord. I was so completely enmeshed that I truly had no idea who I was without him. That's a terrifying feeling: that you might physically disappear without the person. We had held each other together through so much that it felt like even small decisions became impossible without him. Without him, it was as though I wouldn't know how to brush my teeth or spell my own name.

I remember asking my brother, 'How can I sing without him to sing to?'

To which Ben wisely replied, 'You sang before he came along, and you will sing long after.'

But I couldn't hear him. I was blindly panicking. At the time, I thought that was love. That if the thought of losing him so deeply pained me, then that meant this was worth fighting for. There was love there, of course, but it was more like how a newborn needs their mother for survival. Everything our relationship had become fed into all my deepest insecurities, the main one being that I am and always have been irrefutably unlovable. So, when the gorgeous guitarist in my newly formed band told me I was lovely, I fell right into his arms. (Yes, I'm that cliché.)

I cried every time Jiang complimented me for the first few weeks because I couldn't believe how foreign the words sounded. It was like pouring water over a wilted desert flower. The part of me that I hadn't realised was slowly dying was being given new life, and it felt good. Ashamedly, I wished it was Simon saying all those beautiful words. Jiang was everything Simon wasn't, which wasn't necessarily a good thing, but it was everything I needed at the time. He talked to me, and he looked at me, and sadly that was enough.

Jiang and I would spend hours in his flat drinking red wine, listening to James Vincent McMorrow and talking. We talked about big things like the meaning of life and little things like our favourite recipes and musicians. I arrived at his small inner-city apartment one evening (lying to Simon that I was visiting a friend) to find him perched over his sink, taping large pieces of paper to his window. He had written in black marker, 'What were you listening to last night?' and directed the words to the apartment block opposite his own. He had overheard his neighbours playing a funk album at full blast, and instead of being incensed by the act, he stayed up all night listening with them. They later replied on post-it notes, 'Uptown Special – Mark Ronson'.

I'd intermittently sneak away to the bathroom to snort an oxy. Jiang knew I leaned heavily on my pain pills, and while it's one thing to know something in theory, it's entirely different to witness it. So, I kept it private, afraid of being seen as dirty or pathetic. These stolen bathroom moments were my solitary forbidden pleasure, escapism within escapism. I've been asked over the years what it feels like to take opioids. I think the best way I can describe it is 'hopeful' – a hit of hope for the hopeless. I sensed that I was more emotionally powerful and stronger than my reality. I was no longer the beaten-down child that wanted to give in: I was tough and ruthless. I was a survivor. In many ways, I owe my life to that drug. It didn't matter if the world shunned my ugly depiction of grief because I had oxy to support me. It wasn't vulnerable to death or loss. It would forever take care of me.

When I returned to Jiang in the kitchen, we would go back to singing our poor rendition of *Drops of Jupiter*. I would perch on his bench top while he stood at the stove cooking okonomiyaki in a singlet. I'd watch him, remembering how he had been at 16 – his floppy dark hair always hiding his eyes and his guitar like an extra limb, accompanying him everywhere he went. A year above me, I had thought he was the coolest guy at school. Way too cool for me. But instead, he was silly and weird. He was warm – a refreshing delight in a sea of mundanity.

With Jiang, nothing was off limits. The more esoteric the concept or deeper the emotion, the better. On warm summer nights, we would go on walks to his favourite places, stopping to look at city lights or stars. It was wonderfully cheesy and devastatingly romantic but always tinged with sadness. I had this deep ache in my chest as I remembered what it was like to fall in love with Simon. I was guilty, but more than that, I was disappointed about how toxic Simon and I had become. I couldn't understand how we had ignored this disease festering between us for so long.

Simon and I had never looked at the night sky together, and whenever I tried to open up philosophical conversations, I would be met with confusion and resistance. I couldn't even fantasise freely about travel without being shut down as Simon decided it was pointless unless we were actively planning a trip. We were trying to meld my world of serial fantasies with his of pragmatism and reason. The truth is neither of us was right or wrong. We were just profoundly incompatible, and neither of us wanted to admit it. *Humans of New York*'s Brandon Stanton says, 'If you can love the wrong person so much, imagine how much you could love the right one.' For a long time, our love was enough to cloud the fact that we had nothing in common, but no longer. Sorry John Lennon, but I've come to disagree – love is not all you need.

To survive my oxy addiction, I would try to ration my pills to dedicated intervals throughout the day. Inevitably, I would ignore my own rules and have the entire day's stash up my nose by early afternoon. While opioids got me through the day, I used alcohol to survive the nights. It was much easier to hide an opioid addiction at uni and work than a booze habit. My car was never without a wine bottle rolling around in the passenger's footwell. My alcoholic beverage of choice was usually white wine –easier to cover the smell on the breath and no stain on the lips. Screw top, of course, so that I could hide it under the seat at a moment's notice sans spillage. By now, I was a regular smoker, an offence that could get me kicked out of uni, as they would see this as not taking my health and nutrition studies seriously – which I wasn't. I was suicidally depressed. Prolonging my life with turmeric extract wasn't exactly at the front of my mind, although I often washed the wine down with freshly squeezed, organic OJ. Vitamin C was useful in combatting the detrimental effects of smoking. *#nutritionist #inspo #walkingcontradiction.*

Before heading home, I would stop at the bottle-o and buy a single sachet of wine in a squeezy bag to drink on the train ride home. Advertised for cooking, these sachets were 250ml of putrefied piss. But they were my drink of choice as they were subtler than a bottle in a brown paper bag. I wasn't one of *those* people. *Heavens, no!*

Simon eventually worked out what was going on with Jiang, but he didn't care. You've never seen anyone care so little about discovering infidelity. We didn't even break up – we stayed together in mutual resentment, loathing and need. We even invented a word for it: 'late'. Love/hate. 'I late you,' he'd call as he ran out the door for work. 'Late you, too!' I'd reply, blowing him a kiss. We joked because confronting it was not only difficult, it was impossible.

If I'm honest, aside from the sneaking around, I never felt bad about my relationship with Jiang. I was so angry with Simon. Sam, my favourite person in the world, was dying, and not once in three years had he asked about her. Not once. Had he asked, I would have told him her life was coming to a close; she was dying, and my heart was breaking. Instead, he sat idly by, watching me kill myself with addiction, screaming for help as I snorted lines in front of him while never questioning why I was so pained. He lived with the intimacies of my psychosis and depression, and rather than care for me, he left me alone to fend for myself. My mental illness was seen as my problem, not ours to weather together. It was so painfully lonely that, in the end, cheating felt good. Like punishment for his abandonment, I wanted him to hurt how I did.

Nonetheless, I stopped seeing Jiang, hoping I could patch together the tatters of my relationship with Simon, thus removing the only person in my life who brought me joy. Jiang was disappointed that I would cling to someone who seemingly gave me so little, but he didn't really have a leg to stand on. He had always claimed he didn't 'believe in monogamy', avoiding any commitment. I agreed that it was a man-made construct keeping us trapped because it suited my current juggling act. But, really, I was looking for love from two men, neither of whom was capable of loving me.

Everyone was miserable. Simon and I stayed together for another year because neither of us had the necessary energy to do what was needed. Nothing is so painful as sleeping next to somebody who once loved you and feeling their animosity sear into the back of your head.

Girl, where do you think you're goin'?

Soundtrack: *Lady Gaga – 'Joanne'*

Sam's family had long been dedicated to finding the best possible oncologists for her, flying her around the globe to access the most cutting-edge medical experts and treatments. And it worked for a while. Sam was relatively well, in cancer terms, for the first three years after her diagnosis. That's unheard of in brain cancer. Throughout those years, even on her worst days, she was still charismatic and captivating in her usual outrageous way.

It wasn't until her fourth-year post-diagnosis – after five brain surgeries, an impossible amount of lost hope and severe, chronic nerve pain – that it became harder to have quintessential Sam moments. At first, it was hard to spot her deterioration because, in many ways, it presented like a superpower. She would claim to see a beautiful blue light, an angel who danced playfully around her room at night. Things that would have terrified me seemed to humour or comfort her. At one point, she even perfectly described what her fiancé, Aiden, was doing on the other side of a wall. She had gone to the bathroom and, while drying her hands, she could see him waiting for her on the other side. She saw him standing with his hands clasped behind his back, gently swaying from side to side. This was an unusual stance for him. She came out of the bathroom, equal parts amused and alarmed, asking, 'Were you just doing this?' She acted out his movements with precision. His face said it all, 'How did you know that?' None of us could make sense of Sam's new superhuman abilities, and I didn't really want to. I liked to imagine she herself would become a beautiful blue angel one day.

Gradually, things started to shift as she had more surgeries and lost vital parts of her brain. The first time I noticed it, I had turned up at her place, ready for our weekly TV binge and bitch sesh. I knocked on the door and waited for the signature shriek of, 'Coming, Schmooooomyyyy!' as she bounded to the door like an overexcited puppy to greet me. Instead, I heard a sleepy, 'Come in, Schmoo. I'm on the couch.' I don't remember her ever calling me Kirsty; I was always her Schmoo-Monkey. I let myself in, assuming she was having a difficult day. But in fact, it was the beginning of watching my favourite person in the world start to die.

We were hanging out in her parents' hot tub about six months earlier, drinking vodka cruisers. She made some silly comment, and I responded with a chuckle and flippant, 'Ahh, get fucked.' Not an unusual interaction between us. We were always teasing one another, but this time she went quiet. I was sure she was faking and would turn around at any moment and start laughing – but she didn't. Instead, she put down her drink and walked inside without saying a word. I was left sitting in the hot tub, replaying what I had said and trying to figure out what I had done wrong. I dried off, waiting for her to come around, but an hour passed, and she still wasn't talking to me. She wouldn't even look at me. She was so angry. I removed myself to another room, where Sam's mother, Linda, found me despondent. 'Are you okay?' she asked.

'I don't know what I've done.'

'I know. It's okay,' Linda said, hugging me. 'The last surgery changed Sam quite a bit. She's still our girl, but she's much more sensitive now. She's lost the part of her brain that deals with reasoning, so when she hears something like "Get fucked" said in jest, she doesn't understand it's a joke.'

'Oh, shit...'

I should have known better. Brain diseases are cruel and unruly by nature. After surgery, Simon's mum could be aggressive and say nasty things that she would never have said otherwise. But I had only heard about her outbursts second-hand. I'd escaped the hurt of having someone I know intimately transform into a different person before my very eyes, until now.

'She's still our girl,' Linda reiterated. 'This is just our new normal. She's reactive in the moment, but she's forgiving. Go give her a hug. It'll be okay.'

I walked tentatively over to the couch where Sam was watching TV. I really hoped this would work so I could join her in watching *Teen Mom*. I crouched down next to her, 'Sorry, Baddie I didn't mean it. I love you.'

'Love you, too, Schmoo-Monkey,' she mumbled grumpily. She then waited a few seconds before following with, 'Want some M&Ms? It was a mixed pack, but there's only crunchy left.' She scrunched up her nose in disdain.

I smiled with relief, 'Gimme.'

As a child, I remembered sitting in front of the TV watching re-runs of *The Nanny* with the whole fam – a rare program we all mildly enjoyed. Between Fran Fine's squawking and Mr Sheffield spawning my attraction to avoidant men were commercials for Bana-nan-a-naa-naa-nan-na-naaa's, Furbies and cancer stats. 'One in three people you meet will get cancer at some stage in their lives,' a scary male voice decreed into living rooms across Australia. Those figures have since grown, of course. I felt guilty because I wasn't scared, and I didn't really care. Mostly, I was thinking about how unfair it was that Elsa, a fellow classmate, was allowed a Furbie, but I wasn't because my parents thought they were creepy. Looking back, I'm pretty sure Furbies fed on the nightmares of children, so it was probably a good call.

I didn't understand what cancer was or what I was supposed to do about it as an 11-year-old girl whose biggest concern was how I was going to meet cute Nick Carter. I knew it was a bad thing that grew in your body, and if you got it, you died, but I didn't know what that looked like. Movies would have us believe that once you have cancer, you get a bit of a cough and a funny tummy. You lose all your hair, but pull it off with Amber Rose-like unyielding beauty and perfect skin. Then, suddenly, you're hospitalised before finally dying peacefully, surrounded by loved ones. It looks simple. Sad and tragic, but simple. In reality, there is nothing simple about cancer progression. Not at all.

You don't see the elation when tests return a positive result, followed by the devastation when they take a turn for the worse a month later. Or how the tumours shrink and regrow again at a rapid pace. Or Sam becoming so accustomed to this that she could read her own scans as she taped them to the window, allowing the light to illuminate the dark spots of her brain. You don't see this process play out over and over again until all hope is lost.

You don't see the many times the patient is in and out of the hospital, fighting for their lives, and the numerous times family and friends collectively prepare themselves for goodbye. The bond I had with the select hospital few was one of immense closeness and equal sadness. They were the only ones who knew what it was truly like. The amount of times one grieves before losing a loved one is shamefully exhausting. You are forever on borrowed time. It's as though you're supposed to be grateful if the prognosis is three months and they survive for four, clutching at life. Gratitude fades, and fear grows daily like a ticking time bomb. Every day you're terrified. You find yourself waiting for something to happen to relieve you of the fear, one way or another. You become disgusted with yourself for needing relief at all.

What you don't see in the movies is the process of the body shutting down, first in subtle ways that are easy to miss if you're not watching closely. They become weak and tired, and their once ravenous appetite is now birdlike and scarce.

Sam, who used to order the scrambled eggs with extra bacon and mushrooms on the side, was now struggling to finish half a slice of peanut butter toast. We brushed it off as the side effects of the medication – maybe that means it's working. After all, we also needed protecting. Over time, plans to meet up were cancelled more frequently, until I'd wait until the very last moment before leaving the house just in case they were postponed again.

We adapted. We all did our best to keep things as ordinary as possible. We still joked together, and we still laughed. Only, her laugh got weaker, and an occasional cough crept in. I started to think I should be taking more photos, capturing a glimpse of her essence in a still, but I couldn't bring myself to do it. I didn't want her to know how scared I was. I didn't want her to think I had given up hope.

We began adjusting to our new normal on a weekly, then daily, basis. Until one day, you see your friend, who you remember jumping off boats in string bikinis, dancing on tables with you at clubs and crying with laughter at your shitty jokes, struggle to understand simple concepts. Her breathing laboured, and appearance very different from the cancer patients you were shown on film. You catch yourself struggling to recognise your friend in the face staring back at you, focusing on her eyes. She's still in the eyes. Soon she will no longer be able to walk, and again we will adapt, but even though she rocks her shiny red electric wheelchair like the badass she is, it's harder to pretend that everything will be okay.

Then finally, I find myself sitting beside my best friend in her hospital bed, telling her how much I love her. She responds with a weak, 'I love you too, Schmoomy', as I try desperately to hold onto the sound of her words exactly as she's said them, because I am terrified of what the next adaptation will be.

On the 8th of November 2015, I sat by her bedside, gently clasping her swollen hand. It was my 27th birthday. I wore a dreamcatcher necklace that had been a birthday present. I knew she would like it, so I displayed it to her proudly. She reached for it with one weak arm, then pointed to a card on the flimsy hospital shelf, which was obscured by vibrant flowers from all the people whose lives she had touched. The flowers were so plentiful they spilled over onto the floor. I opened the card to see it was for me: a birthday card. She was going to die – there was no longer any doubt about that – and she'd had the forethought to give me a beautiful, heartfelt birthday card. No doubt she had one ready for the following day when it would be her brother's birthday. *Who thinks of that?* Sam. Sam did.

I remember the final time I got to tell Sam I loved her. I was talking to her, telling her how beautiful she was and giving her a gentle kiss on her forehead. I remember the freckles lining her nose and the weight of her plump cheeks in my hands. She could no longer speak, and the muscles in her face and eyes were too tired to function. Her eyes welled up as I spoke, and I noticed the tiniest amount of tension visible between her brow. 'It's okay, Baddie. I know you love me too,' I assured her. Her brow softened, and she closed her eyes. My heart fucking broke.

We lost Sam on the 12th of November when she was just 31, four years after being diagnosed with stage four glioblastoma. I was down the hall of the hospital when I got a text from her hairdresser-turned-friend of ten years, Jay, revealing the news. He had been to visit but was now back in Melbourne. I don't know how he became the person to tell me what had happened, but suddenly my phone dinged and there on the brightly lit screen were Jay's words, 'Our girl is gone'. A text message. I learned my best friend had died through a fucking text message.

All I remember is this guttural scream bursting free of my chest as another group of hospital visitors looked on. I tried to stand up, to run to her bedside, but my legs buckled beneath me. I fell to my knees as Simon weakly patted my shoulder. *There, there.* Sam's courageous friend, Alana, flew down the corridor and scooped me up from the hospital floor. I buried my face in her cushiony chest and sobbed. She held me, rocking my shocked, limp body as Simon shuffled awkwardly in his seat. In that moment, I hated him.

I don't know if he hated me back, was overwhelmed by the stark similarities to his mother's passing, or was so emotionally stunted that it came across as heartless and cruel. But that night, as I mourned alone in our soulless hotel bed, he sat in the lounge room watching the footy and eating takeaway. I clamped my eyes shut, clenched my fists and screamed into my pillow in silent rage.

I wished he had never come, leaving me to grieve alone in the strange hotel room because that would've been easier than drowning out the emptiness of the next room. I held my head in my hands and squeezed, trying to stop the images of myself holding him to my chest as we received the news of his mother's passing. I squeezed so tight my hands shook and my nails dug painfully into my scalp, but I could still see myself singing *Panis Angelicus* at his mother's funeral, wondering if he was ever going to cry. I wanted it to stop. I didn't want to hate him for his ineptitude. I didn't want to think of him as a stone-hearted robot. I didn't want to think of him at all. All I wanted was to let my heart be with Sam, but my grief became confused with my anger, and I couldn't untangle what I was feeling.

How had I, a girl who feels everything, ended up with a man who feels nothing? It made no sense. How could Sam be gone when she soaked up every last moment of her life with vigour, and he was still alive, blinking at the TV as if the world hadn't changed forever? Could he not see that? Could he not feel that? It was all I could feel. The shift in my world felt like tectonic plates grinding beneath me. Suddenly I was being shown, clearer than ever, who I had spent the last six years of my life with. *It should have been you.*

We rarely talk about friends as life partners. We put all that pressure on romantic love. But that's what Sam was to me – she was my soulmate. She made me better, happier. The strange thing about losing your closest friend is that they are the only person you want to talk to about it. It doesn't make any sense, but the minute I found out Sam was gone, I took my phone out to call her and tell her the news. I wanted her to tell me I would be okay, even if she didn't believe it. I wanted to tell her how useless Simon had been and hear her chuckle at his emotional incompetence before telling me to dump his sorry arse. I wanted her back. I still want her back.

For months after her death, I would crawl into bed and scream, 'Help me! Help me!' between heavy sobs. At first, I didn't know who I was directing my pleas to, but now I know I was calling for her. I would imagine her next to me as I lay in the foetal position, wailing into my pillow.

I even started repeatedly calling her mobile just to hear her voicemail, 'Hi! You've called Sam. I'm either sleeping, meditating or can't be bothered talking, but leave your name and number, and I'll get back to you!' It killed me to hear her voice like she was still here, but it was better than accepting she wasn't.

As the next year went from bad to worse, I began to question whether she could hear my cries. I remained in touch with her family and developed friendships with Jay and Aiden. We all carried little pieces of Sam with us in our mannerisms, humour or appearance. It felt comforting to be surrounded by Sam, even if only in half-developed snapshots.

Her family and loved ones would tell me warmly about their spiritual interactions with her, but as hard as I tried to look at every passing butterfly as a sign of her presence, or rainbow as a symbol of hope, I still felt completely alone. I couldn't feel her with me and I took that as rejection. *Why won't she visit me? Am I not enough?* It sounds irrational but that's grief. There are no steadfast rules for what it should look or feel like. I took it personally and began to question what our friendship had meant to her. To me, she was my soulmate, but maybe to her I was just her 'cancer friend' helping her feel less alone. In order to protect myself and preserve her memory, I was forced to conclude that there is no afterlife. Sam lives on through me and everyone who loved her.

I've thought a lot about the best way to honour her memory. I'm not sure I'm doing her justice. I got a replica of her colourful butterfly tattoo, symbolising the first year she survived her diagnosis. She planned to get a new butterfly each year. When she showed it to me, she said, 'So when I'm 90, I'll be covered head to toe in butterflies!' and laughed. We released butterflies at her funeral as they played Emeli Sande singing *Free*. They played it three times. Everyone noticed and no one said a word. I simultaneously wanted to laugh and scream, but did neither. I just stood there in a rainbow skirt that I know she would have loved and thought about how, if she was here, she would've stormed up to the person in charge of music and comically, yet sternly, asked them to play the next track. She would've done something, but none of us could move.

I try to honour her by wearing her jewellery, and when asked where I get my incredible pieces from, I proudly relate, 'They were Sam's.' But the best way I have found to keep her spirit alive is to love myself the way she loved me. To work toward my most absurd and wild dreams without fear. To be bold, assertive and unafraid to take up space. To practise the art of 'More is more!' when it comes to fashion, and to laugh as loud and as often as humanly possible.

I love you and miss you dearly, my friend.

I'll kill her

Soundtrack: *Soko – 'I'll Kill Her'*

By December 2015, Simon and I had lived through a tumultuous year of breaking up, taking 'breaks', and getting back together. He never officially dumped me; I was just systematically uninvited to family events. Christmas at his dad's house was the first to go. Then the upcoming weddings of siblings I had spent the best part of my 20s getting to know. These weren't a hi-n-bye level of relationship either; these people were my family and suddenly they were just gone. No, they were fine – I was gone. I couldn't even tell you when our relationship was over because I feel as though I was the last to know.

Having given up our flat, I moved back into my childhood home. Mum was spending half the year in Toronto to be with her centurion mother, and Dad was still working in the UAE. I was back in the tiny bedroom I chose at four years of age because it had musty pink wallpaper on the walls. My brother had lived right across the hall from me my whole adolescence. I would listen to him chuckle to himself as he watched TV before bed each night. I loved that sound. Being in this large house on an acre block in the suburbs now felt so quiet. I never heard myself laugh. I would binge-watch hours of *New Girl*, *Unbreakable Kimmy Schmidt* and *Crazy Ex-Girlfriend* (which was rudely relatable) in the hope that I could emulate my brother's laughter to *South Park* or *The Simpsons*. Instead, I just stared blankly into the screen, willing it to suck me into another world. Sometimes I would catch the sadness on my face in the reflection of my laptop and just cry.

The house that was so full of life, love and people throughout my adolescence was now an old empty building disintegrating around me. The only thing with a heartbeat in there anymore was me, and it was taunting. The constant thumping in my chest was a reminder of how I had destroyed the only thing that truly mattered to me: love.

By January 2016, I was still under the illusion that I was in a relationship. A fractured relationship, sure, but *my* fractured relationship. Simon and I drove over two hours to a remote country town outside Melbourne to mend the gaping wound between us. We sought couples' counselling from a kind-hearted hippy woman, Susan, who I'd met at the cancer retreat. Both Sam and I had seen her for counselling, meditation or miscellaneous healing sessions over the subsequent years and felt a strong affinity with her. Even Simon, who was reluctant to open up to anyone, felt comfortable confiding in her about his mother's death. Perhaps it was because she shared his mother's name and was similarly patient and warm-hearted. I was hopeful the woman who called herself a healer could revive our very sick relationship.

I spent all morning primping and preening, knowing I had the opportunity to spend several hours alone in a car with Simon. I ensured I was primed in that effortlessly beautiful way that actually takes hours of preparation. I hoped that all the reasons he no longer loved me could be swept away with a good hair day and fresh Kylie Jenner lip kit. He said nothing; I felt pathetic. We didn't speak for the entire drive, and I came to understand how silence can be truly deafening. Within the quiet of that car were all the answers we weren't yet ready to admit to ourselves or each other. He couldn't tell me it was over, and I would have been unreceptive had he tried.

I was desperate for his love to the point of humiliation. This would become obvious over the course of the next few hours as Sue dug deep into our relationship. My infidelity. His lack of emotional expression. My toxic lashing-out. His neglect. My clawing need for his attention. His neutrality towards me. My rage at him for not loving me. His guilt about it.

At one point, Simon revealed that the reason he didn't talk to me anymore was that I would get too upset. I was upset. Almost seven years of our lives together, *gone*. It was upsetting. Why wasn't he upset? He had mastered the art of suppressing his pain to the point where anyone else's was uncomfortable and unwelcome. We were two ends of the emotional spectrum. He sat next to me like a stone while I vibrated with rage, jealousy and fear, ready to boil over at any moment. I wanted to shake a reaction out of him. Pry a single tear from his starkly dry face, even if I had to peel his eyelids open and take it for myself. Feel something!

The three of us sat in Sue's sun room, looking out onto a dry paddock with one solitary grazing horse. I wondered if the horse got lonely out there but pushed the thought aside, realising I didn't have any room left to carry his sadness, too. It was summer, so the Sun slanted in through the large glass window, highlighting my own darkness. Sue had prepared camomile tea to calm our nerves. Simon thought this was wonderful. I thought it was fucking pointless. I was already dosed up on lethal amounts of oxy, and that barely touched the sides anymore. I hugged the warm mug in my shaky hands and smelled the earthy, sweet camomile. *Ergh. Who likes this shit?* I gulped it down anyway, desperate for its herbal magic.

After listening to us debate the quality of our relationship for two and a half hours, she said the words that made me despise her. 'Your relationship is toxic. You need to grow apart.' *Fuck you!* 'Perhaps you will come together again in the future, five years or so down the track, when you are different people. But, right now, this is causing too much damage.' *I hate you.* I began to sob. *Why did she put a timeframe on it?*

I witnessed the wave of relief course through Simon as I felt my entire body get hot and prickly. I wanted to rip my skin off like a scratchy woollen jumper, but instead, I sobbed uncontrollably, unable to catch my breath. I knew how my desperate brain would interpret her words. Now that she had voiced this arbitrary number, I would obsessively hold onto that with hope, prolonging my own suffering for the next five years. *What have you done, you stupid hippy bitch?*

There, gazing out at Sue's picturesque view, I had a panic attack. I was sobbing, hyperventilating and gulping for air. My chest hurt. It was as though my soul was trying to rip free of my body. I could feel the heartbreak. Sue turned to Simon and said in a patronisingly calm tone, 'Is this what you mean?' He nodded solemnly. That's when I realised that for them, I was the problem. It wasn't *us* that was toxic. It was *me*. Simon was the long-suffering partner who had borne the burden of me for far too long. They both knew it; they were just waiting for me to catch up.

I thought back to myself as an eight-year-old, to a time when I confided in my teacher that my two best 'friends' were bullying me. The three of us were called into the teacher's office to discuss what had been going on. As I tried to explain how the girls had been teasing and excluding me, my voice shook and I began to cry. I was annoyed at myself for showing weakness, knowing it would only fuel the fire. I reached for a tissue and it ripped as I pulled it out of the box. I tried again and the same thing happened. *Cheap-arse one-ply tissues.* The girls began to laugh openly at my struggle. I looked to the teacher for support but caught him smirking along with the girls. 'Is this the kind of bullying you mean?' he remarked, trivialising my genuine concerns. *No, Sir, I'm not upset about a fucking tissue. I'm upset that my 'friends' are laughing at, and adding to, my distress. I'm upset that you, as my teacher and protector, don't seem to understand that, and I'm frustrated because when I have been strong enough to fight for myself and stand my ground, I am told I am 'too sensitive' and 'can't take a joke'.* But I was eight, so I just looked at my feet in shame.

At 27, things weren't much better. Once again, I was left to feel as though my emotions were extreme and invalid. My school friends, my teacher, Simon and Sue were right. I was wrong. Maybe I am crazy. Maybe I do feel too much. How would I know? Or maybe my heart was breaking in so many directions that I didn't know what to do.

Having met with Sue a handful of times, this would be our final session. It was clear to all, except my denial, that it was over. I had been hopelessly invested in our therapy. I scribbled in my notebook each session, studying our love like it meant something. Like I could learn all the right answers and put us back together. Simon was less enthusiastic about the future of our relationship, and the coming weeks would show me why – he was already in another one. Just like his dismal attempt to support me in Sam's final days, these sessions were not an indication that he was standing by me; these were attempts to placate and pacify me while he moved on with someone else.

Elizabeth. Say it with me: E-Li-Za-Beth. Lizzy. Liza. Beth. Betty. Bitcharseslutarsewhore! Ugh, who cares what she goes by – she's not me. She's blonde, because of course she is. Straight hair, too. You never have to worry about getting tangled in her mess of curls. Light, creamy skin. No blotches of fake tan around her wrists or adult acne around her chin. I wonder if she's younger than me? Or older? I'm not sure which is worse. She's thinner, so I guess she wins. She's unlikely to be clinically insane, either, because she works for a fucking children's charity. *Well, good for you, Lizzy. You're a great person and I'm a psycho, junkie bitch. We get it!* It was at that point of pettiness I realised how deep down the spiral I had fallen. I mentally took a step back from Facebook-stalking to think, *She looks happy. She looks like a nice, normal Aussie girl, who won over my boyfriend with her talent for happiness, and for that, she deserves to die.*

Mum was my lifeline and would answer the phone at the drop of a hat. I would call her at all hours, hyperventilating down the phone line as she tried her best to calm me down at 3 am Canadian time. She reminded me how loved I was and that, despite the distance, I was not alone. Dad and I were still talking weekly. Every Thursday afternoon, he would call me without fail. He, who had fluctuated from driving me insane to inspiring me with his genius, was now (the only person) showing me that others had felt this level of despair and it was possible to survive it. Others would poorly hide their expressions of concern, confirming my suspicions that I had crossed over into 'unhinged' territory. But not Dad – Dad got it.

I found out about Simon and his new gal pal from a cheery little Facebook post of the two of them together. I was never able to call her his girlfriend; I was his girlfriend – my brain never quite made the jump. Simon had long since blocked me on account of my regular drunken rage blackouts, where I would tag all of his photos with descriptive genital terms. However, on this day, a concerned friend thought it would be helpful for me to see how well he was doing without the old ball 'n' chain and sent through some screenshots of his page. 'It's better you hear it from me. Soz, Sweetie! Hugzzz. xoxo' Those were the last words I read before I turned into a homicidal maniac.

I opened my phone to find a montage of photo booth shots. You know, the ones that were cute back in the 90s when teen rom-coms depicted 'true love' by strategically placing one of those rolls of film on Jennifer Love-Hewitt's mirror? There it was in black and white: confirmation that he was happier without me. He'd never done a cute photoshoot with me. Maybe she brings out the fun side in him. Does he even have a fun side? I'm a goddamn laugh a minute! Why didn't I get 'fun Simon'? How dare they be happy when I'm crawling out of my skin with grief? I think that's one of the cruellest things about a breakup: someone will always be happy again first. It had been two months since the death of my best friend and only weeks since her funeral, yet here he was, flaunting his happiness online. *He sat next to me at Sam's funeral, holding my hand. Was he with her then?* I have never hated anyone more.

I called Mum in Canada at the sight of the new couple's smiling faces. When she answered, I was crying so hysterically that it took several attempts of me screaming, 'HE HAS REPLACED ME!' down the phone line before she finally understood what I was trying to say. I couldn't breathe – it was another panic attack. By now, they were happening multiple times a day. Even at uni, I would have to sneak away to the disabled toilets to sob my heart out on the floor, trying not to faint from lack of oxygen. I would hold my hands tightly over my mouth, run the taps and flush the toilet so that no one could hear the sound of my heart breaking.

My shaky hands would open an oxy and rack out a line or two, which I would inhale with a sigh of relief. *Please help me*, I'd beg the thin white lines. Then, after a few minutes, I would stand up, straighten out my crisp white lab coat and go back to treating patients for their irritable bowel syndrome and psoriasis.

I cried so much I didn't even know where the tears were coming from. I was sure I would dehydrate from a lack of fluid. The breaking of my heart was a physical searing in my chest and convulsive gripping in my gut. I felt like I was dying – like I was terminally ill – but there was no disease to treat or broken bone to mend.

Mum stayed on the phone while I used the landline to call my psychiatrist. He organised a bed for me at the psychiatric hospital for the following day. We arranged for my brother to come and stay with me for the night so I wouldn't be alone. My psych sent the CAT (Crisis Assessment and Treatment) team to my house to assess how likely I was to kill myself. Answer: very. I wanted my parents. I wanted Simon to tell me it was all a misunderstanding and he was coming back. I wanted Sam to show up on my doorstep with magazines and peanut M&M's, making it okay. I wanted any part of my life to be recognisable again.

When the CAT team arrived, they started asking me questions about my past. They were particularly interested in my history with anorexia; the recovery rates for people with severe eating disorders are so low that the fact I was able to recover displayed a certain level of strength. I didn't feel strong; I felt like a shell of a person, but maybe they were right. Overcoming anorexia had felt like an impossible task, but somehow, I'd made it. Could this be the same? I had no idea, but seeing as no one was going to let me kill myself today, I had no option but to believe.

They then started to talk to me about where I would be staying. They offered me a room at a public residence and gave me the address – which sounded familiar. I confirmed the location on Google Earth only to have my horrifying suspicions confirmed. In typical disaster movie fashion, the facility was directly in view of Simon's house. I don't mean down the street and around the corner. I'm saying I could see his bedroom window from the ward. *What in the actual demonic bullshit is that?* What if I'm sitting in bloody art therapy doing some docile finger painting, and I turn around to see his new girl pull up outside his house for date night? Am I just supposed to sit here and not commit double homicide? *WHAT DO YOU MEAN?* 'Dear God, um yeah, hi, it's me. I was just wondering, WHAT IS YOUR TRAUMA? Sincerely, Kirsty.'

To protect myself from a murderous rampage, I decided to forgo the free public residence available within my jurisdiction and instead spend all my savings on a private hospital stay a few suburbs away. Here I was, asking for help, and it was as though the universe itself was laughing at me. 'How far can we push her before she snaps?' *I've snapped. Jesus, I concede!* I was no longer just being tested; I was being baited. 'Kill yourself, kill yourself, kill yourself,' the universe whispered maniacally. These words rang on repeat in my head for months on end. Sometimes I'd even whack myself on the head in an attempt to dislodge the words, like someone you'd see lurking around North Richmond station. But nothing worked. They were here to stay. *I want to,* I'd reply.

Within 24 hours of calling Mum, she was on a plane home from Toronto, and I was setting up in a psych ward a safe distance from Simon's place. I looked at my small, lonely hospital bed and imagined Simon being held lovingly in his king-sized bed; a warm body next to him, protecting him from feeling this hell. The sense of injustice transformed my despair into an adrenaline-fuelled rage. I had lost everything. Every. Fucking. Thing.

> The last six months had been a storm of shit so powerful that when asked how I was coping, I would have to pick and choose which tragic events were significant and which the masses could do without. For example, my general reply might include the loss of Sam, followed rapidly by the breakup. These were the big hitters, but a concurrent shitstorm would kick me to my knees every time I attempted to stand. This is what had me convinced I was Kirst. Sorry no, that should be *cursed*.
>
> For instance, my childhood cocker spaniel, Yoda, needed to be put down. He was elderly, in pain and could no longer walk. This is

a devastating event on its own, but compared to watching your favourite person deteriorate and die, then getting your arse dumped weeks later, it pales. I sang gently to him as he was given the lethal injection and slipped away from us.

To fill the space of Yoda's little footsteps through the house, I'd adopted two rescue kittens, Kiisu and Meemo. They would sleep snuggled up on either side of my neck and remind me I was loved. They served as a tremendous aid in getting me up in the morning. Even if I did nothing else with my day, I knew that I needed to feed those furry munchkins twice a day without fail. They gave me purpose and a glimpse of joy. These kittens were the only thing keeping me going – until Kiisu disappeared.

I waited, hoping she had gone out hunting for mice or skinks and would eventually come back, but days passed without a sign of her. Two weeks later, I would start to smell the very distinct stench of rotting kitty from beneath the house. Later still, a handyman would find her and proudly remark how he had just found the biggest dead rat he'd ever seen. I laughed in horror because I didn't know what else to do. It was like I had acquired the world's worst superpower, and everything I touched turned to dead.

It didn't end there; my grief was complex, incessant and seeped into every aspect of my life. I continued to get angrier and more erratic, unable to separate my pain from my work, studies and friendships. I couldn't relate to anyone around me anymore – these enthusiastic, active people who cared about things like health, climate change and social justice. I couldn't care for myself, let alone the whole fucking planet! It seemed elitist and privileged even to be capable of caring. I was angry at them for having free space in their minds and hearts for others *over there* when I was drowning in front of them. *What about me? Help me*.

I had been given a coveted position at a yoga studio and was desperate to make a good impression, but I was a wreck. I would drive to work, smoking out the window and sobbing uncontrollably the entire way. I wished I had windscreen wipers on my eyes to help me see the road as I drove. I could no longer listen to music – sad music broke my heart, and happy music mocked me. It would be four whole years before I could listen to music again. When I got to work, I would quickly snort a line and take a few slugs of leftover wine that was still in the fridge from the Christmas party. Then I would chew down some mints – a pathetic attempt at masking the smell of booze and cigarettes – and splash cold water on my face, followed by a little concealer, then practise smiling a few times in the mirror. *It's show time!* I don't know if you have ever attempted to stand on one leg while drunk and high, but the fact it took me several months to get fired is a testament to my balancing act. Truthfully, I was relieved to be let go. Can't pour from an empty cup 'n' all that hippy shit. So, as an act of goodwill, I kept that cup full to the brim … with double vodka crans.

In an effort to heal, I organised to see a new psychologist. I was on my way to our initial session, hopeful that someone new might save me. I had just been to a meditation class and was feeling about as centred as possible. To get to the appointment, I had to drive past both Simon's and Sam's streets, which gave me intense anxiety. I tried to breathe through it, holding onto the remnants of calm from the class. *Inhale calm. Exhale stress. Inhale calm. Exhale stress. InhUUUUUUCK!* I slammed on the brakes as my wheels screeched violently against the road. The airbags slapped me in the face as the car came to a dead halt. I looked out of my left side window to see that a blue sedan had T-boned my little Suzuki Swift – 'The poor man's mini,' Sam used to tease.

I quickly assessed whether I was dead and realised, disappointingly, I was not. *Why?* It didn't make sense to dangle death right in front of my nose like that and not commit. *Just do it!* When the ambulance and police arrived, I was trapped in my car, screaming at the top of my lungs. It was like I was trying to exorcise a demon that had latched onto me and wouldn't let go. I screamed because I was alone in the world. I screamed because I was alive. I screamed because I felt like a goddamn puppet. And I screamed because even my fucking depression kitten died. I just fucking screamed. You know that scene in *Ozark* where Ruth realises she has nothing left to lose and ends up screaming at the top of her lungs, 'If you wanna stop me, you're gonna have to fuckin' KILL MEEEE!' I found comfort in that. It made me feel seen.

My car was rubble, but I was unharmed, and the ambos kept asking, 'Who can we call to come and get you?' They asked me over and over again as I cried, 'No one! I have no one!' The police wouldn't take me home because I lived out of their district, but they felt sorry enough for me to try and flag down a taxi. After 20 minutes of failed attempts, they asked me to book an Uber. The driver tried to make small talk but I couldn't hear him. I stared numbly out the window, listening to the blood pulsating between my ears.

A week later, when I was able to get to my psych, I asked her in earnest if this life was nothing but a cruel joke, or perhaps I had died and this was Hell. I wanted answers for why things had taken such a dark turn with no sign of relief. I needed to know if I would be given a chance to heal or if suffering would keep coming.

She replied, 'Unfortunately, there is no finite amount of suffering a person can experience. We like to tell ourselves things like "bad things come in threes", or "everything happens for a reason", but the truth is that life is mostly random. Some people will experience a lot of suffering and others travel through life without much at all.'

Within a year, I had lost my relationship, my Sam, my home, my job, my dog, my kitten, my car, my sanity, and, to top it off, my album launch, which had a decent turnout, brought no career reward. I had nothing, and when you have nothing left, nothing matters. When you don't value life, you can do anything because the consequences don't bother you. I was hopeless, but I was free. Free to look crazy, to be violent, to take the pain away in any self-destructive way I needed because what's the worst that can happen? I die? Ha! Who gives a flying fuck? If my life was going up in flames, I was taking the world with me.

Stage direction: *Pulls hoodie over head and stares down the barrel of the camera, a la Elizabeth Moss at the end of every episode of The Handmaid's Tale.*

Bring it.

A fucked-up holiday

Soundtrack: *Lana Del Ray – 'Gods & Monsters'*

Psychiatric hospitals are curious places. This particular one was a smallish, private facility starting from $2500 a week, so it was the top in town. I found the price disturbing, considering it was old, dark and quite sterile. The musty aqua walls were reminiscent of something you might find at a swimming pool in the '80s. I wasn't expecting much, but to me, it was a regular hospital, only smaller, with gnarly old carpet that might have been blue once upon a time. There were a couple of private rooms, but most patients shared two or four-bed dorms. I was guided to a two-bedroom by a tired, wiry nurse with a stern face. Thankfully my roommate wasn't arriving until the next day, meaning I could settle in without someone's polite attempts at small talk. I wondered what to expect from my roomie as I ran through the characters from *Girl, Interrupted* in my head.

Upon arrival, I was asked to hand over any cords or laces I had brought with me – anything I could potentially hang myself with. I can honestly say I had never thought about hanging myself with a shoelace until that moment and didn't find it at all practical. All technology was labelled, and phones or laptops were charged under watch at the nurses' station. I will never forget returning to uni weeks later and being praised for having a sticker of my name and phone number stuck to the front of my laptop. 'See everyone,' the supervisor announced to the final-year nutritionists. 'Kirsten has labelled her laptop, so there is no chance of it getting mixed up with anyone else's. Good job, Kirsten.' I smirked and thanked the supervisor, knowing there was no chance I would be praised for my organisational skills again.

Sharp objects were not permitted, so no shaving or manicures for me. That was fine; I had already gone to seed months back. Finally, we handed over our medication to be distributed at dedicated intervals. I enjoyed handing over my entire life to other people who would tell me when to wash, eat, sleep and take my meds. The simplicity was important.

Ben had driven me to the hospital. He stayed as they checked me in and asked questions about why I had come. I remember groggily answering as if I were a corpse having my jaw controlled by someone else. Kinda like if *Weekend at Bernie's* were a true story (which, can we just acknowledge for a second, is a horrifying concept). I remember having to answer vulnerable questions in front of my brother. I felt the familiar prickle of shame searing my cheeks. I didn't want him to hear me confirm all of his fears.

'Are you a smoker?' asked the intake nurse.

'Err, yeah, I guess. Just the last two years.' I felt ridiculous. Who picks up smoking in their late 20s?

'And why do you smoke?'

'What?' I glanced at Ben as I chewed at my ragged cuticles. My nails were painted beautifully. They had tiny little flowers on them, a remnant of the Fijian wedding Simon and I were supposed to attend together. Although he had pulled out to avoid sharing a room with me, I decided to go alone – a misguided attempt at being a strong independent woman. Big mistake. *Huge.* The torrential rain meant everyone hid in their rooms. So, I stayed in the double bed that was meant for *us,* getting drunk, crying hysterically, taking oxy and sending Simon abusive texts until the picturesque holiday was over.

'Sorry, why do you need to know that?' I asked the nurse.

'It just helps us understand you and how we can help.'

'Oh.' I took a moment to literally swallow the last of my pride. 'Okay, well, I smoke because I want to die, but seemingly no one will let me kill myself. So, I smoke so at least my life won't last too long.'

'Okay, thank you,' replied the nurse.

Ben's eyes were glassy with tears. The boy we joked about having two emotions – contentment and slightly annoyed – was hurting because of me. *I'm the worst person in the world.*

Once Ben left, I sobbed silently into my pillow, not wanting to alert the nurses to my distress. They would only try to comfort me, a futile task. How could I look a nurse in the eye and tell them, straight-faced, that I had been set off by a box of tissues? The brand name was *Scott* – Simon's last name. They would look at me like I was insane. Which I clearly was. I wanted to hurl the box all the way across the room, but I couldn't because tissues were the one thing I actually needed: one single, useless ply attempting to soak up the tsunami of mess that was me.

By day two, my roommate had arrived. I automatically felt the need to play hostess and appear saner than I was. It reminded me of visiting Grandma at her nursing home in Canada. The woman was a billion years old, yet without fail, would offer us her liquidised lunch of pureed salmon, mashed potatoes and mushy peas, just so we didn't feel left out. I'd occasionally joke with her, 'Maybe I'll be as old as you one day!' and she'd reply, chillingly, 'I hope not …' *Girl, same.*

My roomie was a middle-aged woman with a kind face and gentle persona. She had been dropped off by her lovely, supportive husband, which gave me a pang of jealousy. She seemed too stable to be here. Later, she would inform me she suffered from Major Depressive Disorder and PTSD. So at quarterly intervals, she came to the hospital to get transcranial magnetic stimulation (TMS), a type of magnetic vibration to the brain for the treatment of mental illness. This was a top-up. I felt even more pressure not to sob loudly after that. That night, we fell asleep in our respective beds with nothing but flimsy, teal curtains between us. I cried silently in the dark and was eventually rewarded with rest.

All of a sudden, I was woken by her piercing screams. It was still dark. I froze, trying to work out what was happening. The woman next to me was sobbing uncontrollably, but between cries, I could make out, 'No, please don't! Get off me! Get off me!'

I tried to talk to her from my bed, to wake her up, 'You're okay, you're having a nightmare. You're at the hospital.' I lay frozen in my bed, just as I had done when I was a scared little kid hearing a bump in the night. I didn't want to approach her if she was having a flashback. Her screams were so visceral that I started to worry someone might actually be there with her.

'Get away! I'm only seven! I'm only seven!' she continued.

Fuck, okay. Get up, Kirsty. Move. I convinced my legs to move and hurried to get the night nurse. It must have been 2 am. He sat by her bedside and woke her gently. She was still in her nightmare as they spoke, 'You're having a flashback. You're safe. There is no one here.'

'He ran off! You need to find him. He's still here!' she cried. 'There are other young women here. You need to keep him away from them. Kirsten? Is Kirsten okay?'

Behind my curtain, I was holding my hand over my mouth, trying not to let my panicked breath worry her. 'I'm okay. I'm fine. It's all okay. I'm right here.' I made my best impression of someone who is anywhere but a fucking psych ward frozen in horror.

'Are you sure?' she asked the nurse. 'Did you check the bathrooms?' The nurse sat by her bedside, reassuring and soothing her until she fell asleep. I lay awake the rest of the night, shaken and devastated for that poor little girl.

It was 5 pm the next day and dinner time before I could drag my heavy body out of bed. I didn't change from my pyjamas, but looking around the small, aged cafeteria, it seemed to be the dress code. Here we all were: a group of dangerously sad and messed up people, chatting and acting normal in our PJs. Pretending that each of our individual lives had not left us on our knees, praying for mercy. I wasn't the only person confused by this. From the hallway, I could hear a new arrival crying and yelling, 'They're all laughing. They're all talking and having fun!' She was right: it was fucking weird. But as I took my tray of scalloped potatoes and broiled chicken breast, then sidled up to the only semi-attractive boy in the joint, I realised we were all doing the same thing. Looking for a distraction from the pain of being buried alive by our misery.

Some people say they feel numb when they are depressed. I imagine I looked numb on the outside. My eyes were dead, my face expressionless, but I wasn't numb. I *dreamed* of numbness. Inside, it felt like all of my cells had a heartbeat, and each one of those tiny little hearts was breaking. My body didn't know how to express my agony effectively, so it gave up trying. It's no coincidence that a girl like me, broken-hearted and in need of saving, attracts an equally broken boy within days of arrival. Boy meets girl. Girl needs to feel as though she is worthy of love. Boy needs to feel that he isn't the useless piece of shit he grew up believing he was. Ta-dah! A love match is formed. It's the perfect combination, made in co-dependent fucked-up heaven.

In the evenings, those interested would gather in the common room and put on a movie. The boy, who I had come to know as Evan, remembered they had *Requiem for a Dream* from his previous stay. They had a random collection of DVDs I can only assume were handed down from the staff or picked up from local op shops over the years. Between *Babe: Pig in the City* and *Requiem*, Jared Leto won out. Days earlier, I had been on the phone confessing to Mum (still in Canada) that my drug and alcohol abuse had gotten out of control, and now I was watching Ellen Burstyn spiral out in a way that was terrifyingly relatable while my new saviour and I snuggled under an old brown blanket on the scratchy carpet of a psychiatric facility.

Later, the stern nurse would come to my bed while I watched *The Real Housewives of Atlanta* on my laptop. She asked me if I thought it was a good idea to be leaning so heavily on Evan. *Yes, obviously.*

'Isn't that what got you into this mess?' she said, trying not to sound condescending and failing miserably.

I stared at her. *No, it's completely different. Everyone else left me! But Evan is trapped here; he can't leave me!* I was embarrassed and annoyed. How dare she shame me for trying to hide from my pain. Besides, Simon was doing it, too. He couldn't be alone. He was just fortunate enough to find someone to hang out with outside of hospital confines. Some people have all the luck.

A month after leaving the facility, I learned that Evan was engaged to a woman he had just met. Rather than being surprised, I understood. At the end of the day, he, too, just wanted to be saved.

The people I met during my week as an inpatient were wonderful. They were people of gentle hearts and poetic souls, people who tried TMS in the hope of finding something liveable on the other side. We didn't dare pursue something as intangible as happiness. Instead, we merely desired contentment. They are people whose mental health conditions made them outcasts to the masses but who also resonated with me more than anyone I'd ever met 'out there'. They were kind because they knew how incredibly cruel life could be.

There was a man in the ward who I would be unlikely to meet out in the wild. He was over six feet tall and a heavy-set guy. He wore thick coke-bottle glasses and walked with a hunch from back problems. He leaned heavily on a walking stick when he was forced to move, which was seldom due to his terrible pain. 'Bone grating on bone,' he would say. Years back, he'd had a spinal injury that never healed properly, and he had become addicted to the painkillers. He needed them desperately, but he also suffered from severe depression. The combination was devastating. He was in his 30s but looked decades older. Despite his suffering, he was always the first to offer someone else a seat or cuppa. Often, we would sit around smoking cigarettes and playing music from someone's phone. He always kept track of whose song choice was next so that no one missed out. I still smile when I listen to *Gods and Monsters* by Lana Del Ray, a favourite of us both. He taught me that it is possible to be compassionate, regardless of how bad your own suffering is.

During our tri-daily window of prescription relief, we would line up like drug-fucked zombies waiting to feed. Shuffling forward in pyjamas and slippers, I would try to hide just how much every limb of my body wanted to move and twitch from premature withdrawals.

My skin felt itchy with anticipation for that small paper cup filled with two rattling parcels of encapsulated bliss. I'd watch the nurse fumble for the key dangling from the fob on her neck and become irrationally frustrated. I would fantasise about breaking into the vault and wonder how many boxes I could grab before I was thrown into the rumoured padded room.

Oh my fuck, how long does it take to get some pills? How hard is it, Janice? Take key. Open latch. Count remaining pills. Place in cup. Check patient ID. Hand cup to me! SIMPLE.

Every time, I felt like I was about to break down and have a full-blown toddler tantrum on the floor. Within the safety of my mind, I would become increasingly belligerent. *Nobody else has to wait this long. It's not fair. They are punishing me coz they think I'm an addict. Fuck! Just give me the fucking …* 'Oh, thank you.' I would smile extra brightly so they didn't notice I was squirrelling my oxy away in my cheek like a clever chipmunk hoarding for the winter. Only I was just hoarding until I could escape to the bathroom three feet away. I wasn't about to waste my precious oxy on a monitored gulp in front of a nosey nurse. I needed privacy. I needed ritual. I needed a fucking line.

Alone in the bathroom, I would spit the capsules into my hand. They would have softened from the sip of water I'd used while pretending to swallow. This meant the two halves of the capsule casing were now glued together, making them harder to open. Harder to open meant more risk of getting caught and, worse, more risk of spillage. I had to be careful not to waste this moment worrying. I needed to keep calm and enjoy my process. Put *that* on a tote bag: *Keep Calm & Rack a Line.* I found I could lightly bite the end of the capsule, creating a miniature lid. From there, I would pour out the life-saving white powder onto my phone screen. This was the cleanest shit you've ever seen or breathed into your body. There was no pain or burning like street drugs. Just pure sweet heaven. I piled up two nice, even lines and took out the five-dollar bill I kept just for this occasion. I smiled softly in anticipation. This was how it was supposed to be taken. Now I could relax. Now I would be okay, and for a few minutes, I wouldn't wish I was dead. For a few minutes, I had something to live for.

There's a starman waiting in the sky

Soundtrack: *David Bowie – 'Starman'*

Mum arrived home from Toronto. When she got to the hospital, she found me yelling profanities at my psychiatrist. 'How can you think about sending me home? I just told you how I'm going to fucking off myself! What is wrong with you? I want another psych. Can I get another psych or what?' He wanted to send me home on the proviso that Mum could be on suicide watch. I didn't want to leave and was furious at the suggestion. *Does he think I'm okay? Is this what 'okay' looks like?* In the hospital, I felt the same all-consuming heartache I did on the outside, but I knew I was safe. I knew I wouldn't die here, and I couldn't be sure of that anywhere else.

His advice felt like another rejection. I couldn't keep a man, I didn't have any friends, and now I was being asked to leave the hospital that I had paid the best part of three grand to put up with me. Was I that bad? I couldn't be the worst person they've had through these doors. I was being treated like an unruly teen on *Dr Phil*. Well, in that case, 'Cash me outside, how bou' dat' I stayed for a few more days, mostly out of spite, before finally heading home.

Mum's return had disrupted several plans. She had been in Toronto to spend time with her mum, who, being 101, she was unlikely to see again. If she was torn about which terminal patient to choose, she hid it well. I would've loved to have been big enough to tell her to stay and be with her elderly mother, but the truth is I needed her more than I've ever needed anyone.

My parents had also arranged their first-ever holiday, sans kids, in 30 years. Dad had handed in his resignation from his job in the UAE because he felt the work environment was driven by threats and manipulation. So the 'rents had decided to meet up in Portugal for a two-week adventure before Dad returned to Melbourne.

When I got sick, Mum came home, leaving Dad to holiday alone. This wasn't unusual for them. In fact, my parents travelled alone so often that my grandma would continually ask Mum how her 'ex-husband' Philip was. 'Such a kind man. He still visits me despite your divorce.' To which Mum would reply and remind her that they were still together, and she was just fiercely independent and didn't feel the need to follow her husband everywhere he went. Grandma did not believe her.

I emailed Dad from the hospital to let him know where I was. Despite his own battles with bipolar, I had no idea how he would respond to my being in a psych ward. He simply replied, 'If you had a broken bone, you would be in hospital treating that, wouldn't you? I see no difference. Stay as long as you need, K. Rest up.'

When I arrived home, I was still a wreck, but I had Mum, and that alone was nothing short of life-saving. Between myself, Mum and one remaining feline, there was life in the house again.

Mum would try to distract me by playing TV programs I used to enjoy. I realised I would have to rediscover an entirely new set of interests because the music and TV shows of my past were now tainted. I stopped listening to music entirely. I couldn't even watch *MasterChef* without bursting into tears, remembering Simon making his daft impressions of George Calombaris: 'It's just so ... *searches for word, searches for word* yummy.' Have you ever watched an amateur chef plate up slow-cooked beef cheeks with cauliflower puree and started to cry? Or heard Ke$ha on the radio singing about brushing her teeth with 'a bottle of Jack' and wanted to die? Because I have. A lot.

I had asked Mum to help me with my rampant pill addiction by giving her control of my pain medication. Opioid addiction is tricky because you genuinely need the drug for your pain but have zero control once it's in your possession. Imagine if an alcoholic broke their leg, and the cure was to drink one sip of alcohol four times a day until it healed. Yeah, not gonna work. The other quirk of opioids is that they are incredibly effective in the short term, but long-term use can actually increase pain. Your body becomes so reliant on the drug that it begins to create pain and sensitivities in order to encourage you to take more. An addiction specialist framed it to me like this, 'When you are dehydrated, it's not one part of your body that is thirsty; every cell of your body is signalling to your brain that you need water. For the rest of your life, your entire body will crave this drug like water.' *Oh good.*

My brain, heart and body would all call for the pills. Crazed, I would scrounge through Mum's drawers and pockets of her clothing to find her ever-changing hiding spots. I watched myself sneak around and felt disgusting, but I knew as soon as that pill was in my system, all my guilt would melt away. This was when I started to *really* feel like a junkie, but by then, I was in too deep and wouldn't have known how to stop had I wanted to – which I didn't. I would have happily let those pills kill me. Even writing this now, my chest is warm and my mouth is salivating for one more taste. It was different to anorexia because I desperately wanted that to end. This addiction felt like my only saving grace.

Since arriving home from the hospital, I hadn't heard from Dad. He had missed his usual call for suicide watch, but Mum and I agreed he was probably having too much fun in Portugal and wasn't thinking about his phone. This was a man who only got a mobile under duress for work and barely knew how to use it. He was neither reliable with keeping his technology charged nor checking for Wi-Fi at hotels. In fact, he loved being off the grid.

Two weeks passed without hearing anything. He hadn't emailed, called or been in touch with anyone else in the family. I had a low-grade sense of dread, and I could see Mum, too, was beginning to worry, which concerned me even more. I had hoped my grief was making me paranoid and her comfort would reassure me. Then the call came.

I had been out for the evening and came home to find Mum talking quietly on the phone. It reminded me of being a kid and overhearing adults talking in that low, hushed tone that alerted you to something serious. Mum hung up the phone and let me know the person on the other end would be calling back soon with news. She looked at me, concerned but not crying. *Mum cries at everything,* I thought. *That's good. That's a good sign.*

'Dad was meant to go back to work yesterday. He never showed. That was his colleague checking to see if we had heard from him.' Although Dad had handed in his resignation, he still had loose ends to tie up before he returned home. 'They are sending someone to his apartment to check on him,' she continued. I cuddled up to Mum on the sofa; we held each other. A few tense minutes later, the phone rang. We held our breath for the possibility of life-altering news. I couldn't hear the person on the other end, but I read the entire conversation on Mum's face: listening attentively, shock, trying not to cry, tears and heartbreak, before ending the call. Watching her restrained tableau, I understood my dad was dead.

My father was found in his bed, his suitcases packed for his morning flight to Portugal, which he had never made. We would learn of the taxi arriving to take him to the airport, the driver honking the horn and banging on the door. No answer. He drove off. Dad never made it to Portugal, meaning my wonderful, brilliant, strange and fascinating father was dead for two weeks before anyone went looking for him. How does that happen? He is suspected of having died the night before the holiday but, being unable to know for certain, his death certificate was 'round-abouted'. An entire life of nearly 60 years on this rotating rock and his final moments were an estimate.

There's a lot of confusion surrounding the details of my dad's death. We were told he had a heart attack, which would be easy enough to explain by his epilepsy and stressful workload. But I'm not convinced. The number of conversations we had about his toxic work environment, how he didn't trust his boss, and how Dad was the only one privy to certain important issues makes me uneasy. The company didn't want Dad to leave – he knew too much, and they still required his services – but he'd had enough of the bullying and corruption and wanted nothing more to do with it. He wanted out. Looking back on our conversations, I do think he was nervous about leaving. I wish I could remember the specifics of our conversations that make me feel so sure something was wrong, but I had just been diagnosed with bipolar disorder, and my head was a wreck with grief.

I wasn't alone in my concerns. There were heated discussions around the dinner table between my paternal aunt and grandfather, who, like me, were worried there could have been a motive to 'get rid' of Dad. These were generally shot down by Mum rather quickly, probably because she didn't want Ben or me to think about anything untoward, and I'm sure as a form of self-preservation. I understand that need. I want to believe it was a heart attack – a swift, quick heart attack with minimal pain. I need to believe that because the alternative makes me sick.

Years later, while cleaning the kitchen together, I would ask Mum, 'Do you think something bad happened to Dad?'

I fully expected her to be offended and blow me off, but instead, she took a deep breath, a long pause, and said, 'Maybe.' She told me that in the months following Dad's death, she had found copies of emails to his employment agent that began, 'If anything happens to me, please make sure my wife gets everything.' Was Dad being paranoid or responsible? It was generally a fine line with him.

Losing three of the closest people to me in the space of six months bore a deeply complex grief. Like hundred-year-old tree roots, it weaves and winds from one loss to the next. I cannot grieve my father with love in my heart without a flood of rage rushing through me, recalling Simon's betrayal. I can't retrieve a happy memory of Sam without feeling the hole my father left behind. I carry guilt for being unable to grieve my beloved pets and elderly grandma, who passed away only a few months later, because I had reached full saturation by that stage. Even now, part of me has shut down to caring too much, building walls sky-high to protect me. I have learned that it is not safe to love because the loss hurts more than the memory of love could ever mend.

PJM

I run to him with arms outstretched
Through frenzied crowds I weave, lest
He who gave me this life
Forgets his precious spark.

Sometimes I get near close enough
That one more step and I could touch.
Fling my arms 'round his large frame
Restless heart be tamed.

Light trickles through in another world
Volume dies, I go unheard.
Colours fade to sepia.
Don't leave your precious spark.

Eyelids flicker to meet rude daylight
Perhaps he'll come again tonight…
This time he'll stay long enough
To hold this weary spark.

You shoulda seen the other guy

Soundtrack: *The Weeknd ft. Ed Sheeran – 'Dark Times'*

As a teenager, watching the kids of *Skins* and *The OC* made 'wiling out' look exciting. *Wait, is Mischa Barton the cause of all my problems?* Partying always looked so fun and glamorous, as did the TV celebrities, stockbrokers and beautiful party girls who would use cocaine to heighten their already-booming careers and incredible social lives. Stoners and burnouts made relaxing without an overriding sense of guilt seem attainable for my anxious mind. Smoking cigarettes and drinking black coffee wasn't a smelly, bitter way to stain your teeth; it was sexy. It was 'French'. And alcohol didn't make you piss yourself from one end and vomit from the other, or wake up shivering and damp in a dark alleyway. It just fuelled the party until you found a lovely, captivating boy to go home with. You and this boy would share hours of passionate sex, complete with mutual orgasms, then stay up 'til daybreak enthralled in stories of each other's lives. (Instead of the reality where he jizzes in some miscellaneous spot on your bed, passes out almost immediately and wine-snores for the next eight hours until he's conscious enough for you to kick out.)

I became terrified of the outside world, paranoid of running into anyone who knew me from the 'before times'. So, within the acre block of my family home, I spent all my time within the four walls of my childhood bedroom. The now-bright-blue walls assaulted my already hyper-vigilant senses. Within my room, I was confined to my bed, where I lived for months, only leaving for vodka refills and pee breaks.

I was on break from uni, meaning I had no purpose other than running away from my pain. I found it too hard to think about food, what to buy, cook and eat. I didn't even have the energy to put on pants. I wasn't about to leave the house to shop and risk running into anyone. To protect myself from the great unknown, I used my patchy nutritional knowledge and made one smoothie a day stuffed with every supplement I could think of. I'd make sure to add a tonne of chia seeds and protein powder for bulk, and *voila*, the burden of hunger was gone. Fucking genius. I kept my base survival needs mostly met, and the rest of the time, I drank, smoked, slept and cried. *#LyfGoals*

However, on days when I was so achingly lonely that even knocking myself out with booze or benzos wouldn't work, I had another option. It wasn't pretty, but it was different, and even a different kind of suffering is a relief in times of desperation. Within the safety of my bed, I would drink myself into a bold enough stupor to put on some clothes and leave the house. From there, I would head into the night, somewhere I knew people would be, and try to find some strangers to spend time with. I've discovered that the saddest, loneliest people in the world are found wandering the streets, looking to continue the party at 3 am when everyone else is home, tucked safely in their beds. Those were my people.

Like this guy I met on my way home one night who lived in a minuscule apartment at the YMCA. At 45, he didn't look a day over 60. Not wanting to go home and be alone with my shame, I decided to go up to the stranger's room. I watched as he scrounged in his drawers for the coke he was supposed to be 'saving for the weekend'. Meanwhile, I mentally calculated how much flirting I would need to do to make him believe I could fuck him but that I definitely wasn't going to, just so I could score more gear. I looked around the room for tools I could use in self-defence if things got out of hand. The choices were limited to an empty water glass I could hit him over the head with and a butter knife I could jab him with, making him slightly uncomfortable. *Oh well,* I decided, *if I die, I die.* This broke-down, sleazy old dude who walked with a limp and a cane was my best opportunity for distraction, and that's what I needed more than anything. More than safety. More than dignity. More than the scarce amount of money I had left. I weighed it up and decided that even if he killed me, that would be okay.

On another such night, I went out in search of distraction. I wanted to get fucked up on lethal amounts of alcohol, get high in dingy club bathrooms and be validated by stupid boys. The problem is that when you imagine these nights, you see the coloured lights pulsating in the darkly lit club. You see yourself dancing in slow motion, hair in your face and sweat on your brow, smiling as if you're in an LMFAO music video. You see cheeky giggles as three people squeeze into a bathroom stall to do things that make you mentally apologise to your mother. You see a glorified version of what you imagine fun looks like. In reality, you are in a filthy room with a bunch of people who are also running from themselves, breathing stale air that smells like BO and cigarettes, and the old sleazy deejay who has his eye on you will be too cheap to even buy you a drink. So, you will not only wake up with bad skin and self-loathing but also be broke.

I went home with the geriatric deejay, not because I found him attractive or thought he was in any way interesting, but because the thought of the night ending and tomorrow beginning was too much to bear. I had hoped to still be drunk enough by the time I got to his place that fucking him wouldn't completely destroy me, but I wasn't. *Oh well.* I tried to remember if I had ever had a one-night stand before. I had been with Simon for so long. I was only 20 when we met. Jiang and I had slept together a handful of times, but I loved him. This was different. This was soulless. This was a hairy, sweaty body I didn't know flapping around on top of me. I was disgusted by it, by him and by me.

Obviously, he didn't make me cum, or even try to. The entire experience was a gift for him, not a thought given to the girl behind the pussy. Afterwards, he got out a piece of paper that, on closer inspection, was his clear results for a recent STI test. I suppose he thought I would be grateful. I looked from him to the results and felt the rising urge to both vomit and cry. *Is this my life now? Is this what being single looks like?* I felt my eyes start to fill with tears and excused myself to the toilet, where I wept quietly. From the bedroom, I heard him chuckle, 'The girls usually wait 'til they go home before they start crying with self-loathing, babe!'

I looked at my mascara-stained cheeks in the mirror and splashed some cold water on my face. Slowly, I walked back into the bedroom to gather my things and ordered an Uber as the Sun was coming up. *Don't you judge me, Sun.* The Uber pulled up and I slumped down into the back seat. As the deejay waved me goodbye in his torn boxer shorts, I rolled down the window and fibbed, 'Oh, you never asked about *my* sexual health. Yeah, I have herpes. 'Kay, byeee!' His face fell and he started yelling expletives at the car as we drove off. I hung my head out the window like a dog searching for fresh air and weakly smiled, a small win in a night of failures.

After many years working as a policeman and magistrate, my grandpa would conclude that 'rage is a temporary form of insanity'. It chemically alters your brain and your rational responses. I was fuelled by blind rage. I believe it was my body's way of protecting me from feeling the enormity of my grief. The rage was all-consuming, but at least it was powerful. It was an interesting time because I wasn't afraid of being unlikeable; I relished it. Like a school bully, it gave me a false sense of strength to act like I didn't give a shit. So, I pretended I didn't give a fuck how crazy I looked and became free in my insanity.

My anger so controlled me that my psychologist decided it was a good idea to prepare an action plan for how to avoid physically attacking anyone. Specifically, Simon, if ever I ran into him. The crux of the plan was to run swiftly in the opposite direction, but I wasn't convinced I'd be able to follow through. All I could see was that he had left me when I needed him most. He left me and chose someone else. Rationalising our split didn't change my emotional reaction one iota. I wanted to kill him. I wanted to kill him with my bare hands.

Whenever I felt anything, sadness, anger, loneliness, all I could see was his face. He was the living, breathing representation of all my pain, and I hated him for it. His only crime was being alive when Sam and Dad weren't. For years, I would go to sleep with violent images scrolling through my mind, like scenes from *The Purge* playing on repeat. I would see my hands covered in blood and hear bones cracking under my animalistic strength. I felt the metallic taste of blood line my teeth. It was visceral and right there whenever I closed my eyes. At night, adrenaline surged through me as I tried to sleep. My heart would race, I would cry, groan in pain and desperately try to eliminate the images of death from my head by listening to some soft-spoken yogi deliver *Meditation for Anger* on YouTube. I would listen on repeat for hours, willing myself to sleep, hoping that something in my brain was absorbing her soothing words.

Following one of my nights out, I brought home a stray. When going to sleep, I reflexively put on one of my 'relaxing' soundscapes and watched the guy almost jump out of his skin.

'What the fuck is that? It sounds like someone banging pots and pans!' he screeched. Being judged by a man who only hours ago was drunkenly taking his pants off in a public bar was upsetting, to say the least. I reluctantly turned off *Train Sounds #3*, which in hindsight, was just metal grinding aggressively against metal. His questioning of my musical tastes made me examine what I was listening to and how much of a war zone my head must have been to find loud, erratic, clanging metal soothing enough for sleep.

I began to date, regularly meeting men from Tinder and other dating apps. My goal was not to sleep around or have one-night stands. I desperately wanted to meet someone special who would love me back to health. I wanted to find my soulmate and shove my happiness in Simon's face, just like he had done to me. I wanted to win the breakup.

Instead, I found men, and men are not like women. Men do not find a broken woman and lick her wounds. The men who are attracted to broken, vulnerable women are the worst kinds, and I was attracting every last one of them. Simon may have left me heartbroken and alone, but the subsequent men took the last of my dignity, self-respect and power, and laughed at me on the way down. These experiences only fueled my anger at Simon, knowing that he was being cared for by a woman – a beautiful woman with all her innate warmth and compassion. He would be patched up and coddled, and I would be used as if I was nothing but a human Fleshlight.

One night, when I was crawling out of my skin with loneliness, I took myself out on the town and ended up at a small, familiar bar. I chose this specific bar because I remembered it as a lesbian bar. I wanted to be surrounded by raucous female energy, not slobbery fuck boys. Unfortunately, I had misremembered, and rather than being a purely queer bar, they just hosted queer events on 'FriYay' nights (as they called it). It was mid-week, so the crowd was sparse but for a spattering of men surrounding the bar.

I sat at the end of the bar and ordered a drink. I stared down into my vodka orange as if I was an old, weathered man in a saloon, swilling whisky and thinking about his old flame. The group of three sidled up to me and started making conversation. They weren't funny, but they believed they were, and I was lonely, so I played along, pretending they were the most fascinating people on the planet. One group member had a deck of cards that he would intermittently attempt to perform magic tricks with. He was so bad at this I questioned if he had ever seen a deck of cards before.

They were sloppy-drunk, rude and arrogant. I didn't like them, but I wanted them to like me or at least spend time with me. I think they could smell my desperation like sharks to blood because as the hours passed, they became more blatant with their sexism and jibes at my intelligence. I laughed everything off, just as I had in school, when I was repeatedly reminded how fat I was while the boys assured me they were 'Just joking!' in both situations. I wanted to cry.

One of the boys was very good-looking. He was in his late 20s and had a toned physique, striking blue eyes and a powerful jaw. I wasn't attracted to him – he was a self-absorbed knob – but objectively, he was hot. He was charming enough and flirty, but best of all, he bought rounds of drinks and paid me attention, which was really all I wanted. Cheekily, he leaned into me and told me to follow him as he got up and walked to the bathroom. I didn't know if he wanted to have sex, do drugs or just have me there to witness him taking a slash, but it didn't matter.

A few seconds later, I got up and followed him in. He grabbed me and pulled me into a toilet stall, where he kissed me with intent. It was exciting, and although we were making out in a dingy bathroom stall, it was hot. Then he got out a little baggy that looked like cocaine but, he informed me, was ketamine. I never understood how a horse tranquilliser, or any tranquilliser for that matter, would enhance an experience, but I wasn't about to turn down an offer to shove some poison into my face.

We both did a bump, and as he was lifting the key to his nose, I noticed something shining on his left hand. 'Is that a wedding band? Jesus, are you married?' I pulled away from him in shock. *How had I not noticed? Ew, am I at the age where I have to check for wedding rings now?*

He rattled something off about it being a green card wedding, which I'm pretty sure is just something he heard in an American film, and left the bathroom. I stood there perplexed, annoyed and warm and fuzzy inside as the ketamine took hold.

I stood in the bathroom stall for a moment, questioning my life choices leading up to this point, and then walked out. Upon my return, I saw my married lover not-so-stealthily sneaking out of the bar with chuckling mates in tow. I was speechless. They were literally doing that thing mean girls do in primary school, where they run off on one girl leaving her confused about why she wasn't in on the joke. It was live-action ghosting. I wasn't expecting him to leave his wife and start a new life with me, but to not even give me the courtesy of a goodbye after trying to fuck me in a toilet only moments ago? *The fucking audacity!*

'HEY!' I yelled, as I caught them outside waiting for a taxi.

'Err, hey? Do you want something?' Jawline replied, acting as if he had never met me before.

'You don't say goodbye to someone who, only moments ago, you were fondling in the bathroom stall?' I enquired.

He looked at his friends, embarrassed and taken aback, before shrugging me off. 'Pfft, that never happened,' he rolled his eyes, indicating to his mates how unhinged I was to fabricate this entire story in my head.

Oh, you have no idea, buddy.

I felt my eye twitch. The three of them stood there smirking and looking at each other as they all pretended they hadn't just spent hours talking, drinking and playing dumb-arse magic tricks with me. It was the most blatant gaslighting experience I have ever seen, and it Pissed. Me. Off.

I stepped forward to stand eye-to-eye with the pretty boy, his cronies on either side of him, backing him up like two dopey bouncers. My eyes were wide, and my nostrils flared with rage. Simon had been ignoring my existence for months, pretending our entire life together had never happened. His family and our many mutual friends erased me from their memories overnight. Sam wasn't giving me a single sign from the afterlife, and some self-important bully in a place I can barely pronounce 'allegedly' murdered my father, cremated him without our consent and walked away scot-fucking-free! Nothing made me crazier than being erased without a thought: *Hell, nah!* This guy picked the wrong psycho to fuck with.

I was so mad that I'm reasonably sure there was actual steam coming out of my ears. I felt like screaming every profanity in the world into their smarmy faces, spitting and scratching at their eyes like a rat, but I didn't. I channelled *Meditation for Anger* and took a few deep, centring breaths, bringing myself back to my body, now quaking with rage. I was intensely connected to the enhanced physical sensations in my body: the tingling of my fingertips, my hair all standing on end and the heavy thumping of my heart as it powered my limbs with fresh, fiery blood.

I looked into his black eyes and saw every man who had ever fucked me over, lied to me, mocked me and made me feel less than. I was sick to death of insecure little boys using women to inflate their fragile egos. Thinking it's funny to leave us more broken than they found us. And I was really fucking pissed off that every one of my female friends had lived this moment more times than they can count. What silly little women we have been to think a man would treat us with respect, without expectation. It's our fault they leave, hurt, humiliate, use, degrade, rape and murder us. It's our fault because it certainly couldn't be theirs.

My body was pumping adrenaline through every limb, and I felt my fingers slowly close into a fist by my side. I was completely focused as I zeroed in on his jaw. *Am I really gonna do this?* Then, suddenly, I saw my fist flying through the air and landing SMACK, right against his perfectly chiselled jaw. *Fucking ouch fuck!* I had never punched anyone before, not even a wall in anger. It was like punching cement. I internally celebrated that I hadn't missed and stood in front of him, panting like a rabid dog. I may have actually snarled. It was fucking fantastic!

The group of boys stared at me in shock for a moment before turning and running away like the 'little girls' they loathed so much. I felt so powerful I wanted to beat my chest and scream like a banshee, calling all my sisters to unite against the patriarchy! I waited until they were out of sight, then realised I had just committed assault (so much for my psychology training) and quickly got in a cab to flee the crime scene. I smiled all the way home.

When I got home, I crawled into bed with Mum. She put her arms around me in her sleepy haze and asked if I'd had a good night.

'Well ... I punched some guy in the face.'

'Did he deserve it?' she asked groggily.

'Yes.'

'Alright then.'

She squeezed me tightly and held me as I fell asleep. In the morning, I filled her in on the whole story. Without judgement, she simply added, 'Well, I hope it left a bruise for his wife to find.' Best. Mum. Ever.

He swims in my eyes by the bed

Soundtrack: *Amy Winehouse – 'Wake Up Alone'*

In November 2016, by some incredible act of fate, I managed to finish my degree and obtain my Bachelor of Health Science in Nutrition. *Hey, Dad, I'm a scientist!* Did I forget to attend my graduation because I was in a whirlpool of depression and drug abuse? Sure. Nonetheless, I got that certificate. To this day, I have no idea how I managed it. I'm either really lucky or some kind of genius because my brain was mush. My final year is a blur of re-reading the same line from *Benefits of Fish Oil in the Treatment of Bipolar Disorder: A Study*, telling patients to drink more apple cider vinegar and ensuring my nose was clean of white powder before consulting with my lecturers.

I didn't tell any of my supervisors about my grief. My musical upbringing taught me never to apologise for mistakes or announce if you are under the weather. It gives the audience a reason to look for faults they might otherwise never have noticed. So that's what I did. I squashed my misery with drugs and booze and dragged myself, bloodied and bruised, into the clinic every day. *Break a leg.*

It wasn't until I was sprung crying silent tears in an empty treatment room that I confessed I was struggling. My friend Ally had found me. She was the only person at uni who knew the layers of my grief. We shared a lot during our years of studying together. We had celebrated her long-awaited pregnancy – jumping up and down in the bathroom together like school girls at a Harry Styles concert – and we had cried together when she learned that her baby was so sick it would die at birth if brought to term. She knew my heart was shattered and that I was attempting to paste it together with something as useless as Clag. When I confessed to her once that I had filled my water bottle with wine and OJ *(yummo ... *gag*)*, instead of judging me, she looked at me and said, 'Oh man, I've been there!' *Thank you.*

'Hey, what's happening? Are you okay?' she asked tentatively, sitting beside me on the client massage table.

'Erm, yeah. I'm just having a panic attack.' I was shaking and crying, but the cubical walls kept me from fully expressing the heavy sobs building up inside my chest.

'It's okay. You're okay. Just try to breathe.' She paused for a moment, then continued, 'Do you think we should call an ambulance?'

'Huh?'

'Do you think you should go back to the clinic?'

'Oh, no. I'll be fine. I just need to go to bed *(for a year).*' She had caught me off guard. This had become a regular daily occurrence for me that, until now, I had been able to hide from view. But to Ally, my sadness was so intense it warranted a trip to the psych hospital. In a way, it was validating – she bore witness to the anguish tearing me to pieces every second of every day, and it scared her. It scared me, too.

I remember walking into the common area with my two-for-one Red Bulls from 7-Eleven, only to be met with looks of horror from fellow classmates. They were more partial to coconut water or Fairtrade matcha latte with ethical almond milk and stevia. I survived on energy drinks and ten coffees a day. *Can you say stomach ulcer?* I needed them because I never slept. I would cry until I passed out, often in my mother's arms like a baby. Then I would dream, and dreamland was just as exhausting.

I would dream about seeing my father through busy crowds. I'd weave and elbow my way towards him, only to have him disappear when I got to where he stood.

I'd dream about Simon. The images would be brutal: blood and gore were recurring themes. While wielding a samurai sword, I would say everything I'd failed to in waking life. 'I'll kill you! I'll kill you!' I'd scream as he stared back at me numbly, saying nothing. Empty and robotic, even in my dreams. However exhausting, these were the bearable ones. They gave me some sense of redemption upon waking.

The dreams in which Simon was loving and gentle destroyed me – they would stay with me all day. He would come to me. He would find me. It wasn't me playing the 'crazy' ex-girlfriend who turned up drunk on his doorstep in the dead of night, or stalked his new girlfriend, kidnapped her and slowly mailed him her fingers one by one. He would seek me out and tell me he loved me.

In my slumber, I could feel Simon's strong, comforting arms as he pulled me close. The bristles of his untrimmed facial hair would brush my cheek as I burrowed into the crook of his neck. I could smell him. *His* smell. When I looked at him, his blue eyes would swallow me up like pools of water. I could see his every freckle and the deepening crinkles around his eyes from all the times I'd made him laugh. I could see his sadness and his fatigue. I could feel his fingers grip me tightly, keeping me safe and reminding me I was his. He wore his real clothes. Not make-believe outfits I had concocted in my mind. *His smell. His clothes.* I didn't know dreams could be so visceral.

Then he would speak. He would say my name the way only he could. The way that reminds you that you belong to someone, that you are important. The way that shows you they have said it, let it roll around their mouths and truly felt it thousands of times. It's not even a name anymore; it's just you. He would grip my face with his slightly weathered hands and say, 'I love you.' That was it. He repeated it, torturously, over and over, 'I love you, I love you, **I love you**.' Each time, he said it with more certainty, desperate to convince me of the truth behind his words. And with my eyes closed in my nostalgic dreamland, I believed him.

The recreation of his voice was faultless. Every inflection. Every pause. The warmth, the timbre, the depth. It was perfect. I was jealous of the words for getting to live in his mouth. Of all the things he could have said, he chose to say my name. I felt special before realising my mistake. I was just a sleepy girl slowly waking up, repeating her own name to herself in the dark, trying to make it sound just right.

I had a decent support network at uni, but no one truly knew the extent of my pain and, certainly, not the ways I was trying to soothe it. The coursework was difficult and extensive, and it was taking its toll. I was wasting away, my appetite suppressed by cigarettes and suicidal depression. Eating was a chore. I wasn't actively trying to lose weight, but I'd be lying if I said I didn't get that familiar jolt of achievement whenever someone remarked how tiny I was, with worry in their eyes. I never weighed myself for fear that reading the number on the scale would solidify a new goal to strive for forever, but there was no hiding the rapidly declining size of my pants. Looking back now, it's so clear that I was skin and bones, but at the time, my anorexic inner voice would chime in as effortlessly as ever to assure me I wasn't getting smaller, my clothes sizes had been mislabelled or stretched in the wash.

When I first met Sam, she used to call me Tiny as a nickname. For a while, it confused and even offended me. I thought she was using one of those opposite nicknames, like when you call someone with red hair Bluey. Looking back on photos from that time, I can confirm I *was* fucking Tiny! Anorexia is such a persistent disease. Here I was, in recovery for almost a decade, and as soon as my life was in turmoil, my old friend Ana reared up her ugly head and showed me how to feign control over my life again. *Welcome home, old pal.*

My drug dealer was a doctor

Soundtrack: *Macklemore & Ryan Lewis ft. Ariana DeBoo – 'Drug Dealer'*

It had been over a year since my breakup with Simon, yet it still felt as fresh as the day it happened. I was sure I would never feel at peace again. I was struggling my way through my final semester at uni when I decided the answer to all my problems was falling in love with someone else. Enter Alessandro. Alessandro was a family friend from Toronto. We had reconnected via Facebook, as per most romances born of desperation and loneliness. Growing up as the migrant kids on their street, Alessandro's late mother and my own were best friends. My mum was the child of Estonian refugees, and his was fresh off the boat from Calabria. The girls bonded as five-year-olds whose pickled fish and smelly cured meats were too confronting for the other children. They enjoyed 60 years as friends before his mother sadly took her own life due to mental illness.

Alessandro swanned into my dysfunction with all his charm, cheek and good looks. Right away, he spoke about our lives together like they were set in stone. Like it was a given that we had a future together. When he spoke of home, it was ours to share, not his and mine. From day one, our separate entities had gone, and I was part of a 'we' again. For a year, I had been walking around feeling non-existent in my own skin, in a body I didn't recognise without Simon beside it. Suddenly, here was Alessandro telling me that I wasn't alone anymore. And I felt whole again. My entire existence rested on the shoulders of this new man. In all those years with Simon, I never had that security. I was never allowed to fantasise about our wedding day or the family we may build together. I never even felt assured enough in our own home to decorate. I bought a single throw cushion, that was it. So, when Alessandro swooped in and started creating this world of 'us', it felt amazing. It felt hopeful.

I was convinced Alessandro was the one I had been waiting for. He was 17 years my senior, at 44, which added to my sense of security. He was Canadian-Italian, tall, had gorgeous olive skin and a smile that could melt an iceberg. He had a young son from a previous marriage but had long since been divorced. He communicated well and was both funny and impossibly sexy. He spoke (at least) four languages and even went to therapy. *Swoon! Boys, if you're reading this, take note: nothing gets a girl going like a man in therapy.* He was perfect, and *damn* was he smooth.

Despite the 14-hour time difference, my intense study load and his corporate job, we chatted all day, every day. We were addicted to each other. I lived on four hours of sleep a night just so I could stay awake until two in the morning talking to him. It was exhilarating. I lived for the hours we were both awake at the same time; the rest of the day felt meaningless and wasteful. In my final month of uni, my supervisors and classmates would see me gazing obsessively into my phone and could tell how my day was going based on my reactions. If my desire for affection and attention had been met, I would go bounding into the clinic like a kid at Christmas. If his tone had changed or he wasn't responding as quickly as the day before, I would be plagued with panic and completely distracted. I'd suck the energy out of the room so fast you could swear I was a Dementor in training.

Only days into our online communication, we had already said those three little words: 'I love you'. I couldn't focus to save myself, but I didn't care. I had *lurve,* and that was more important than any degree. Love would pave the way to my future.

After a week of talking, we booked two tickets to Tuscany for the type of romantic, month-long holiday that dreams are made of. *Our first date.* It was all I could do not to burst out of my skin. I even forgot about my heartache; I had something to look forward to again. Nothing could ruin this; nothing could burst my bubble.

Every day I would count the days until it was time to board the flight that would take me to the man of my dreams. Perhaps it was a little strange that the first time we met, I was 11 and visiting my grandparents in Canada, and he was pushing 30, but any oddities were easily overridden by the pure fact that this was fate. All the pain and suffering of my previous relationships – of my previous life – had guided me to this very moment.

We became so close so quickly that I didn't worry about telling Alessandro about my mental health issues; he had his own troubles, after all. I had already advised him about my addiction, but looking back, I don't think he really heard me. Just as I had when I was on the verge of paralysis with my spinal tumour or wasting away from anorexia, I looked relatively normal. I was thin, and if you got too close, you would see a film of sweat lining my skin and the glazed-over look of my eyes. But when I left the house, I would dress in slacks and a shirt for uni and slap on some make-up. Like everyone else in their final year of study, I looked tired and stressed. I needed to look a certain way, or my doctors would have figured out that I was hiding a crippling addiction a long time ago.

Two weeks into our long-distance romance, I spilled everything to Alessandro.

'Oh, hey, you should know I have bipolar. I mean, you obviously know I'm grieving, but yeah, I guess you should know about the bipolar, too. I'm on medication for both anyway, so it shouldn't be a problem.'

'Oh right…okay…'

'I mean, I've been diagnosed with every mental illness under the Sun. It's not like they are all happening at the same time, all of the time. Besides, I'm starting to question whether I'm actually that sick or if the world just wasn't built for people like me. I would be really content if I could live like a cat, but we are supposed to contribute to society.

Boo! Cats contribute to society by being super adorable. I'm amazing at that!'

'Ha ha, yes you are weirdo.'

'So anyway, I thought you should know. There is a bit of speculation around whether or not I have Borderline Personality Disorder, too, but...'

'What?'

'Yeah, it's kinda like bipolar but like ... on steroids.'

'No, it's not. You have BPD?'

'No, I just mean it has been bandied around as an op ...'

'What the fuck, Kirst?'

'What? What's the big deal? You were cool with me having bipolar two seconds ago!'

'BPD is different. You should've told me before!'

'When? We've only been talking for two weeks! Do you want me to drop my mental health shit on day one? Are *you* mental?'

'You tricked me. You have been lying to me! It's messed up.'

'Um ... no. I'm telling you right now. Besides, I'm not even officially diagnosed! It was a flippant remark. For fuck sake, I wish I didn't say anything!'

'Whatever. Even the thought that you could have it is bad.'

'Where is this coming from? I'm so confused right now.'

'I don't want to talk about this anymore. I've gotta get ready for work. I dunno, maybe we should just cancel the holiday.'

'What, no! Please just talk to me.'

'I've got to go. I'll talk to you later.'

He wouldn't talk to me again for three days. Nothing. Dead silence. I panicked as I saw yet another man driven away by my intensity, driven away by my *me*-ness.

Not this time, I decided, with a terrifying level of tenacity. I wasn't letting this one get away. I would make him love me whether he wanted to or not! You know those Australian koala souvenirs that wrap around the end of a pencil and hang on, clutching for dear life? Yeah, so that was my entire plan. We would meet in Tuscany, I would wrap myself around his neck and he would have to pry off my cold dead hands if he ever wanted his freedom back. Simple, romantic and not at all a symptom of BPD. *Awks.*

Before the flight, I needed to organise all the medications I would need for a month away. This was no easy feat as it would include over a hundred opioids, daily anti-psychotics (which were clearly working a treat – see above), and my weight in anti-depressants. By this stage, I was also using a walking stick because my health was declining from stress-induced fibromyalgia and the painful cravings my body produced from oxy withdrawal. I was in constant pain and chronically exhausted.

I had tried to warn Alessandro about all of this, but he, like me, was blinded by fantasy and told me to leave my 'pimp cane' at home. I had concerns about being left to walk in pain or be weak with exhaustion, but the sheer fact that I needed to believe Alessandro would take care of me quickly dismissed them. All I wanted was for someone to take my life in their hands and nurse it back to health like a baby bird. I don't think either of us thought that we would end up walking the cobbled stone streets of Montepulciano while he supported my entire body weight on his arm because I was both too weak and too pained to stand on my own.

Getting the medication for this holiday was a mission in itself. My GP was starting to catch on to the fact that I had an issue with these meds, but rather than refuse my prescription, he chose to make sure I would be safe while away. We would deal with my little problem when I came home. As he so generously put it, '*You* are not a problem, but *this* is a problem.'

As far as he was aware, Mum had successfully taken care of my medications for months, and all was relatively under control. Sure,

I was reliant on my weekly OxyNorm prescription, but it wasn't out of control. He certainly didn't picture me waiting impatiently for the pharmacy to open at 8 am, gripping my hand tightly around the end of my walking stick so I wouldn't feel it restlessly tickle and shake from withdrawals. He didn't imagine me fiendishly scraping the tiny granules of white powder off public bathroom floors after I'd foolishly knocked the phone I'd been racking on off the large silver toilet paper holder at the crack of dawn right before treating patients. That wasn't me. I was sweet Kirsty, who he had treated for ear infections as a child, as he pretended to look for possums between my ears. I was the girl who survived spinal cancer that he'd discovered. I was ashamed, but not enough to stop. In any case, it's not like I had another option. The alternative was to feel everything that bubbled and brewed just below the surface, which was unbearable even in its dulled state.

My desperation to obtain the meds and fly to Alessandro outweighed any hint of shame. Besides, soon everything would be fine. Alessandro was the answer to all of this. Heartbreak had destroyed me, and love was the cure. To gain access to the medications, I had to adhere to several rules that proved I could look after myself for the duration of the trip. I had previously asked Mum to be in charge of my pill supply, hoping this would derail my addictive tendencies. So, Mum was required to accompany me to my next doctor's appointment and agree that she felt completely comfortable with my capability to self-dose – despite the fact she had caught me stealing my tablets from her hiding spots multiple times. Then she would have to call Alessandro and make sure he knew exactly how much and how often I was to take my meds, now that he was my newly assigned carer. It was like 'the adults' were talking, and I was the naughty teenager being sent away to the grandparents' house for the summer to get my shit together. *Hot.*

Imagine my delight when we passed every test and were given all the prescriptions my junkie heart desired! Boxes upon boxes of those orange and white capsules. *Decadent.* Now, imagine how Alessandro was feeling. Something I didn't consider at the time but now imagine was similar to that YouTube clip of the little girl whose mother feeds her wasabi for the first time. The three-year-old unsuspectingly tastes the green mush, and we watch her transition from shock/horror to betrayal as her entire face catches on fire. She's in so much agony she can hardly speak. Somehow, she manages to squeak out a solemn plea for help. It's as cruel as it is hilarious. But my gut was telling me this sceanario leaned more toward cruelty than hilarity.

The day had finally arrived, and I was in the sky on my way to a brand-new life. My excitement was palpable and contagious. I told anyone who would listen about my romantic journey to love! But the 22 hours of travel gave Alessandro the space he hadn't had in weeks – to think. *Don't think; never think!* I needed to get there and suction myself to him like a barnacle before more damage was done. By the time I was halfway and could check my phone between change-over flights (*totes not obsessively*), his texting style had changed significantly. He was now indecisive about meeting me at the airport in Rome and was no longer convinced we should stay in the same room. He even started to claim that when he had said he loved me, he had meant it 'as a friend'. Not that he was *in* love with me but that he had love *for* me. *Cool, thanks bud.*

I was confused, scared and unravelling with anxiety. Had I made up the entire thing? I couldn't have. Who plans an entire romantic escapade to Tuscany with a mate? No, he was pulling away, and I could feel it over the Pacific Ocean. I spent the next ten hours drinking tiny bottles of ice-cold red wine and lamenting the fact I had left my boxed-up oxys in my luggage, having already made my way through the flight rations. I watched *A Star is Born* three times and cried so hard that the young boy sitting next to me tugged at his mother's sleeve to ask if I was okay. I simply gestured to the ruggedly handsome and relatably fucked up Bradley Cooper on my in-flight entertainment, which was met by an understanding nod from the mother. *Nailed it.*

Fuelled by lack of sleep, copious amounts of alcohol, oxy withdrawals and panic that Alessandro wouldn't show, I crawled off the flight with a mixture of dread and excitement. I hurried straight to the bathroom to take a whore's bath with wet wipes, change my in-flight undies and slap some make-up on my face to pretend I am always this effortlessly stunning when coming off a long haul flight. Collecting my baggage, I was sure I would be stopped for drug trafficking with the amount of medication I had with me. My doctor had even written individual letters for myself and Alessandro, just in case we got pulled up carrying my supplies. But all was well, and I made my way through the departure gates, heart racing. I walked through the large automated doors, following the hordes of weary travellers before me. My eyes darted about rapidly to try and find him as I held my breath in anticipation. *There he was.* My guilt-tripping had worked: he was here and all would be okay.

As I walked towards him with my bags in tow, I anxiously wondered if he would kiss me, hug me, or tell me he was sick of my bullshit and put me straight on a flight back home. To my delight, he took me in his arms and gave me a big kiss. I'd never been so in love.

The following days were spent in our gorgeous Italian cottage, surrounded by olive groves and rolling hills. We zipped from Arezzo to Volterra in our hired Fiat 500, stopping only to drink provincial wines and gorge ourselves on tortellini al brodo and wild boar ragu. In the afternoons, Alessandro would sip his espresso like the real Italian he was, and I would order a macchiato or, god forbid, a post-midday cappuccino, much to his embarrassment. He taught me the correct way to twirl my spaghetti so I wouldn't draw attention to the dirty fact that we were tourists.

'What are you doing?' He leaned in and hushed his voice in a way that made me positive I had committed a terrible crime. *Did I forget to wear pants again? Shit.*

'What?' I replied, a mouth full of spaghetti al limone.

'Have you never eaten spaghetti before?'

'Erm … I'm eating it right now. It's delicious. You want some?'

'Oh my god, stop.' *Is he serious?* 'Here, let me show you.' He took my plate and put it down in front of him for my lesson on how to feed myself. Something I had been somewhat successfully achieving on my own for the past 28 years.

He took a small amount of pasta, twirled it around his fork, and then popped it in his mouth. 'See?'

'You did it all by yourself! Good job!' I said as if praising a baby because, well, you get it.

'No, you have to take a small amount to the edge of the bowl and then twirl. Not from the middle like you were doing. That's how you don't get too much.'

I took a deep breath and a large swig of the perfectly selected white wine that accompanied my pasta dish. 'Not all of us spent every year between 10 and 18 summering in Calabria, you know,' I teased, taking my dish back.

'It's a basic life skill.' *It's really not.*

'Has anyone ever told you that you are the single most pretentious person on the planet?' I asked, now twirling my pasta with precision technique.

'Very often, yes. But now look at you! Perfetto!' he said, kissing the air. It was infuriating how much easier his technique was.

I began to notice, more and more, that he was embarrassed by me. I laughed too loudly. I talked too much. I pronounced Nutella like an Aussie bogan [Nut-ella] and not with the Italian flair of Sophia Loren [noo-TEL-a]. The wines I enjoyed were déclassé, and I was forbidden from cooking out of fear I would ruin a perfectly good meal. Cooking with and for another is a passion of mine and a sincere expression of love. He felt suffocated by me. I *needed* him too much. Which I did. He was my only means of connection to the people of these remote villages, most of whom did not speak English. Even as he flirted at length with the lusciously curvy, brunette concierge of our Albergo, I turned a blind eye because I didn't want to feed into the narrative that I was unstable and jealous (which obviously I was).

Later he would mock me, 'Ha! You didn't even know we were flirting right in front of you! She invited me to her family's cottage, and you were just standing there clueless.' To argue that despite not understanding the langue of Italian, I did understand the language of love would have been useless. He wanted me to be jealous and possessive, so I would be neither. Instead, I excused myself to the bathroom to be with my true love. *sniff* Ahhh. Safe now.

He was responsible for maintaining my failing health and well-being and for soothing my heart. It didn't take long before he was exhausted and resentful about being stuck with me.

It would have been impossibly hard. I was unwell in every imaginable way, and here was this man who, from nowhere, suddenly had the weight of my world on his shoulders. Like me, he had entered this relationship excited for a future of love, relief and happiness following a difficult break-up. He was hopeful that I would be what he had been waiting a lifetime for. He was a romantic. Before he met me, I guess he pictured this woman who was damaged but in a sexy/moody, 'Lana Del Ray' kind of way. He hadn't considered the extent of my anguish and how desperately I needed him to save me. But he was learning.

I watched as he discovered that he was not cut out for the job. I don't know who would be. I needed a tribe of doctors. I needed full-time care, with my mother on standby. The last thing I needed was a middle-aged man who lived on the other side of the world and carried the baggage of his own past traumas to add to mine – but nobody could tell me that at the time. A few brave souls tried, but it fell on deaf, volatile ears.

I felt Alessandro's growing hesitation. It panicked me, but I had all the answers in several hundred little pills rattling around in my suitcase. He had been advised by me, my mum and my doctor to hold onto the medication and monitor its usage, but this didn't happen. Probably because I was very good at pretending I was totally in control and would pathologically lie about how much I was taking. I even stopped monitoring myself. Why would I? I had an entire pharmacy at my fingertips! I was convinced that even though I was prescribed four low-dose oxys per day and I was taking well over double that, I would never run out. Besides, Alessandro was bound to notice eventually, right? Like I'd done with Simon, I allowed myself to get worse and worse, willing him to notice. Soon he would see. Soon, he would sound the alarm and stop me. *Please.*

It was a cold November in Italy, but my withdrawals made sure I was always coated in a thin layer of sweat. Overnight, as the time between oxys peaked, I would have severe hot flushes that drenched my clothes and soaked through the bedding to the mattress. I would wake up in the night shivering from the cold air hitting my damp skin and have to change my clothes. There were times Alessandro and I would be making sweet passionate love in our romantic Tuscan villa, soaked in wine and natural oxytocin, and I would become so sweaty I'd have to grab on to him for dear life. Letting go would surely mean flying, slippery and naked, across the room, like a surprised seal being flung off a rock by a large wave. Not the most graceful way to start a picturesque *Under the Tuscan Sun*-style romance – rained upon by foul-smelling sweat emanating from the very depths of liver toxicity and imminent death. Onions. He told me I smelled like onions. Suffice it to say that is not what I was going for.

Despite his growing disdain and fear of my ever-increasing erraticism, I desperately wanted to earn back his love. He sniffed out my desperation and made me work for his affection by openly flirting with attractive waitresses and concierge people right in front of me. Speaking in Italian, I suppose he thought he was getting away with something. It was a twisted display of power and narcissism. To not fuel the fire, I stood idly by and said nothing. I didn't want him to know how much it hurt and embarrassed me, and I really didn't want him to realise that his stupid little game was indeed working. I felt him slipping through my fingers but knew that if I could just keep hold of a single grain of hope, maybe he would relent. Only weeks ago, I was his lifeblood! Love couldn't dissolve that quickly, could it?

Ten days in, and he was hardly speaking to me. His sweet nothings had transformed into the grunting and snapping of a teenager when asked 'how was school', but in public, he would come alive. Then, I became the light of his life. He would buy me fancy dinners and expensive handbags as he proudly exclaimed that I was his *raggazza*, and just like that, my dream of us would be restored. Privately, he made no effort to disguise his resentment and disappointment that I wasn't the girl he'd imagined, yet he was still sleeping with me regularly. He still seemed to desire me. This wasn't the selfish, just-because-I-was-there type of sex. No, this was the most passionate, intense, fulfilling, multiple-orgasming sex of my life. If he was using me as his personal wank sock, he disguised it magnificently.

Alessandro's duality played with my head and heart in a way I wasn't used to. I would swing from loved to despised and back again in a single afternoon. To cope, I took more painkillers until, before I knew it, with over two weeks left of the holiday, I ran out.

I searched every inch of my suitcase and begged Alessandro to do the same, but neither of us had a single pill stashed away. I had been taking at least ten painkillers a day and would now have to go cold turkey. I had been taking these pills for seven years to soothe the ache in my body and heart, and now I had nothing to lean on. I was already getting withdrawal shakes, debilitating exhaustion, hot sweats, joint and muscle aches, suicidal depression and homicidal aggravation, and that was just between doses on any average day. This was going to be bad. Alessandro regularly reminded me how grey and clammy I looked in my current state. How would I win back his affections while potentially foetal, sickly green, and heads or tails over a toilet bowl? *Buckle up, motherfuckers!*

'Do you have any of my oxy left anywhere, my love?' I asked, trying to sound calm and coming across as wildly unhinged.

'Check your daily pill box.'

'Yeah, I have. '

'It's Wednesday.'

'Yeah, I know, but …'

'What did you do?'

'No, nothing. Nothing, really, but I accidentally did take some of the other days.'

'Fuck, how many?'

'Oh, um ... *pretends to count* just ... all of them?' I hoped turning it into a question would change the outcome.

'All of them? What do you mean all of them?'

'Oh, just ... all of them. I know it's really bad, but you have some stashed away, yeah? You put some in your suitcase?'

'What? No. That's what was in the pill box! Have you hidden some? You've hidden some away, haven't you?'

'Alessandro, I promise you if I had, I would not be having this conversation with you right now.' Now I was beginning to panic. I was sure he had an extra box in his suitcase. Did I just fantasise about that in my fucking hot-flush fever dreams?

'Well, have a look in your suitcase. Show me you're not hiding any!'

'Sandro! I have just been through every single fucking inch of my bags like a goddamned maniac. You were my last resort. Fuck. I'm fucked. Oh my god, this is bad.'

'Ah, yeah, it is.'

'You were supposed to help me!'

'You lied to me! You didn't tell me you were this bad!'

'I didn't know! Fuck. What the fuck are we going to do? What am I going to do?'

He was pissed, I was a wreck, and we were both freaking out. I knew I couldn't be trusted with my own dose management, but he hadn't wanted to listen. He didn't want to know who I really was, how sad I really was. He just wanted me to be his sexy little gypsy girl. Well, he was about to learn how sexy I could be without my drugs and my fucking walking stick, which, by now, I was definitely regretting leaving at home. If he had been using me as arm candy, he was in luck because I was clinging to him like my human cane. As the days wore on and my pain and exhaustion worsened, I relied more and more on him to support my dead weight.

In an attempt to prevent my falling into fatal, or just plain disgusting, withdrawals, Alessandro and I spent two days driving around quaint

Tuscan villages in search of a doctor who would provide a random Aussie junkie with opioids. This came with several layers of difficulty. One was that I only spoke enough Italian to ask for 'gelato al pistacchio' or 'un altra bottiglia di vino rossa per favore' and certainly not enough to manipulate a non-English speaking doctor into trusting me with schedule eight drugs. Another is that Italians, in general, are very strict with medications. They aren't all that keen on paracetamol or ibuprofen, let alone something as addictive and dangerous as my meds.

We had no idea how to locate or book to see a doctor in one of these tiny old villages. The way I understand the medical system in Italy is that residents are allocated a local doctor as their GP without a choice. So, as tourists, we didn't belong anywhere. The hospital probably would have been our best bet, but we were hours from any major city, and I was deteriorating rapidly. My depression and fatigue worsened by the hour, my hands began to tickle and shake, and all over my body, muscles cramped without relief. My right knee began to throb and buckle out from under me.

Alessandro chuckled, 'It's funny, isn't it?'

'Excuse me?' I winced in pain, rubbing my knee.

'You know, how your body is actually making more pain.'

'What the fuck? I'm not making this up.'

'No, I know you don't think you are, but it's all in your head.'

I stared at him, willing an anvil to fall from the sky and squash him.

'You do know that literally all pain is generated in the mind, right?' But he didn't listen. I began singing Fiona Apple to remind myself that all boys are this stupid. It's not his fault. He can't help it.

He said, 'it's all in your head,' and I said, 'so's everything,' but he didn't get it. I thought he was a man, but he was just a little boy.

In order to protect his sanity and stop my incessant complaining, Alessandro worked hard to find a doctor that would see us. Thank fuck he could speak fluent Italian. Without him, I am positive I would have ended up either in the hospital or dying from heart failure. I wanted to punch a wall, vomit the contents of my guts and sleep for 14 years, but I didn't really understand how dire the situation was. I didn't realise how close to death I came.

Three villages and much googling later, Alessandro found us a tiny doctor's office in Lucca. It was a hole-in-the-wall, ancient, one-man operation that I was so grateful for I could've kissed the cobblestones. We walked in to join the four other patients in the waiting area. They were all over 60, and I'm pretty sure one of them was a nun. *Forgive me, Sister.* The assembled stared at me, intrigued. I tried to smile to hide the fact I was a feral drug fiend here to pollute their town with my presence. I swear there is nothing that makes you question your life choices more than an 80-year-old Italian woman looking into the depths of your soul without saying a word. *I'm sorry, Nonna. I promise I'll be better,* I thought, bowing my head in shame. As we were called in, Alessandro turned to me and said, 'Don't say a word.'

The doctor was sitting behind a large leather-topped desk. I felt like a naughty schoolgirl who had been called into the principal's office. I sat quietly, trying to look sweet and nice, preventing my involuntary twitches by holding my hands together tightly in my lap. Alessandro was talking quickly in Italian; I couldn't understand a word. The men would turn to me every now and then, and Alessandro would translate a question. I replied, and he translated my words back to the doctor. I smiled softly the entire time, despite the thick tension in the room. If I just kept looking doe-eyed, he couldn't possibly think I was here to score. *Please, sir, I need your help. I am but a poor and sickly travelling beauty lost in this strange and wondrous land.* Damsel, distress, etc. Alessandro's plan was to focus on my spinal surgery and drop the cancer card. *She's a cripple with rods in her spine. Her very existence is agony. Take pity, kind sir.* At least, that's how I imagined it.

After a lengthy discussion *about* me but *without* me, the doctor finally pulled out his prescription pad. I held my breath in anticipation. *Please, please, please.* I crossed my toes beneath the table, praying for oxy and not some other watered-down shit. Alessandro turned to me and said slowly and calmly as if talking to a toddler who had just scraped their knee, 'It's okay, we got it,' before he instructed me to leave the room while he paid the nice man. Inside, I was quietly celebrating. I focused intently on my facial expression, making sure I didn't lick my lips in anticipation. As I walked to the door, I couldn't contain the excitement any longer, and my face burst into a wide smile. He'd done it. He'd actually done it.

Alessandro stayed, talking to the doctor for another 20 minutes or so. I sat outside the office, letting all the twitches I had suppressed earlier come out in full swing. One foot tapping the floor and the other leg jiggling rampantly. Likewise, my eyes and mouth would twitch and stretch intermittently, and my hands were fiddling with something on my face or scratching one of my many bodily itches. That was one symptom of opioid addiction that I never got used to. Your entire body becomes itchy as though your skin is crawling with a thousand tiny ants, creeping and crawling just under your skin. You can scratch and scratch until your skin is red-raw, but you never find relief. I have woken up some mornings with bruises or having drawn blood from scratching in my sleep. It almost made it not worth it. Almost.

When Alessandro emerged from the doctor's office, he looked a mixture of concerned and pissed off. Rightly so, but I was more interested in getting out of there and straight to a pharmacy. He said nothing as we drove home and nothing for the rest of the day until the evening when he was ready to talk. 'So, that doctor's worried about you, ya know.'

'Yeah, him and the rest of the world.' I rolled my eyes, sick to death of everyone's concern.

'So, what did he say?'

'He doesn't think your doctor at home is taking care of you.'

I tried hard not to snigger rudely at this, knowing I was the charlatan in that relationship.

'Oh yeah?'

'You're on too many different things.' *No shit.* 'Why are you on both long and slow-release OxyContin? He said you don't need both.'

'I need both.'

'But ... you don't.'

I stared the very definition of 'if looks could kill' at him and said, slowly, 'I. Need. Both.' He stared back, unwavering. He was angry, and I felt caught out. I felt like yelling, 'You know why! I'm a fucking junkie with chronic illness and chronic grief. I need it all, and, in fact, I need more!'

But I didn't need to. He was learning it for himself in real-time.

High all the time

Soundtrack: *Tove Lo - 'Habits (Stay High)'*

'Are we there yet? Are we there yet? Are we there yet?' my brain asked on repeat for the next 24 hours, waiting to get to a pharmacy. I was desperately trying to be patient and give Alessandro time to make sense of what was happening, but I also really needed my fucking drugs. The next day we tried three pharmacies, as Alessandro drove from town to town only to be refused at each one. I sat in the car and waited so I wouldn't muddy the 'deal' with my me-ness. None of these small Tuscan towns had any need to stock such a strong drug and would normally only order it in as needed. Most people could wait the few days it took; we, however, could not.

The next day was much the same. We drove for hours, trying one Tuscan pharmacy after another, until finally, on our fourth try, we found one that could provide.

The relief and excitement of seeing Alessandro walking out with that white paper bag of goodies was palpable. My heart pounded, and my mouth salivated with anticipation. He gruffly handed me a single slow-release blue pill and put the rest in the trunk. He wasn't taking his eyes off them this time. These were not my first choice of oxy, and certainly not in this quantity or at this dose, but they would reduce my withdrawals, and that was all we could hope for at this stage. The doctor had refused to match my prescribed dose strength, which I was, of course, already doubling. So we were in for a rocky ride. As the

Italian doctor told Alessandro, 'She is going to have withdrawals; there is no preventing that. All I can do now is give you enough to survive the rest of your trip. Best of luck.' The doctor was just as concerned about 'Sandro as he was about me – perhaps more so.

Honestly, I don't remember the withdrawals being the worst part of this trip. They sucked – I was moody, emotional, tired and achy – but it was bearable with the slow-release tablets somewhat tiding me over. What was worse was the relationship between Alessandro and me. He realised it might have been a mistake to invite a young, suicidal drug addict on holiday. *Weird.*

I watched him enter his fear response. His emotional reaction was that of someone seeing a snake, freezing and then slowly backing away, one slow step at a time. Joke's on him, though, because I was a mother-fucking boa constrictor, and I was about to love him to death! The more he pulled away, the more desperately I attached myself to him. Everything about it was reminiscent of my entire seven-year relationship with Simon but condensed into just four weeks. *Fun!*

I estimate that I nearly died around three times that trip. I'm very lucky not to have overdosed or gone into fatal withdrawals. I'm fairly certain Alessandro hovered a pillow over my face at least twice as I slept. Then there was the day we followed the GPS down a muddy embankment and into oncoming traffic. We were on our way to visit my friend Grace and her husband Federico, who lived in a small town outside Bologna. Alessandro was driving. He was getting confused by the directions and constantly grumbling at the GPS lady for butchering the Italian language with her American twang. 'Why don't they just program her with an Italian accent? Can't Zuckerberg do something about this? It's offensive.' I didn't think it was really Mark's domain, but I thought it best to let him vent. The GPS was giving instructions that didn't seem right, but as we were new to the area, I told him to listen to the lady in the computer.

We arrived at a dirt road surrounded by tall, unkempt grass. Alessandro was hesitant, but I assured him the nice lady wouldn't lead us astray, so we followed her advice. Several metres on, the road started to get thinner, the grass taller, and we were now encased in trees on either side. What had been a rough gravel road quickly became wet and muddy. There was nowhere to turn the car around, and stopping would mean getting bogged in the deepening mud, so we ploughed on with arseholes clenched. We were in deep shit physically and metaphorically as we slid down the muddy embankment on our way to certain death. 'Follow the GPS, she says! Follow the goddamned GPS!' Now I was in the bad books again, along with the GPS lady.

I held my breath and gripped the sides of the tin can with wheels, just like Mum does every time she enters a vehicle with me. Alessandro was now swearing loudly in multiple languages as he tried to stabilise the car, 'Ah! Minchia! You motherrrr FARRNK-CULO!' I stayed very still and quiet while remembering the scene from *The Office* where Dwight and Michael drove their car into a lake following the GPS. *Am I at their mental capacity? Am I ... dumb?*

As we slid down the hill, holding on for dear life, we began to hear traffic through the trees.

Oh good, the hill is coming to an end! Oh shit, the hill is coming to an end! We both braced ourselves and went forth blindly. As we reached the bottom of the hill, Alessandro – smooth as anything – slid out onto the main connecting road. The only reason we are alive to tell the tale is that there was no immediate oncoming traffic. It was pure dumb luck.

Alessandro was clasping the wheel for all he was worth while I stifled my laughter. *Why am I like this?* I was so pumped full of adrenaline that I wanted to punch the sky and scream out the window, but next to me was an angry six-foot-three Italian man squished into the world's smallest car, clinging for dear life. His face was red, and his nostrils flared as he stared straight ahead at the now beautifully paved road. I turned to him and opened my mouth, ready to apologise with my perfect Urkel impression. *Did I do thaaaat?*

'Don't,' he cut me off. 'Just ... don't.'

We got through the rest of the trip only because Italy is the single most wonderful place in the world and the true love of my life, but it certainly wasn't what either of us had envisaged. Despite the varied array of near-death experiences that took place throughout the trip, I still believed the relationship was salvageable. Alessandro was constantly frustrated and annoyed by me, but he continued to reciprocate my affections and tell me how much he loved me. I believed him because I needed to. Right up until I boarded the plane home, he held me, kissed me and whispered 'ti voglio bene' in my ear.

It wasn't until I talked to Grace months later that she told me what he had really been saying. In Italian, there are two ways to say 'I love you' – one for family and friends and the other for romantic partners. Guess which one I was getting?

Every time I expressed my love, Alessandro would take my face in his hands, gaze deep into my eyes and reply, 'Ti voglio bene. Ti amo.' *'Ti amo'* means I am *in love* with you; 'ti voglio bene' is for friends and family. While I was bravely opening my bruised heart, he gave me the equivalent of a pat on the back and a 'good on ya, mate!' He knew exactly what he was doing. I don't understand people who can fake their emotions like that. In primary school, I was known as 'the Girl with a Thousand Faces' because I couldn't hide how I felt to save myself. Once, during a one-night stand, this guy asked me to tell him I loved him. *Gag.* I couldn't even do it to make it end faster, and god knows I wanted it to end! That was one single night. Alessandro had been pulling it off flawlessly for a month.

I called Mum a few days before the flight home to ask her to make a doctor's appointment for me on my arrival. I needed to renew my script as soon as physically possible. She told me she had been putting something away in my drawer when she came across dozens of loose pills. 'Plenty to get you through until your next appointment,' she said nonchalantly. My stomach simultaneously fell to my feet and leap-frogged out my mouth. Remember that old health insurance commercial where the little boy says, 'My legs went that way, and my head went that way'? That was me.

It was over – I had to tell her.

'Mum, I still need a doctor's appointment, okay?' Shame leering at me from the sidelines.

'I'm telling you, Kirst, there are heaps here. You will be fine.' Oh my fuck. I'm really going to have to just lay it out in black and white.

I started to become confused myself. Why wasn't she questioning the fact they were out of their pill sheet? What kind of oxy addict just accidentally leaves 20 pills rolling around in a drawer and forgets about them? It has literally never happened in the history of time. I kept the pills hidden in my underwear drawer once I had opened them up and snorted the powder inside. I kept the capsule casings because I didn't want anyone – specifically her – finding them in the bin or floating in the toilet (they were too light to flush, because yes, of course, I had tried) and worrying that I was up to no good. *Which I clearly was!*

'Mum, listen, *please*.' I needed to get this out quickly, or I would never say it.

'Honestly, babe …' she continued.

For god's sake, Mum, they're fucking empty!

'Mum … they're empty.' I felt winded, like when Ben would double-bounce me on the trampoline as a kid. I'd go flying through the air before collapsing against the hard, dry earth, struggling to breathe.

I let my words hang in the air, awaiting any follow-up questions, but they never came.

'Oh, haha,' she chuckled. 'Okay.'

'O … kay?' I replied, with complete and utter confusion, but not wanting to rock the already-sinking boat. 'Okay! Well, great. Cool. Coolio.' *Too far.*

'What the fuck is happening?' asked my internal monologue to herself. *I dunno, brain; just go with it.* Mum went on to make the appointment for me, and we never spoke of it again. In hindsight, her brain was likely fried from the recent loss of both her husband and mother in rapid succession, and she simply couldn't weave together all the pieces of my sneakiness. But whatever the reason, I was grateful for the lack of interrogation.

Mum met me at Melbourne International Airport on December 12th 2017, after 30 hours of travel. Exhausted, I walked through the automatic double doors with my luggage, the familiar twitches of withdrawal now kicking into overdrive and yet another broken heart trailing behind me. I saw my beautiful mum's smiling face as she looked at the daughter she recognised through only a mother's eyes. Her eyes still lit up when she saw me. Her arms still opened, welcoming me in any state. I dropped my luggage and flew into her arms, my home. I had been looking for a man to provide the love I needed to heal me, but my home was here; my safety blanket was here. I took a deep breath, withdrawing from our lengthy reunion hug, 'Mum, I think I want to go to rehab.'

'Okay, babe. Let's get you home first,' she said, holding my hand.

The next day I went to the doctor to renew what would be my final script before they weaned me off at rehab. I took it to the pharmacy that now knew me by name and went to the supermarket bathroom to snort my first pill, unable to wait until I got home. This was my regular process. Soothed, I went home and started researching drug and alcohol rehab facilities.

As it turned out, detox centres and rehabs are not cheap. Similar to psychiatric facilities, they can't be claimed on health insurance, and you are usually looking at a minimum of ten grand for your 28-day stint. I was so hopeless I even begged my psychiatrist to perform transcranial magnetic stimulation, but he refused, saying, 'It won't work. Your depression is caused by your maladaptive personality disorders. It only treats clinical depression.'

'My depression is my personality?'

'In a word ... yes.'

'But I've been sad since I was a little girl.'

'Exactly. That is not clinical depression. It is not normal for children to be depressed. That is the result of environmental factors which caused you to develop coping strategies that no longer serve you as an adult.'

'Oh.' There was a long pause before I asked, 'So if this is just who I am, does that mean I'm going to feel this miserable forever? Because if that's the case, I can't do it. There's no way. I can barely get through this sentence, let alone the next 50 years. Shit, if I'm anything like my grandma, I'll live to be 101, so you're telling me I'm fucked for the *next 70 years?*'

I broke down and sobbed. I wanted to get on my hands and knees and beg him to lobotomise me. Just shove a pin through my eye socket and end it all. Make me a vegetable, please! But instead, I slid back into the oversized leather chair and let it swallow me whole.

He droned on, explaining the myriad medications and psychological techniques I could learn over the forthcoming months and years to make my life somewhat bearable. Many of which I had already tried or been working on for the past decade. Any remaining hope was fast dwindling. I'm sure in the right circumstances, with a willing participant, his suggestions would have been helpful, but being told you have to learn, practise and be patient when you are so suicidal your entire body feels like it is on fire isn't helpful. All you want is a quick fix, a cool bucket of water dumped over you to soothe the immediate danger.

Being suicidal is not just a prolonged sadness that eventually goes away. It is an all-consuming rotting from within, as though your very soul is being shredded. It is the sense that you will never feel anything but despair, darkness and devastating loneliness for the rest of your life. It is heavy and gnawing, and you can feel it physically in the twisting of your gut, the aching of your heart and the exhausted dragging of your limbs. It is desperately trying to stay alive when your entire being is begging to be put out of its misery every second. There is no release. Pure and simple, it is hell on earth. It takes effort to maintain a healthy mind, but when you are so deep down in the pits of psychological distress that you can't remember the word for the stuff you pour on your cereal of a morning, you sure as hell don't have the energy or mental capacity to work on yourself.

During depressive episodes, I used to complain to Simon that I hated my brain. To which he would reply like someone who has never experienced mental illness, 'How can you hate your brain? You *are* your brain.' I thought that was the meanest response in the world. My brain is evil and cruel. She's dangerous and spiteful. How could he say I am she? But what this doctor was saying was worse than that. He insisted Brain was the good guy. It was me who was fucked.

I reached out to a couple of friends who I thought might be able to help. It was Sam's brother who recommended a facility in Sydney called South Pacific Private. There were certain prerequisites to getting in, which made it feel exclusive, like I was applying for my Masters in Self Destruction. South Pacific, or SPP, is a mental health treatment facility specialising in addictive tendencies. It appealed to me because its goal was to get at the *why* of addiction, not just manage the detox and withdrawals. Their aim was long-term healing. They covered all kinds of addictions, from eating disorders to substance abuse, gambling, and – my bread and butter – co-dependency. In order to be accepted, you had to have both an addiction and a diagnosed mental illness. *Ding ding ding! Thank you!* Finally, I was excelling in something. I applied and was accepted for December 26th – a Boxing Day miracle! Now, all I had to do was wait out the two weeks before I could attend without killing myself.

This was exceedingly difficult as Alessandro had pulled 'a Simon' and fucked off. Since I had touched back down on Victorian soil, he had stopped replying to my messages and answering my calls. He had walked me onto the plane with promises of everlasting love, and **poof!** He disappeared as soon as I was a safe distance away. My rage hit new heights, and I became truly insane. I felt like I was living in the fucking *Twilight Zone*. Had I entered some kind of alternate reality where men were so completely terrified of conflict that they simply 'block and delete' instead of having difficult conversations? Have we seriously been mollycoddling them for so long that they have lost all human decency and the ability to say, 'Sorry, this isn't working out'? Because it really seems that way.

I knew I needed help. I knew I was unravelling faster than Luann de Lesseps could slide out of handcuffs in the back of a police car, and I knew a healthy relationship was well beyond my current capacity, but I didn't realise that expecting to be told I was dumped was too much.

This is why there are so many stories of men killing their wives and children so they can start a new life with someone else. It is actually easier for them to murder their entire family, chop them up into tiny pieces and dump them in a water tank than it is to have a difficult conversation. *Fuck. Ing. Hell. #nOtAlLmEn*

The not-knowing was agonising. My guts churned with anxiety as I cycled through all the potential reasons he wasn't responding. He doesn't love me. He hates me. He's not okay. He's been in an accident. He's dead.

Losing Dad the way I had left me on high alert. When I don't hear from someone as readily as I usually do, I automatically expect tragedy. It causes an entire emotional upheaval, as I am taken right back to the days following Dad's death. I am inconsolable, and the anxiety does not end until I have an answer. In Alessandro's case, this would last the entire two weeks.

Help, I have done it again

Soundtrack: *Sia – 'Breathe Me'*

It was our first Christmas without Dad. In an attempt to minimise the sense of his absence, the extended family decided that we would celebrate at a restaurant rather than at home. Dad was amazing at Christmas. It was like he saved up all his social energy for this one single day a year where he would shine. Each year, we would have the extended family over to our house. Mum and I would cook up a storm, Ben would organise group games, and Dad would greet everyone with bubbly before giving them a tour of the garden and regaling them with stories from the year that was. He was charismatic and jovial. He popped bottles of champagne over the balcony and laughed heartily. Dad genuinely found Christmas magical, and because of him, so did I.

So, when I heard that we would be shifting from our traditional grand English lunch to a whacky German bierhaus, I was perplexed. Mum, Ben and I arrived at the bierhaus for Chrissy lunch, joining the extended family. The restaurant was huge and filled with kitsch German pieces, from giant bier steins to solidified pretzels. If it could in any way be considered German, it was on those walls. The staff were dressed in traditional garb: the ladies rocking their best dirndls and the men lederhosen-ed up. There was a live band playing Volksmusik and Umpapa and a large buffet with everything you could dream of, from goose stuffed with apple and sausage, potato dumplings and Christmas stollen for dessert. Oh, and beer. So much beer.

The scene was completely overstimulating to my already heightened senses, but to make matters worse, I was also coming down. I had finished my new script of oxy 24 hours earlier, and I was crashing. I had assumed I would be okay to hold out for two days until I got to rehab and was weaned off properly; however, I was not expecting to be vomited on by a barrage of German culture. Things I have learned: if there is somewhere you want to avoid while coming down off drugs, it's a German bierhaus on a very popular holiday surrounded by family.

Of the table of 12, only Mum and Ben knew about my addiction. All anyone else knew was that I'd been a wee bit wobbly since 'the deaths', but that I had found love and even travelled to Italy on a romantic escapade. I walked into that 'Haus of Hell' with a painted-on grin, planning to lie my way through the entire lunch and not talk about anything of substance. 'Have you tried the cauliflower? It's deviiiiine!' 'Oh, this old thing?' I'd say, waving at my dress. 'I got it overseas. So, you can't have one. Ha!' Everyone fake laughs. End scene. That was the only way I knew to survive.

I sat between Mum and Ben, my buffers to the table full of questions. I had planned on drinking a substantial amount to numb both the withdrawals and the hyper-stimulation of the room, but my anxiety was so strong I couldn't take anything in. Then my aunty leaned over and asked, with a smile, 'So! Tell us about the big trip. How's the new man?'

My stomach was gripping tightly, and my throat closed in on itself. I swallowed, 'Oh. Um.' *Fuck fuck fuck fuck fuck fuck fuck.* '*Really* great.' I smiled back, displaying all my teeth. I took a deep breath and channelled Christmas Dad. I faked a conversation about the wonders of Italy for a few minutes, then excused myself to the bathroom to cry. The tears started, and they wouldn't stop. I sat on the toilet, my undies around my ankles and crumpled up toilet paper covering my mouth to muffle the sound of my heavy sobs. *Merry Christmas to all, and to all a fuck off.*

There was nothing I could do. I couldn't hide it. I cried all my make-up off until I was red-faced and blotchy like Kim Kardashian ugly crying (if you know, you know). 'Kirst? You in here?' my brother's voice called into the ladies' toilet from the doorway.

'Ah, yeah. Coming.'

'You okay? You've been gone a while.'

I made my way out of the toilet cubicle. 'I don't want everyone to know. I feel like they think I'm a loser.'

'Nah, they just think you're upset about Dad.'

'Yeah? Okay.'

'Do you want a stroopwafel?'

'What? No.'

'Or a yard of ale?'

'Umm ...'

'Or a ... Heisenberg strudel hausen bloch?'

'Are you just saying German-sounding words?'

'Yes. Let's go!'

I smirked, which was a testament to my brother because that was the closest I had come to a genuine smile all day. 'Fine,' I grumbled and walked back to the dessert table to fill the gaping wound in my heart with pastries.

As I neared the table, shoving something buttery and sweet into my mouth, my grandpa jumped up, took my plate and set it down on the table. Before I could resist, he grabbed my arm and flung me onto the dance floor. *Kill me now.* Suddenly, we were the focal point of the entire restaurant, as my 88-year-old grandpa forced me to do the Charleston Shuffle with him. Did I mention the band wasn't even playing at this point? No. He just saw an opportunity and leapt at it. I looked over at Mum in disbelief, my eyes calling out for help. She returned my gaze with a grimace and a shrug. *Jesus Christ, my Lord and saviour, if indeed you are real and have ever loved me, you will do me the kindness of killing me right this instant. Amen.*

I waited all day to hear from 'Sandro. We had wrapped presents for each other before I left and had planned to FaceTime on Christmas Day and open them together. As he was in Toronto, my Aussie Xmas came first. I kept my phone on me all day, but the call never came. Not even a text to explain that he had been captured by aliens and would get back to me as soon as the probing was done (which would be the only acceptable reason for his lack of communication)!

I had bought him a beautiful leather satchel that was way out of my price range and written him a heartfelt letter apologising for being a disaster and reiterating the depth of my love. He got me a generic notebook that read 'Find joy in the ordinary' on the cover and a card with a turtle on it. He obviously didn't know what to say, so he filled the card with turtle facts and signed it, 'You're a wonderful person, love A'. Please note I have never mentioned turtles. Turtles are a'right. That's the entire extent of my feelings toward them. More offensive still, he called me 'wonderful'.

Later, I would read the card to Grace to get her impression.

'Wait, he said what?' she scoffed. 'He called you wonderful?'

'Mmm ...'

'Wonderful?'

'Yup.'

'But ... wow.'

'Ugh. I know.'

'Sorry, but in what world?' By now, she was crying with laughter, which I found a tad rude but also totally valid. 'You are a lot of things, Moo, but wonderful is not one of them. You're exciting, you're fun, you're unpredictable, stunningly attractive and devastatingly thin ...'

'Do go on.'

'... But wonderful? Who does he think he is?'

At 5 am on Boxing Day, I began calling Alessandro frantically, trying to get to him before my flight to Sydney. I was desperate for any sense of closure before my phone was confiscated. No mobile phones in rehab – it distracts from 'the work'.

'Yes?'

'Oh, you answered! Great. Thank you.' I was pathetically relieved.

'Yeah, look, I don't have long. I'm with Josh. It's Christmas.'

'Yeah, I know, we were supposed to ... Did you like your present?'

'It's nice.'

'Good ... good. So, um, okay. Well, I just wanted to let you know that I'm going to rehab. Like, I'm leaving for the airport right now. I'm not allowed my phone, so I won't be able to talk to you for about a month. But, um, they have a pay phone there, so if I can work out the extension, I could ...'

'Yeah, 'kay.'

'So, erm, where have you been? I've been really ... I dunno, not good. Do you hate me? You hate me, don't you? I'm sorry, I ...'

'I don't hate you! Jesus! I'm exhausted, okay? I'm fucking *exhausted*.'

'By me?'

'By all of it! Look, I gotta go. I'm glad you're getting help and that I was able to help you get there. And, hey, I really hope you stick with it. I'd love to meet the real you one day.'

'Huh?'

'Merry Christmas, weirdo. Bye.'

'Goodb...' He hung up, and I was left standing in my bedroom, wondering why he thinks he is my saviour when he nearly let me die under his care and knowingly triggered my very raw abandonment trauma. *'Oh hey, by the way, I never loved you! Byeee!' *slams door** Not one single person has contributed less to my wellbeing than Alessandro. It's truly amazing how he got there. Is it narcissism, or is it just the patriarchy? Someone send help: call Clementine Ford or Roxanne Gay. The boys are not alright.

I don't ever want to drink again ... I just need a friend

Soundtrack: *Amy Winehouse – 'Rehab'*

It was Boxing Day, and I was in a taxi from the airport on my way to the Sydney rehab facility. With nothing better to do, I decided to lighten the mood by texting Mum and Ben. 'They tried to make me go to rehab; I said yeah, yeah, yeah!' Mum replied with the face-palm emoji, and Ben LOL'd, but in a way that made me feel sad. Well, shit, if I couldn't lighten the mood with a little dark humour, I had truly exhausted all my options.

I arrived at the facility, which was a stone's throw from Curl Curl Beach. It was small but appealing, and all of a sudden, I felt like I was Lindsay Lohan recovering from 'exhaustion' somewhere in Miami. *Get sober and a tan? Don't mind if I do!* I sat in the reception area with two male patients waiting to be admitted – both mid to late 30s. The guy to my right was attractive in a Pete Doherty I-haven't-slept-in-a-week type of way. His eyes were so sunken that his under-eyes were a deep purple.

I would later learn his name was Mike, and he had been a heroin addict since he was 15. He was eight years clean and sober but had since transferred his addictive tendencies to gambling and sex. I liked him right away. He had a gentleness about him that felt familiar. He had that 'tough guy with a heart of gold' thing down pat. I felt safe with him. The other guy, not so much.

He, too, would have been good-looking once upon a time. He was tall, blonde and had a decent face. But of all the residents in the 100-patient facility, he was the only one I was ever afraid of. He was constantly fidgeting and scratching. He would sit down, then get up to pace in circles, and his pupils were dilated to the entire width of his eyes. His very presence was erratic. *Fuck. I just described myself, didn't I?* I had the sense that, at any moment, he could snap and pull out a weapon or run through the double glass doors, screaming and ripping his shirt off. He was intense in a way I had never felt before.

As a kid, I remember Dad telling me not to look wild animals in the eyes because it can aggravate them. So, I sat in reception with my eyes down. I used the last few moments with my phone to chat with Aniibish, AKA Mah Bad Bish and Alessandro's cousin. She's from Calgary, and we became friends through Mum's friendship with her aunt, Alessandro's mother. I kept obsessively checking to see if Alessandro was online, looking for that little dot next to his name to turn green. *'Talk to me. Talk to me. Talk to me,'* I pleaded with the device. *'That's how manifestation works, right? I want it. Now make it so!'* I heard nothing. Not only was I about to enter substance withdrawal but also love-addiction withdrawal. *Fucking ouch.*

In the background, the boys were chatting like two men meeting in a prison yard. 'So, what are you in for?' Mike asked.

'Ice. I'm not even addicted. I have my own construction business, and it helps get me through really busy days, ya know? Anyway, I've got another kid on the way, so the wife wants me to clean up.' He spoke so quickly it took a moment for my brain to catch up, like sound chasing light.

'Oh, you've got kids? Me, too. We just had our second,' replied Mike, unfazed by anything he'd just heard.

'We got a two-year-old boy and another on the way.'

'Nice. We got two girls.'

Me to me: *And I can't even get a text back!*

If it wasn't for Bish, I think it would have been very easy for Alessandro to convince me that our entire relationship was in my head and that I had misinterpreted everything. She was communicating with both of us at the time – a torturous task I wouldn't wish on my worst enemy. From my end, she was hearing the story already relayed – not perfect or pretty by any stretch, but sadly true. From him, the story would change from one week to the next. One minute he would tell her how 'Italy was just meant to be about two old friends getting together – Kirsty got totally carried away' (Note: we were never friends) to 'I was ready to start a life with that woman – I loved her!' (Note: *ti voglio bene* does not count).

A little aside here for the guys: if you happen to find yourself spending time with a woman, telling her that you love her, taking her on romantic getaways and giving her multiple orgasms ... YOU. ARE. IN. A. RELATIONSHIP!

Suffice it to say, if I didn't have Bish's input, Alessandro's confusion and gaslighting would have worked beautifully. I would have gone on to believe I was the entire problem when I was only 78.5% of it. She truly is one of the best people I know. I visited her in Calgary once, many years before Alessandro was even a thing, and the girl picked me up in her truck, playing my own album full-blast. It wasn't even a good recording; it was a demo CD my mum had sent her. 'Get in, biAtch! We're going karaoke-ing!' were the first words I ever heard from her mouth. It was love at first high note. I dare anyone to watch Bish sing *Total Eclipse of the Heart* and not fall in love. It simply cannot be done.

A radio quietly played behind the reception desk, the only place in the facility that allowed recorded music. There was a common area with a piano and guitar that the residents could play, but no devices were allowed. Listening to music through headphones could be isolating and, again, distract from 'the work'. Just as the nurse came to show me to my room, *Back to Black* started playing on the radio. The last words I heard before I checked into rehab were Amy Winehouse lamenting, 'My odds are stacked. I go back to black ...' I tried not to take that as a bad omen.

The nurse that took me through was a large woman with a kind face. She wore colourful clothes and a bold statement necklace. She tried to make me feel comfortable as she showed me to the room I would share with two other residents. Her chipper small talk exhausted me as I forced minimal replies. I had nothing left to give. I was a shell of a person. She asked me to place my bags on the bed and open them so she could inspect them for contraband. She wasn't very thorough, which made me regret not stuffing a flask of vodka in a side pocket, or at the very least, some real coffee. The decaf provided was not going to cut it for my current 10 mug a day consumption rate. I thought about how prepared Sam had been for Cancer Camp and wondered what she would make of my being here. That said, had she been alive, I don't think I would have reached this point. *Where are you, Sam? I need you.*

The nurse's voice broke through my daydreaming, 'What do you think? Do these contain alcohol?' she asked, waving my packet of make-up removal wipes in my face.

'No, I don't thi ...'

'Hmm ... it doesn't say in the ingredients. I'm going to take them anyway. Okay, love?'

'Ah, sure.' I resented the implication that I would use alcohol-based products on my precious skin but allowed her to take them because I didn't want to be seen as the troublemaker on day one.

She continued, 'You wouldn't believe how many patients I've seen sucking on alcohol swabs, wet wipes or drinking hand sanitiser in desperation.' The thought instantly gave me heartburn.

The nurse gave me a brief tour of the facility. She showed me the nurses' stations, the dispensaries, the outdoor ping pong area and 'meditation nook' (a small area with a water feature and wooden bench), and the bathrooms – that, upon entry, reminded me I needed to wear thongs in the shower. The common area was filled with a collection of mismatched sofas, tables and the beat-up piano that needed a tune-up just as much as the patients did. Attached was a balcony that looked onto the beach. For a hospital, it was quite beautiful. There were meeting rooms of various sizes that looked unassuming but would be used to confront our deepest darkest demons – AKA cry, scream and get on each other's nerves – but ultimately develop life-long friendships. The kitchen, which must have been decked out with decorations, had already been stripped of festive cheer. All that remained were a few loose pieces of tinsel under the plastic tables and chairs.

Rumour had it that the no-sugar rule had been broken, and ice cream was allowed as a Christmas Day treat. The kitchen staff had foolishly left the nine-litre tub of ice cream out for the residents rather than serving it. Nine kilos of sugar and cream left, without supervision, for a horde of addicts whose closest sniff of sweetness in weeks had been the dried dates at supper. Allegedly the residents were like hungry zombies, piling their bowls high with scoop upon scoop of vanilla bliss. There had been enough ice cream for each resident to have at least two scoops each, but the hordes were overcome with excitement. Some people were seen taking as many as seven scoops, leaving others with none. Many poor men and women missed out that day. I can't imagine the devastation of walking up to the giant bucket of dreams only to have your hopes shattered as you realise, tragically, it's empty. So sad, so, so sad. When I first heard this story, it made me sick to my stomach, but after a week of living in sugar-free prison, I too would be found loitering near the snacks table at Narcotics Anonymous, trying to figure out how many Tim Tams I could shove into my pockets.

An addiction specialist once told me that the only thing more addictive than heroin (opioids) is sugar. When you have your drug of choice taken away, you start looking for other means to fill the void. It's all about distraction and dopamine. Distract from the internal agony of existence and drive up dopamine to make you feel better about being trapped on this mortal coil. SPP removed all of our distractions upon arrival. We lost the obvious addictions that had brought us there: alcohol, drugs, sex, porn and cigarettes. But, also, more acceptable forms of addiction, like work, technology/phones, TV and, of course, stimulants in the form of caffeine and sugar. We were stripped bare, leaving us raw to the emotions that we had been running from for the longest time. It was like being handed a giant box of all your deepest traumas and being forced to look inside. So, of course, when someone puts a pile of lovely, distracting, happy, smiley sugar in front of you and says, 'Have at it', you're gonna lose your goddamn mind. *Mmmm, delicious distractions.*

My memories of the welcome tour are foggy. I remember feeling as though I was being dragged from room to room, having to feign gratitude when I was beyond exhausted. I remember wanting so desperately for it to be over so I could crawl into bed and cry, but I kept swallowing my tears, not wanting their first impression of me to be the annoying crybaby. As it would turn out, we were all annoying crybabies. It was one of the dominant themes of the place. A few residents looked like they might introduce themselves to me while I was being shown around, but they stopped themselves as my demeanour frightened them off. For this, I was grateful. I didn't have the energy for 'hello'.

Then, 'Hi, I'm Tommy!' A fresh-faced young man bounded up to me with his hand outstretched.

'Oh hey, I'm Kirsty.' I was completely taken aback by his energy.

'Have you had the grand tour?' he asked, gesturing widely. 'I can show you around if you like.'

'Ah, no ... I mean, no thanks. I've just finished it.'

'Okay, well, welcome to the *Big Brother* house! It's a good season.' He was bubbly and charismatic. Funny, even. Why the fuck was he here?

He then turned to the nurse, 'Do you know if my mum sent a package through? I'm waiting on a Turbie Twist for my hair.' To be fair, he did have luscious locks. *Also, wtf is a Turbie Twist?*

'I'll check for you, love, but you need to tell your mum to stop sending chocolate. You know it's contraband.'

'Yeah, yeah, I have.'

As the nurse walked away, he turned to me and whispered that his mum now leaves blocks of chocolate scattered in the bushes at the front of the facility. I was tired and grumpy, and my body ached from my soul out, but at that moment, all I could think was, '*Who is this guy, and how do I make him like me?*'

By midday, I was getting antsy to start the weaning process. That's what they do, right? You see it in films. They wean you off your drug of choice safely and slowly. 'When will I see the doctor?' I asked the nurse.

'Let's get you all settled in first. There are several new patients in today so it could take a while.'

'Right, okay. Can you give me an estimate, though? It's just that I'm really anxious, and I'm in a lot of pain.' I tried and failed not to sound like a jonesing addict.

By now, I was in serious pain. My body felt as if the muscle was sliding away from the bone, like a perfectly cooked lamb shank. My anxiety was so out of control I wanted to bash the thoughts out of my skull with my fist – but it's difficult to do that without looking next-level mental. So, instead, I forced all the feelings deep down within, and my body reacted by lightly vibrating as the feelings tried to break down the walls. You know when a fly gets stuck inside, between the window and the curtains, and in its panic to get free, it bounces itself erratically between the two surfaces? That's how it felt. This wild ball of energy inside me, banging down the walls to get free.

'I'm sorry, love, I can't give you any more information than that, but it will be today.'

I must have looked particularly distressed because she put her hand on my shoulder and looked at me sympathetically.

'What is your drug of choice, sweetie?'

'Huh? Oh, opioids. Oxy. I had a spinal surgery … and anyway, here I am.'

'Sure. I used to be an ICU nurse. We see a bit of that.' She took a moment before she changed tack, 'So, do you work?'

'Ha, no. I just finished studying nutrition.'

'And how did you find that? Using while you were studying, I mean.'

'I mean, not great. I didn't drink while in prac, but I'd snort lines between patients. That's the thing I'm probably most ashamed of.'

'Oh, don't worry, sweetie. We've all got stories like that here. When I was an ICU nurse, I was a heroin addict and used to shoot up in the bathroom during long shifts. I got fired when I was caught slumped over in a disabled toilet with a needle poking out my arm.'

I stared at her, trying to look as non-judgemental and relaxed as possible. 'Oh, I didn't realise …' I replied, one eye twitching uncontrollably.

'Oh yes, most of the people who work here are in recovery of some variety. Co-dependency, mental illness, addiction. That kind of thing.'

I had a splitting headache from keeping all the feelings in. I was sure they would burst out of my sockets, splattering my eyeballs against the wall in the process.

'Cool …' I replied. *Help.*

All I could think about was waking up from spinal surgery and imagining the person solely responsible for my survival was fucked off her nut on heroin. I know I am in no place to judge, ya girl has done some *sheet*, but no one was going to die if I gave them the wrong B vitamin. This woman was literally holding life and death in her fingertips in the ICU. That's some *Dr Death* shit right there.

That was the moment I realised that there is always further to fall. You may think you have reached rock bottom, but the trouble with addiction is the bar keeps moving. Like the world's most dangerous game of limbo, you always find yourself saying, 'Sure, I do this, but I'd never do *that!*' before inevitably doing 'that' and then some.

I thought back to Denise's advice regarding eating disorders, 'Once things get bad, they can get worse really quickly. These things tend to spiral out of control unless you actively put a stop to it.' Like replying to an automated text, you can't just hope it goes away on its own; you have to opt out: STOP. Dear God, STOP.

It was 5 pm by the time I got to see the doctor. It had been nearly three full days without my drugs, and I was white-knuckling it bad. It took all of me to hold on until I got that one little pill. Just one pill to make me feel normal again. I sat outside his office waiting to be called in, legs shaking in anticipation and wondering how many he would give me to start off the weaning process. *Even one baby 5mg would be amazing right now.*

'Come in,' called the gentle Indian voice from behind the door. I walked into the office and was greeted by a man in his late 50s with a thick black beard. He introduced himself and asked me to sit down. I listened to the roundness of the words floating out of his mouth. I had always loved Indian accents and found them soothing.

'Kristen?'

'Actually, it's Kirsten, or Kirsty. Either way, I don't mind. Just not Kristen … ew, I mean, please.'

'Ha, ha, noted,' he chuckled warmly.

'So, opioids, ey? Oh dear,' he said as if I had just told him I had eaten too many biscuits.

'Ah, yeah, I had a spinal fusion about five years ago and, um, then I was diagnosed with bipolar, but some people don't think I have it, but … anyway, I'm on mood stabilisers. Then, like, a year ago, my best friend died of a brain tumour, and a few weeks later, my relationship of seven years ended. Um, and yeah, then my dad disappeared for a while, but it's okay coz it turns out he was just dead.' The doctor looked at me for a beat too long, so I kept talking to fill the space. 'Then I went to Italy with this older guy, and he, well, I dunno what's happening with him. I'm pretty sure he hates me. He's not very nice to me, but then I'm *me*, so why would he be? Anyway, I just really want to kill myself, but my mum won't let me, which is really fucking annoying coz I'm an adult, but also, it's my mum, so yeah. So … are you going to wean me off, or how does this work?'

'So, you are suicidal?'

'Well, yeah. Of course.'

'And how would you do it?'

'Sorry?'

'Do you know how you would do it? Do you have a plan?'

'Oh. Um, yeah.'

'Go on.'

'You want to know how I would kill myself?'

'Yes, if your mother let you. How would you do it?'

I had never been asked that before. I had told so many people I was suicidal. Simon, Mum, Ben, all of my GPs over the years, every psychologist and psychiatrist I had ever met, and no one had ever asked me that question. It felt extremely intimate but also oddly comforting. Someone wanted to listen. *Finally,* someone that wasn't afraid of the depth of my pain.

'Okay, well, I'd take every last one of my pills. Opioids, mood stabilisers, antidepressants, I dunno, fuckin' Panadol, anything I could find. Wash them down with a bottle of vodka and, just to be safe, jump off a building. Voila!'

'I see. Well, that's not going to work, I'm afraid.'

'Huh?'

'Yes – sorry. The most likely outcome of what you have described is paraplegia. You will most likely become a para or quadriplegic, probably with a massive brain injury, and be unable to do anything yourself. You won't be able to wash or feed yourself, you'll likely live in tremendous pain, and you certainly wouldn't be able to kill yourself anymore because now people would be caring for you full time. I'm assuming that burden would fall onto your mother. You love your mother, right? That is why you are still here. So why would you want to do that to her?'

I had no good response. I was stumped. He had debunked my entire plan within seconds, and it was really annoying.

Even then, my brain wanted to problem-solve and say, 'well, I'll just get a taller building then!' but he had sewn a seed of doubt that there was a building tall enough to get the job done.

My options were quickly dwindling. Option one had always been opioid abuse. But now, had I wanted to go back to abusing painkillers, I couldn't. My doctors were all aware I had an issue with them, and they'd red-marked my name across the country, meaning any time I legitimately need painkillers for surgery or anything serious, it is a huge palaver. Addiction = out. Option two was the ultimate backup plan: to kill myself. Now this plan had been debunked, and doubt instilled. Suicide = out. Option three was perhaps the worst of all, and I can't believe I'm actually saying this ... but option three was *to get better.*

Ggahiueghrsgnnoasfuckingjaekenmotheriodsgoggcuntingaliodfshitforbrains! FINE, I'LL FUCKING TRY IT. FUCK!

'Anyway, I'm in a lot of pain, sooo ...' I looked at him expectantly.

'Ah yes, your meds. No, I don't think we need to wean you. You've already had a great head start, with nearly three days clean, so I'm just going to give you some beta blockers to ease your withdrawal symptoms, and you can have paracetamol and ibuprofen for the pain.' *Fucking paracetamol! What am I, a toddler?*

'No, no, no, no. Ha, ha. But no, because I thought ... NO.' I felt the blood leave my extremities, which instantly became cold and tingly. My stomach lurched as if I was on a rollercoaster. All I could feel was blind panic. 'No, because you wean me off. You wean me off. That's what you do. You *wean* me off.' By now, I was in fits of tears. I have this hazy memory of sliding out of my chair onto the floor and sobbing, just like I had done when I received the news about Sam's death. But I think I may have restrained myself from actually doing so; at least, I hope I did.

'Look at the hold this drug has on you. You are crying like I just murdered your firstborn son.'

It felt like it. *Why did it feel like it?* I cried real tears as I lamented the fact I never got to say goodbye to my pills. I never had the ritual of appreciating that final capsule – hearing her crackle as I peeled her open, pouring her out and drinking her in, knowing it would be our final farewell. *Fuck!* Why didn't I treat every moment with her like it was our last?

'This reaction is not healthy. You are a smart girl. You deserve to be free of this drug. I can help you.'

I didn't even bother to wipe the tears from my face, knowing they would just keep coming. I thought about how I had given myself over completely after my spinal surgery and decided I would have to do the same here. This, whatever I was doing, wasn't working anymore. Maybe it had helped for a while, but now it was destroying me. Anything had to be better than this.

'Alright,' I said. 'I'll try.'

I wanted them all

Soundtrack: *Kirsten Moore – 'Incomplete'*

I remember very little of my first few days in 'da hab', but I was terrified – I know that. Having removed all of my obvious addictions, I sought comfort in 'familiar friends' like male company and disordered eating. I had never been one to purge after eating and my anorexia had been in recovery for almost a decade, but without any other release, all I wanted was to hide in the bathroom and make myself sick. I only did it once or twice before I decided this was unhelpful behaviour, but the urge to find an outlet was overwhelming.

I wasn't the only one struggling with this. There was a pretty girl about my age in group therapy with me who had been an ice addict, among other things. She would come to group talking rapid-fire about absolutely nothing. It was excruciating, and clear she was abusing her ADHD medication. She was seriously two-faced and would talk shit about me behind my back, but occasionally she would give me stolen sugar packets, so I let it slide. Once, she came to group with bloodshot eyes and these tiny little red spots all over her face. She said she had been up all night making herself sick, and the pressure in her head was so intense that it burst the blood vessels in her cheeks and eyes. That was the day I stopped purging. My face is the money-maker, I'm not going to walk around looking like a half-baked leper. *No sir!*

Another woman in her mid-40s arrived in my first week. She was tall and blonde, and would've been absolutely stunning before the years of alcohol abuse left her haggard and gaunt. I remember being jealous of her disappearing frame and annoyed at myself for it. She had been to the facility twice before but hadn't managed to maintain sobriety on the outside. Her husband had told her he would leave and take their daughter if it didn't work this time. She was always crying. Every time I saw her, she was in fits of tears, and again, I was jealous. She was bold enough to express what I was too afraid to show, surrounded by onlookers.

She snuck out on her first night. She waited until everyone was asleep and the facility was closed, then she jumped over the side fence and made a run for it. She walked for an hour until she found an open pub. She got absolutely hammered until she was kicked out for being drunk and disorderly, and then she made her way back to rehab. She was caught trying to sneak back in. The next day was very exciting as people were talking in whispers and hushed tones throughout the facility. The rumours were flying about her fate. This incident was taken very seriously as, apparently, this had happened on other visits. Eventually, it was decided that she was allowed to stay, but if it happened again, she would be asked to leave and not be allowed to return.

The next night she did it again.

I attached myself to the men in my group therapy classes – my attempt to fill the void that Simon and now Alessandro had left behind, and probably Dad, too, if we're going to get all Freudian about it. Flirting was forbidden, so I was cautious not to be overt with my attachment style. But going from suctioning myself to men like a barnacle to normal human interaction was difficult because, by day three, I was held back after group. My group therapist pulled me aside, which instantly ruffled my feathers. The only thing worse than being told what to do is being told what to do by a young, attractive therapist the same age as you.

'Yes?' I said, with all the attitude of a 15-year-old girl in a stand-off with her teacher.

'Thanks for hanging back,' she said, smiling. 'So I've noticed you're becoming quite close with a couple of the men in the group. Would you agree?'

'I'm just trying to make friends.' *What the fuck kind of question is that?* 'I mean, I've only been here three days.'

To her credit, I was already exchanging saliva with Evan by day two in the psych ward – only she didn't know that. I was shocked. It's not like I was walking around holding hands or exchanging lingering glances with anyone. I wasn't sneaking away to make out in the disabled bathroom or inviting boys into my room at night. I was behaving to the best of my abilities, which meant that what she was sensing was just me and my innate essence of slut (which is totally the name of the fragrance the 15-year-old I was channelling would wear: *Slut Du Jour* by Impulse). It was humiliating. Could everyone see my desperation? Was I walking around with a sign on my face that read DTF?

She continued, 'In an effort to help you get the most out of the program and address your co-dependency, myself and the other supervisors thought it would be best if you didn't spend time with the men anymore.' *Oh great! So, everyone is sitting around talking about the slut in room 5B.*

'What do you mean?' By now, I was starting to low-key freak-the-fuck-out.

'Remember this is all for your own good, not to punish you in any way.' She was talking slowly and calmly to avoid angering the beast in front of her, but it was too late: my nostrils were already in full flare as I anticipated her next few words. 'We no longer want you to be around the men in any capacity, social or otherwise.'

'Well, I live with them, so ...' I said, burning holes through her head and into the whiteboard behind her.

'Sure. We just want you to avoid talking to and sitting with them. Obviously, in group you will be together but try not to sit with them at meal times or during free time. Avoid walking with them during exercise and avoid eye contact or responding to them as much as possible.'

'Are you serious? I can't look at them? Sorry, but that's some *Handmaid's Tale* type shit.'

'I know it sounds extreme, but I promise this will benefit you. You are only here for a short time, and we want to make the most of that.'

'Whatever,' I replied, *werking* my petulant teenager like the pro I am.

'There is just one more thing,' she said, now looking worried. *Here we bloody go,* I thought, rolling my eyes. 'You will now have to stand up at every morning meeting and read this.' She handed me a small handwritten note.

Every morning after breakfast, all the residents and staff got together for a meeting to discuss the day's activities. Anyone who had broken the rules was required to stand up and 'repent' in front of the entire group. They claimed it was about taking ownership of our actions, but it felt a lot like ritual shaming.

The note read: *I am whole. I do not attract the male gaze for my self-worth.* Which is fine as a private affirmation, I thought to myself, not publicly announced to a group of strangers who I had to live with for the next month.

'You've got to be kidding me. You make it sound like I'm a fucking predator!' Infuriated, I went to storm out but quickly remembered I needed her help. *Shit.* 'Oh, um ... can you sign this for me, please?' I said sweetly, as if I hadn't just taken a giant shit on her desk.

She looked at the form and sighed, 'This is a contact form for your boyfriend?'

'Yes, yes it is,' I said, pretending I didn't notice the blatant irony of the situation. 'It's just you did say I could email him, seeing as he's in Canada and I can't call him.'

'Fine. You get one of these. Okay? One.'

'Yup. Got it.' I breathed a momentary sigh of relief before being flooded with overwhelming shame.

I spent the rest of the day in bed, alternating between crying and sleeping. Occasionally, I would march up and down the halls hoping that someone might ask me what was wrong, but there had been an influx of patients leading up to New Year's Eve and limited staff due to the holiday season, so everyone was run off their feet. No one had time to talk to me, which increased my sense of invisibility. I wasn't allowed to fall into the arms of the men for support, and the nurses weren't helping, so naturally, I lost my tiny mind.

I stormed up to the nurses' station and launched into a full-blown rant. 'So, what? Is no one going to talk to me? Isn't that the entire reason I'm here? I've literally just been told I'm not allowed to talk to any of the residents in the whole facility and now not even the goddamn nurses will see me? Look, if no one has time for me, just give me a fucking Valium. I mean, it goes against all the reasons I'm here but you're clearly too busy to assist me in any other way, so, hey, let's just lean on the drugs again!' This continued for quite some time before they caved and sent someone to talk to me. Just kidding! They gave me a Valium and put me to bed.

It was not a good day.

A few hours later, I woke groggy and puffy-eyed. My stomach gnawed with emptiness, and I had to keep checking my hands to make sure I still existed. I felt like I was fading away – like I was becoming less densely pixelated, and soon I'd be gone. Eventually, a nurse joined me in my room.

'I hear you're having a rough day. What's going on?'

By now, my rage had subsided, and I was left dull and lifeless. 'They've isolated me from everyone. I'm completely alone. I just want to go home.'

'But you're not alone, sweetheart. It's just the men we want you to avoid.'

'Exactly, I'm alone!' *What isn't she getting?*

She paused for a moment, then said, 'What about the other 50 per cent of the people here?' I blinked at her, confused. *Huh?* 'The women?' she added.

My eyes widened with the realisation. The thought had not even crossed my mind. Not for a second.

To say I was unimpressed is an understatement. How would women fill the gaping wound in my heart that had been left there by men? It didn't make sense, but after a few days of hiding in my room and being a bit of a shit, I eventually tried to engage with the women. In fact, I had been so determined not to rely on the women that I found a way to manipulate the system.

Tommy's charisma and animated nature deceived the staff into thinking he was LGBTQI. I decided to use his accidental deception to my advantage and forced him to be my friend. As we walked up and down the beach singing '90s Billie Piper pop songs and talking about what it was like for him to work alongside Leonardo *fucking* DiCaprio – *I know, I fucking know, you guys* – we became besties. I would love to tell you I learned all kinds of sordid celebrity details or got Leo's number and became the next young piece on his arm (LOL, I'm over 25, was never gonna happen), but tragically his NDA (non-disclosure agreement) is stronger than the force of our addictions combined. It's probably for the best, anyway. I don't want Leo learning about the life-sized calendar I had of him when I was 12 or the tiny Leo images I would cut out of *Smash Hits* magazine and Blu Tack to my wall until it was covered from corner to corner.

Reluctantly, I started to befriend the women and realised their stories weren't so different from my own. They were women who had been disillusioned by love, deceived by men and hurt beyond compare. They had experienced the most horrific abuse from the people who were meant to protect them. Many were musicians and artists. They were sensitive and funny and would have me crying with laughter. It's easy to forget how incredibly sensitive addicts can be. We are people who, for whatever reason, struggle with the intensity of the real world, so we search for ways to escape it or dull it down. When I first got clean, I remember feeling like a veil had been lifted and not in a good way. If I had been watching the world through a blurred Vaseline-smeared lens, the likes of which Cher might enjoy, it suddenly leapt into full-blown HD. It was so uncomfortable. Like I was too close to everything. Remember in *Willy Wonka* when Mike Teavee transitions from watching telly to being in the show itself? It was like that. The world was too real, and I felt as though everyone was watching me and knew exactly what I was thinking.

Waking up in rehab on New Year's Eve felt oddly comforting. Perhaps it gave me a way to mentally halt my self-destruction and start the new year with healthier goals, or perhaps it was just the sunshine and soft beach air that made life seem more bearable. Either way, a welcome sense of hope rippled through the facility.

I attended the early morning yoga class, saluting the Sun with pride in my heart as I remembered who I used to be. I thought about the fact that I was here; I hadn't died or given up, which in itself was an indication of hope. I may have felt hopeless, but my actions proved otherwise. There was still a little bit of something left in me. Something that, despite wanting to stay in bed all day, got me up to do yoga on the grass overlooking the beach. 'Spark', my psychologist called it. A tiny little ember that the surrounding darkness hadn't yet snuffed out. And with that tiny spark, there are only two options: let it die out completely or fan the flames and gently encourage its growth.

Some of that hope came from friendship – a bond I had been without for many months. You make friends fast in a place like that. One, because you are living together, and two, because you are sharing the ugliest, most vulnerable parts of yourself in an environment that is without judgement. It becomes very difficult to judge people on their misadventures when you, too, are so deeply flawed. Some people came straight from selling their bodies on the street for heroin, and there were coked-up high-flying movie execs, but we were all in the same place at the end of the day. It didn't matter how rich, successful or well-known you were out there. In here, you were stripped to your core, to your deepest shame, and rather than destroying you, you realised that you were not alone. You were okay, you were understood, and you were still lovable.

NYE was hot, in the high 30s, as we took our afternoon stroll along the beach. Someone was throwing a ball around, occasionally hitting the forbidden ocean edge. We were allowed to get our toes wet but weren't allowed in past our ankles. OH&S BS. We were a group of hooligans, 18 to 60, but the consequences fell on the staff if we got injured.

The ball started creeping further and further into the sea with each throw. We went from ankle-deep water to knee-deep, then thigh-deep, until we reached 'fuck it' levels of wetness and jumped all the way in.

You need to understand that although we were there to better ourselves, we were also a group of troublemakers who resisted authority and got a thrill from breaking the rules. It must be an innate quality of addicts. We do not like being told what to do. Alessandro had even commented that I could be stuck in the middle of the desert, desperately dehydrated, but the moment someone told me to drink, I would rather die than take that refreshingly cool glass of water. Honestly, the best way to get me to do something is to tell me to do the opposite. *I'm the worst.* So something as harmless as having a splash in the ocean on a scorching hot day seemed like a rule waiting to be broken.

We kept pushing the boundary of that ball until ten of us were neck-deep, splashing in the water. The water was cool and fresh, a liniment for our cracked, rusty interiors; its rhythmic waves lapped against our skin, cleansing us of our sins. The communal relief was palpable as we were reborn, baptised by the forgiving ocean. Together, we remembered what it was like to play, to discover that we still had the capacity to experience joy. We could be happy without a substance. Many of us had not felt that since childhood.

We continued to laugh, play ball and catch waves as our supervisor ran, arms flailing, down the beach. Screaming at us to, 'Get out! Get out of the water! You are all out of here!'

The mood instantly shifted as we realised we might be getting kicked out of the program before our new chapter had a chance to begin.

We slunk out of the sea, clothes sopping, as we tried vainly to squeeze any water from our hair and shirts. Moments earlier, we had been body-slamming each other beneath the waves, and now we were trying to dry ourselves in the Sun with seconds to spare. We weren't fooling anyone.

On the walk back to the facility, we snickered at each other like naughty teenagers, but inside we carried a pit of dread in our stomachs. None of us were ready to go home yet, not by a long shot. We were sent to our rooms to dry off.

Later, we gathered in a line of seats in front of the hospital staff, like a firing squad, while they decided what to do with us. We sat anxiously, looking at our feet and bouncing our legs. I was shuffling in my chair and shivering as I felt the water from my wet hair trickle down my back. We sat for what felt like an hour as the staff debated the consequences. They left the room, at which time we all turned to each other and started bitching about how fucked up this all was and how completely underserving we were of punishment, which, of course, was totally untrue. This was rehab, after all.

When they returned to the room, we all sat bolt-upright in our chairs and held our breath. The bravado from moments ago vanished instantly. Now it really did feel like *Big Brother* was deciding our fate. Would we be safe from this week's elimination round? After a long pause, our coordinator announced we could stay. We collectively breathed a sigh of relief before scurrying out of the room, lest they change their minds.

There were whispers that the decision was mostly due to the number of us that had broken the rules. To lose ten patients in one go would not be a good look for the hospital. Thank you, optics! Our punishment was to stand up and announce our wrongdoings to the entire group of inpatients and staff at every morning meeting. More public shaming? No probs! By now, I had mastered the art of coping with 'en masse' daily shaming. Add it to the list.

'Hi, I'm Kirsty. Today I feel … *looks at daily emotions chart* angry and sad, I guess. I am a co-dependent, bipolar, depressive drug addict, and I have two affirmations to deliver today. The first is: I am whole. I do not attract the male gaze for my self-worth. And the second: I am here to heal. I trust in the process and those here to assist me. I do not seek out self-destructive behaviours.' After robotically rattling off my affirmations, I slumped back in my chair and pulled my hoodie over my head in a bid to make myself disappear.

After our day of debauched fun in the water, there were whispers we would be forbidden from witnessing the seven o'clock fireworks display that evening. This was something we had all been looking forward to, that is, until we realised seven o'clock in Sydney during daylight saving time is too bright to see anything but an occasional plume of smoke in the distance. Despite being a lacklustre experience, as far as rehab goes, it was almost as exciting as another ice cream day, so, fortunately, we didn't miss out. We were, however, punished by being forced to stay at the facility for the next week. It's true that most of us were already there against our will, and leaving the premises for other than our 45 minutes of daily supervised activity was forbidden. But there were a couple of nights a week where we would be led 'off campus' for 12-step meetings. This was our only social interaction with other humans in the real world, so it was always very exciting. It was also the only place we had access to caffeinated coffee and sweet biscuits, so denial was no joke.

That evening, instead of going to the town hall for SLAA (the aptly named Sex & Love Addicts Anonymous), we stayed in-house. A group of perverts, myself included, sat pouting in our common area, waiting for the depravity to begin. Of all the meetings I've been to – Narcotics Anon, Alcoholics Anon and CODA (co-dependency support groups) – SLAA was hands-down the best for gruesome intrigue. The stories you hear are such an interesting mix of twisted, horrifying, salacious and sad. Like a car crash you can't look away from.

The first SLAA meeting I attended was a lesson on the differences between men and women. It was mixed, meaning there were both men and women in the group. Our counsellors recommended attending meetings of one's own gender where possible, as women and men tend to have different issues. In all 12-step programs, it is also advised not to date for the first 12 months of sobriety as it can challenge progress. In my limited experience of hearing men's stories, I have noticed that they tend to be much more physical in nature. You get your peeping toms, stalkers, serial cheaters and chronic masturbators. On the other hand, women tend to deal more with emotional issues such as co-dependency, heartbreak, obsession and self-loathing. Bitches may be cray, but men, well, men are downright terrifying.

If you spent some time in those rooms, you began to realise just how fragile we all were. How life can be turned completely on its head by something as elusive as emotion. Self-helpers can preach about willpower, logic and the power of positivity all damn day, but when you are in the heat of the moment, and all you want to do is fight, fuck, hunt or kill, there is no mantra on earth that can save you. You just have to get yourself somewhere safe where you can limit the amount of damage you do.

There was a moment during the in-house meeting when one of the new recruits decided to share. The deal in any of the meetings is that you let the person speak and just listen. By doing this, we let their story remind us why we are choosing a different path or inspire us with hope. When they have finished talking, we don't offer feedback or talk it through as a group – they can do that in therapy – we just move on to the next speaker.

The newbie spoke candidly about the 200-person-deep gay orgies he frequented. Seemingly fuelled on nothing but coke and cum, these men would meet for the ride of their lives. I listened intently, eyes wide in poorly masked glee. I had a million questions and nowhere for them to go. I had to physically hold my hand under my chin to stop my jaw from falling to the floor. He finished his sordid little tale with a flippant wave of the hand and a 'but anyway, we've all been there.' *Who has? Me has?* I looked around the entire group, desperate to catch someone's eye, but no one would meet my gaze. They all nodded in quiet acceptance as we moved on to the next speaker. I sat there for the next hour wondering if I was the biggest prude in this sea of horny rehabians.

That night, I went to sleep trying to mentally work out the logistics of the piles of heaving male bodies. When elephants travel in packs, you know how they hold the elephant in front's tail with their trunk, which continues in a long line of adorable travelling giants? Well, that was the best idea I could come up with... but, like, a lot less quaint.

I gave you all my money

Soundtrack: *Lana Del Rey – 'Dealer'*

Several things happen to your body when you get clean after a long period of using. There are obvious signs, like your eyes becoming clearer and your skin less lifeless and grey, but there are other subtle indicators to show you that your body is remembering how to function.

Within the first week, my appetite came back with a vengeance. After having not eaten a proper meal in over a year and losing over ten kilos from my small frame, my body was ready to gorge. I went from surviving on one smoothie and ten cups of coffee a day to three solid meals and three scheduled snack breaks. Despite that, I would still wake up in the night starving, my stomach crying out for food. My roommate, Li, who had been in and out of the facility for years, offered me an array of snacks she kept hidden in her drawer for just this kind of occasion. Taking food out of the kitchen was forbidden, but she assured me no one ever noticed. From then on, we enjoyed a midnight snack and debriefed about our day's adventures each night before we fell asleep.

She was Filipino and looked 19 rather than her actual 27 years. She was stunning and spent hours every morning perfecting her make-up and fussing over the symmetry of her eyebrows. I felt physically inferior to her despite knowing she hated how she looked. We discussed beauty trends, which therapists we were secretly in love with and played 'fuck, marry, kill' with the other residents until we got in trouble for laughing too loud. We chatted about our personality disorders, and she told me she kept getting dumped by therapists who claimed they 'don't work with borderline (BPD) patients.' This is, disappointingly, not uncommon. And she told me about her controlling boyfriend, who would steal her phone and turn all her friends and family against her. And how he would beat her and drag her by her hair if she so much as looked at another man or reached out for help.

She left the facility a week after me. The day she left, she overdosed on her medication in an attempt to kill herself. Fortunately, she was found just in time and survived, but she had tried before, and I'm certain she will have tried again since. We kept in touch for a while, but I haven't heard anything from her in years. I'm too afraid to check for fear of what I might learn.

It's commonly assumed that suicide is a selfish act, but nothing could be further from the truth. People who are suicidal don't just wake up one day and decide to off themselves. They think about it for months and years until they have every detail planned out perfectly. They may have rehearsed their suicide letters in their heads or even written them out. By the time someone has successfully died by suicide, the vast majority will have thought about it (or attempted it) dozens, if not hundreds, of times. Trust me when I say that being suicidal and not killing oneself is an act of tremendous strength. A strength that most people are never forced to muster in their entire lives. A strength I truly hope I never have to draw on again.

Think about it. From the time we were single-celled amoeba, we were biologically programmed to survive and reproduce. Survive and reproduce. That's our only job. So, for a person to have the desire to take their own life and follow through with it, they must be in such an extreme state of despair – and for a long enough period of time – to override their genetic makeup. That is no small feat. I wish I could say that suicidal ideation was one of the things that healed in the early stages of my sobriety, but that would take a while yet.

Watching the changes in my body as it began to recover was interesting. I expected the mental struggles, but seeing the damage I had done to my physical body made it all so real.

During the 18 months I had been stuffing oxy up my nose, it rarely bled. I remember being surprised because every movie about drug addicts shows them glassy-eyed, gazing into the mirror and washing blood off their upper lip as if they are Eleven in *Stranger Things*. But that wasn't my experience. I took this as a sign that my drug was pure. *My* oxy was better than *your* shitty street drugs. It made me feel like I was a fancy bored housewife rather than a drug-fucked scumbag. But after a week in rehab, my nose started to bleed, and it didn't stop. It bled every day for six months and then on and off for a year. It was scratchy and uncomfortable and affected my breathing, as dried blood would clog my airways. The rehab doctor told me that smoking cigarettes had suppressed the bleeding by constricting my blood vessels. When I stopped smoking, my body was finally allowed to function how it needed for it to heal. He warned me I might even notice my gums or other small cuts and wounds start to bleed. I wondered what else I had been preventing from doing its job. How many areas of my body had I injured irreparably?

The pain in my body was constant. It was like having a pulled muscle in every inch of my body. Not only that, it made me nauseous and beyond exhausted. Several months earlier, I had seen a rheumatologist who suspected I had fibromyalgia. The two major symptoms (of a possible 60) were decreased pain tolerance and chronic fatigue due to overactive nerves. It's as though your nerves are on edge, waiting for disaster to strike at any moment.

The rheumatologist couldn't diagnose me definitively at the time, despite my having all the diagnostic symptoms, because opioid addiction presents almost identically to fibromyalgia. To know for certain if I had fibro, I would have to eliminate the opioids, which at the time wasn't feasible.

There were two types of beds in the facility: ones that had been there for years and newer, much more comfortable ones made of memory foam. I was placed in one of the ancient beds, and it was destroying my back. I complained every day, asking to be transferred to a new bed, but there simply weren't any available. Instead, I was scheduled to speak with a pain specialist to see if there was anything more he could do.

He was a very peculiar man whose voice reminded me of the comic book guy from *The Simpsons*. He looked like a potato impersonating a doctor. He was as round as he was tall, wore large glasses, and buckled his pants right up to his nipples. He dressed like an old man but was only in his 40s. He was so strange that I was distracted during our entire consult, picturing what his life would be like out in the real world. I came to the conclusion that, between writing for scientific journals and treating thankless addicts, he collected doll shoes and hoarded his receipts 'just in case'.

He saw me in an empty patient's bedroom rather than an office.

'You must be Kirsten, mnyes?' he asked in a nasally, drawn out tone while peering at me over the top of his glasses.

'Hi, yes,' I replied, shaking his hand, which he then immediately sanitised.

'You're having issues with pain, mnyes?'

'Yeah, so I am recovering from opioid addiction. I may have fibromyalgia, but we won't be sure until the opioids are out of my system. I was hoping I could change beds to be a bit more comfortable?'

'Hmm, well there are no more beds available right now, but what we can do is put you on a medication called Buprenorphine. It is a slow-release opioid painkiller that you take sublingually. We can supply it to you while you are here, and once you leave, we will provide you with a script that you take to the pharmacy daily. It lasts 24 hours, and you can only collect one wafer at a time.'

I stared at him in disbelief. All I wanted was a better bed and maybe a heat pack. Both heat and ice packs were forbidden due to OH&S, but they were allowed to provide opioids ... to an opioid addict. *MAKE IT MAKE SENSE!*

'Sorry, no, I'm here to come off the opioids,' I said, genuinely concerned he didn't know he was at an addiction recovery centre.

'Yes, this is a very simple treatment. We use it with heroin and prescription opioid addicts all the time. It is similar to Methadone but safer and easier to withdraw from.'

'But … I've already been clean a week. I'm almost through the withdrawals, and the opioids will be out of my system in three more days. I'm just looking for alternative ways to manage my pain. I'll take some Deep Heat if you've got it.'

I was reeling. Rather than looking at me as an individual, he lumped me in with similar patients, giving me his stock-standard treatment suggestions. After the Hippocratic Oath, that's the first thing you learn in any health field. Treat the person, not the disease.

My choice wasn't simple. On the one hand, he was offering me an out. He was right in front of me saying take my hand, and I'll guide you back to the Promised Land. On the other, I was so close to freedom and getting my life back.

At lunchtime, I (lawlessly) told a few of the boys from my group what had happened. They were ex-heroin addicts, so I wanted to get their opinions. Mike looked at me the way I had looked at the doctor, confused and appalled.

'He offered you opioids? Does he even know why you are here?'

'Yeah. It's weird, right?'

'That's messed up. You're doing so well, and he wants to put you on the Bupe? Don't do it, mate. It's a prison sentence. You have to line up every day, like those heroin junkies you see at the pharmacy. You can never go away anywhere. You are literally handcuffed to the pharmacy. I can't believe he offered you that. You're not thinking about it, are ya?'

I was.

'Nah, no way. Fuck that,' I responded.

He didn't believe me.

That night, we piled into a bus and went to an off-site Narcotics Anonymous meeting. We all ended up in those rooms for different reasons, but many of us had one thing in common: crushing loneliness. I didn't resonate with everything the meetings had to offer – a little too many Jonestown vibes for my liking. But one thing they do well is connect lonely people with a community of supportive, understanding folk, and I believe that is where most of the healing takes place.

Someone at a meeting once said, 'There is never any reason to be lonely. If you are lonely, come to a meeting. Talk to people, make friends.' I took incredible comfort from that. I had been achingly lonely for so long. The thought of going out and mingling without booze or my comfy blanket of opioids to support me was something I couldn't even fathom. But in the meeting rooms, everybody was working toward sobriety, and they knew how hard it was to integrate back into social situations. They were supportive, kind, and a little odd, just like me.

We grabbed our cups of tea and snuck our sugary biscuits before sitting down to share stories. A guy from our group spoke. He was in his mid-30s and rocking strong surfer dude vibes. He was also covered in tattoos, which would come to make sense as he told us he ran a tattoo parlour; two actually, one local and another in Bali. Initially, he flew up to Indonesia twice a year to check on the place and make sure all was running smoothly – until he became addicted to Xanax. His Australian prescription was tightly monitored, but it was seemingly a free-for-all in Bali. So, each time he visited, he would stock up. The more access he had, the more he took until he worked through his six-month supply in a matter of weeks. It got to the point where he would fly to Bali every month to purchase hundreds of pills and chew through them in no time. I wasn't at rehab when he arrived, but apparently, he was near-comatose for the entire first week, and after that, he was barely conscious.

Later, a young girl – not from our rehab group – told her story. She was in her early 20s and very 'Bondi', with her bleached blonde hair and natural tan. I expected her to start talking about how she smokes too much weed and takes ecstasy on the weekends, writing her off as a party girl.

Then she spoke, 'So I was at my dealer's house picking up. He just got a new batch of oxy, so we had some before I left. It was kinda expected at this point that he would wanna fuck, but ya know, I got a good deal, so I went along with it. It was nice, anyway, to have someone with me for a while.' As she spoke, she looked both sad and hauntingly disconnected from her words. 'By the time I got back to my car, it was late, around midnight. I was driving home, and I came up to some lights. I don't really know what happened. I didn't see them change to red or even orange, so I just kept going. I was kinda racing home at that stage 'cause the roads were pretty empty, and I wanted to get home so I could get into my gear. Then, out of nowhere, this chick comes out on her bike and ...' She looked down at the floor and, pathetically, clapped her fist into her other palm, indicating a collision. The entire room was silent, too afraid to breathe.

Her voice had changed when she started talking again; it was broken and shaky, and her eyes were misty. All of our eyes were misty. 'She died. I killed her.' She let that hang in the air for a while. We sat wide-eyed, many of us with our hands over our mouths in shock. 'I killed someone. I called for help. I called the ambos, but it was too late.' By now, the room was in tears. 'She was only 22. I stole her whole life because I was racing home to get high. How do you explain that? How do you look her parents in the eye and tell them that? There is nothing I can do to make it better. I've ruined so many lives. So that's why I'm here. Because I never want to use ever again, and I never want anyone else to go through anything remotely like this. There is nothing worse. Nothing. So, anyway, that's my share. Thanks.'

We sat in stunned silence, dabbing at our eyes for what seemed like a lifetime before someone finally suggested we take a pee break.

A small group of us loitered outside for a while, drinking tea and taking some deep breaths. Mike approached me. 'So that must've been pretty crazy for you, hey?'

'Yeah, I mean, I've never heard anything like that before.'

'Nah, man, I meant how she's basically living your story.'

'What?'

'Can't you see how easily it could've been you telling that story tonight?' He started listing the similarities on his fingers. 'Opioid addict, seeks validation from the wrong men. And remind me how many cars you have totalled while using? She's you. You're just lucky you've never hit anyone.'

Mike walked back inside, and I stood in the dark courtyard, cradling my tea, willing it to soothe me from the inside out.

The next day I informed the strange doctor that I would not be taking the Buprenorphine, and instead of regret, I felt tremendous pride. For the first time in about a year, I chose something good for me. I decided to keep trying to make decisions that aided my survival as best I could. Some days, all that would be was staying in bed, watching *The Real Housewives* and ordering Uber eats; other times, I slept all day and brushed my teeth at 3 pm. But, occasionally, I could go to 12-step meetings or therapy or eat something nutritious. I told myself that my only goal was to stay alive, and every day I chose the best way to make that happen, the hope being that, eventually, survival would become simple, and one day I might even live again.

My experience with co-dependency was the most excruciating I have ever had. The pain of losing myself to another person and giving them complete power over my emotions (unwittingly and unwantingly – to them) is the most painful thing I have ever had to drag myself through, without comparison. But if you want to be slapped back to reality, talk to a bunch of addicts about the man you love.

A small group of us were playing board games after dinner one night. 'So what's this dude's name?' asked Mike, as I blatantly ignored my instructions not to associate with the male species.

'Alessandro.'

The group snickered.

'What?' I demanded, spitting out the 't' for emphasis.

'Nothing, it's just ... *Alessandro,*' Mike said, rolling his r's dramatically. 'It's so posh. What is he, Spanish or some shit?'

'He's Italian, actually.'

'*Don't call my name, don't call my name,* Alessandro!' sang Tommy, blatantly taking the piss.

'Really?' I asked, rolling my eyes.

'*I'm not your babe, I'm not your babe, Fernando,*' another chimed in.

'Oh my god.'

'*Alessandro, Alessandro! Ale-ale-sandro. Ale-ale-sand-ero!*' The group chorused together before erupting into laughter.

'I mean, that's not even the words. You're misrepresenting *the* Stefani Germanotta but whatever.'

For the rest of my time at the clinic, Alessandro was only ever talked about with a strong accent that fluctuated between Italian, Spanish and French. Nothing cuts a guy down a few pegs more than a bunch of hooligans serenading you with Lady Gaga every time you mention his name. Well, almost nothing.

I was in a session with my stupidly attractive rehab psychiatrist. *Talk about transference! All psychiatrists and psychologists should have to be hideous potato people.* He was talking to me about co-dependency and the effects of love addiction.

'It's interesting you've chosen opioids to become dependent on.'

'Oh?' I replied, barely listening as I played with a loose string on my jumper.

'Yes, you know OxyContin mirrors love in the brain. It acts as oxytocin, the "love hormone".'

I looked at him. 'I'm sorry, Kirsten, but you cannot replace the love of a human being with the love of a pill.'

'*Watch me,*' I thought bitterly. By now, I had wrapped the string around my finger so tightly I could feel my heart beating in my fingertip.

I was so broken, my heart so crushed, that I tried to replace the love of a significant other, a best friend and a father with that of a chemical. Had it worked, I never would have stopped.

'Why do you think you let this bloke get to you so much?' he continued.

'Erm, what?' I said, entirely offended by the use of such casual language in reference to the man of my dreams.

'This guy, Alessandro. What makes him so great?'

I couldn't believe what I was hearing. How dare he speak about him like he's just an average Joe.

'Do you know why I'm calling him a bloke?' he asked, doubling down.

'No,' I said, reeling.

'It's because you have him on a pedestal, but, in reality, he's just a guy. Just like any other guy.'

No, he's not.

'He's not even particularly nice to you, yet you talk about him like he could solve the world's problems.'

He could!

'That is addiction. It is obsession. And it is *not* love.'

No, but ... huh?

'Love does not fluctuate between astonishing highs and devastating lows, hour by hour. It does not disappear and result in suicidal thoughts when you go without contact for a day.'

It doesn't?

'You do not need to cling and claw at love in desperation.' The term 'clawing' made me aware of my hands, which were indented by my fingernails as I had been digging them into my palms.

'That is fear, not love. Do you feel afraid?'

All the time. 'I dunno. Maybe.'

'Love is peaceful, gentle and comforting. It comes from deeply learning who someone is. So tell me, this bloke, what is it you love about him?'

Everything. Just like, ya know, the way he ... Shit, wait.

My mind was blank. I knew I needed him, and that need felt so powerful that it must be my destiny to be with him, right? But when presented with this seemingly innocuous question, I couldn't think of a single thing I actually liked about being with him.

'I, um ... I really like it when ... It's just that he's ... Fuck.' I sighed.

I was coming to the end of my 28 days. The final week was tough as I watched the friends I had connected with start to leave, one by one. For many of them, it would be easy to catch up on the outside and attend meetings together, but I was going back to Melbourne, where I would only be joined by a few stragglers.

When Tommy left, the facility instantly became a lot quieter and duller. We made plans to keep in touch on the outside, and, despite him being in Sydney, we became very close very quickly. Once I'd left and was reunited with my phone, we would message each other every day. We developed a ritual of 'date nights' where we would press play on *Ru Paul's Drag Race* and *Vanderpump Rules* and watch together as we laughed about their dismal outfits, Adderall addictions and poor life choices. *Totally un-relatable!*

We both adore animals, great and small, and would talk at length about them. He's the only other person I have ever met who saves insects that have become trapped in pools. This is something I have also done since I was a very small child, unable to watch beetles and flying critters struggle to breathe as they hit the water for a drink, only to drown. I would scoop them up in my hands and gently guide them to safety. Relieved, the insects would wait a few moments for their wings to dry before flying to freedom. Mum always told me to be careful saving the bees and wasps, but I never worried. They were grateful and never stung me. Tommy has a heart that I understand. He is sensitive and kind beyond most people's understanding. He is my people.

Mike left a week before me. That was hard. We had come in together, and I felt safe and secure with him around. We had been in group therapy together and attended the same meetings, so we learned a lot about each other. He saw past the make-up and the flirting and saw the real me. Not only that, he liked who he saw. The day he was leaving, he found me to say goodbye.

'Ey, I'm leaving soon. I just wanted to say goodbye and wish you luck.'

I loved listening to him talk in group. To look at him, you'd expect him to be rough around the edges, but the years of therapy and self-improvement had worked wonders. He wasn't at all afraid of open and honest communication. He showed his bravery through vulnerability, not stoicism.

'I heard you were leaving today. That sucks. For me, I mean, I'm happy for you.'

'You'll be good. You just gotta keep going to meetings on the outside and don't fuck with boys for a while.'

'Ha, ha, wise words.'

'Anyway, I wanted to give you this.' He handed me a small book of *Daily Reflections* by AA members for AA members. He took it everywhere with him, and whenever he felt wobbly, he read a few pages. I thought it was a really sweet gesture, but a little bit like giving me a bible I would never read.

I gave him a hug. 'Keep in touch, okay?'

'Sure thing, mate. You got this.'

As he left, I opened the book. Inside the front cover, he had written a message:

Kirsty,

You are a funny, beautiful, talented girl with a heart of gold. Thank you for the belly laughs, games of 'adult Pictionary' and inappropriate beach walks. Wishing you the very best in your recovery, one day at a time.

Your friend, Mike

Here was a man, maybe the first, who saw my worth without wanting or expecting anything from me.

Here was a friend.

I'm ready to release

Soundtrack: *George – 'Release'*

Although the mixed-sex SLAA meetings were rather traumatic, I found the female ones incredibly important. These groups helped me see the value of having a community of women around me, as I had previously always leaned on men for comfort and protection. I've always had female friends, but my eyes hadn't been open to seeing women for what they really are: insanely strong, quietly wise, deeply emotional, intensely fierce and nurturing healers. I can't believe it took me until I was 28 to realise that women are the backbone of the world. That's how strong the patriarchy is; it convinced me as a little girl that women were lesser than men and that we needed them to live, breathe, and exist. *Ugh!* I was a child misogynist, and if that could happen to me – someone raised by a staunch feminist and parents in unconventional roles – it could happen to anybody.

I continued going to meetings on the outside. SLAA was only held once a week, and even then, I would have to drive for almost an hour to get there. But these meetings – or gatherings of inspirational women of varying degrees of fracture – were instrumental in my healing. I would meet Jess, my friend from rehab; we would share our stories and struggles, listen to the other women share theirs, and then the two of us would debrief over Vietnamese noodles. I would want to drink with my meal so badly, but we could resist the urge because we had each other. It was a gentle transition into the world of sobriety, which might be the key. I have no idea. I won't pretend I know the answers, but I know that the transition from simple old habits like having a cold beer with spicy noodles on a warm Summer's night to enjoying a meal with your girlfriend while sipping a Sprite is no small feat. It requires strength to ignore the refrigerator of sparkling bottles dripping with condensation and say, 'not today, Satan.' Strength and sass – you *gotta* have sass.

There was a beautiful woman in her mid to late 30s who attended our group. She had long brown hair, was tall with legs up to her armpits, and these enormous doe-like eyes that softened her sharp cheekbones. She could have been a supermodel in another life, but here she sat in the group, shrouded in baggy clothes that hid her tiny frame, and collapsed into herself as if trying to disappear. She looked how I had felt a year ago. Before she even said a word, you could see that her pain was eating her alive. She was entirely broken. It was tragic, but it was also awakening. Before I saw her, I felt like my anguish wasn't shifting, and I would live at the same level of despair forever, but looking at this shivering lamb in front of me, I realised I had grown. I may not have been #livingmybestlife, and I may still have cried every day, but I was not where I was a year ago, and that was progress. That meant change was possible.

I supplemented my SLAA meetings by attending NA (Narcotics Anonymous) several times a week. These were mixed meetings and came with their own difficulties. There were generally more men than women at NA, and despite everyone knowing dating hinders the recovery process, I would still occasionally be hit on and ogled during meetings. Going to meetings and having the same men staring at me every week was very uncomfortable and started putting me off attending. Meanwhile, many of the well-behaved men from rehab, having left the prying eyes of our supervisors, were inappropriately messaging me. It was clear they had relapsed and, after a few drinks or nine, were trying to remember which of the female rehabians had been identified as sex and love addicts. Maybe they, too, were feeling wobbly in their recovery and thought their urges and 'her' self-loathing could line up for one magical night – before the regret set in, that is. *Boys, I understand you were struggling, but your selfish contact derailed my progress and broke my spirit. Not cool.*

After a while, I had to stop going to NA. Being clean and hearing everyone's insane drug stories, or knowing someone in the room had used as recently as that morning, became triggering and unhelpful. Not only that, I began to see people I recognised. People I had partied with on nights out while running from ourselves, and yet here we were – lost, hopeless and wondering where the fun had gone. We would sit in these meetings checking each other out and trying, foggily, to remember where we knew the other person from. *Are they from TV? Did we go to school together once upon a time? Oh, right, that's that dude I went home with to do lines until I was kicked out at 8 am 'cause his baby mamma was dropping off his kid soon.* These were the true FML moments. F my F-ing L!

I was outside taking in the sunshine during a break at an NA meeting when a dishevelled, tired-looking 40-something-year-old man approached me. He'd admitted in the meeting that he had used heroin a few hours ago, but I respected that he was still here and trying. Trying is really fucking hard. His name was Nate, and I had already worked out that I knew him from a rough night out. We met the night Alessandro told me not to come to Italy. I'd been distraught and spiralling in rejection, so naturally I got absolutely shit-faced and went on the hunt for anything that would distract me from the added welts to my already-beaten heart.

> I had met Nate and his buddy Zack at a bar in St Kilda. I connected with Zack over our shared love of Amy Winehouse. When Amy's rendition of **Valerie** came on over the loudspeakers, we held each other in the street and cried because we just missed her so much – that and we were completely fucked off our nuts. He told me he had regularly served her while working at a bar in Camden. He even said he had slept with her a few times. When I asked how it was, he replied, 'How do you think it was? Really sad.' I have no idea if anything he was spouting was true. My lucid brain would guess likely not, but at the time I believed him.
>
> There was a moment that night that made me realise how hyperaware addicts can be, especially when it comes to recognising another addict. I was drawn to these guys because I could see they were trouble, and

I'm sure they were drawn to me for the exact same reason. Zack had looked deep into my eyes and asked, 'So what are you withdrawing from?' It had been several days since my last oxy, and I was desperately waiting until Monday to pick up my new script. It's asinine because we were connecting over addiction, but in a year of feeling like I was fading into oblivion, he made me feel seen and understood. This random junkie, who looked like Ryan Phillippe crossed with one of those goldfish with their eyes on the side of their heads, was the only person who could recognise the war going on behind my eyes.

I must have looked sceptical because he continued, 'It's cool,' 'I'm a recovering heroin addict.' He pulled out a thin foil packet containing what I now know to be a Buprenorphine wafer.

Been about six months on these.'

'Prescription opioids for me,' I replied.

'Ha, really?' he chuckled.

'Er, yeah …' I replied defensively.

'That doesn't count.'

'Excuse me?'

'You're not a real junkie.'

Me to self: Do I want to be a real junkie?

'Okay, well, it's got the same chemical make-up as heroin, just without all the rat poison 'n' shit. It's literally known as hillbilly heroin.'

'Nah, man. Doesn't count.'

'Okay.' I resigned, rolling my eyes. I wasn't about to spend my night arguing over who was the 'better' junkie. **What is my life?**

I promise you this was not an unusual conversation. Just as there are surprising judgements and hierarchies in the 'peace and love' yoga community, the same is true among drug addicts. **Who knew?** Later we made out because I wanted to feel close to Amy, and then he stole my money to buy drugs. An eventful evening all 'round!

'Hey, do you remember me?' asked Nate, sidling up to me during a break at one of our NA meetings.

'Yeah, hey, weird seeing you here. I mean, it's good. It's good for both of us.'

'Well, I won't be back for a few months. I got into The Buttery halfway house in the country. Gonna be there for at least three months shovelling horse shit and whatnot.'

'That's awesome. I really hope it helps. I just got out of treatment, too.'

'I just can't keep doing this, ya know. I'm fuckin' 40, dead broke and I live in my mum's basement.'

'Mate, I hear ya.'

'Anyway, that's not why I came over here.'

'Oh?'

'I know what my mate did that night, taking your money 'n' shit. Anyway, here ya go.' He handed me a 50-dollar note.

'Seriously?'

'Yeah, man, what he did was fucked. I'm sorry I don't have more. This is all I got.'

'No, I really appreciate it. Thank you.' We had a quick hug and he left, not returning for the second half of the meeting.

I'd always thought of money in these situations as collateral damage. If I went out looking for trouble and happened to find it, I couldn't be too upset about the type of trouble I found, but that incident had left a bad taste in my mouth. I had gone home feeling the usual shame and self-loathing of a night out but with the added sense of deception and manipulation. It felt icky. Nate giving me 50 bucks didn't make up for the money Zach stole back then, but it helped mend some of my distrust in humanity, and for that, I was grateful.

I haven't seen Barbados, so I must get out of this

Soundtrack: *Tori Amos – 'Me and a Gun'*

Callous laughter rings through empty streets,
Gentle summer breeze, stinging blistered feet.

Run, run, fast as you can,
A fist of ginger hair caught between cruel hands.

Cold car bonnet, shocks warm cheek.
I pray that I'm asleep, got lost counting sheep.

Old friend fear shows who I really am,
And I smile in the knowledge I'll one day kill this man.

Leaving rehab left me restless. Despite being made aware that my obsessive, addictive version of love was unhealthy, it didn't stop me from feeling the devastation left in its wake. Falling for Alessandro had been a thankful diversion from the torment of losing Simon, but now that he had also rejected me, it all came flooding back, stronger than ever. The pain in my heart was so physical that I was sure it would kill me. I was waiting for the moment when my heart would give way and I would follow in my father's footsteps.

I began obsessively looking to replace the emptiness I felt with men. Horrible men whose pain was masked by rage and sex. Men who hated women. These men weren't pretending to care about me, which felt safer than being fooled into love and, ultimately, heartbreak. I wanted someone to tell me I was pretty and hold me as we fell asleep. Strange men won't hold you without sex. The awful, selfish, meaningless sex is the price of human affection, and I was willing to pay that price in the hope of a cuddle.

I had been swiping away and organised to meet up with someone called Amir from a dating app. He was nothing like the men of my past, and that intrigued me. He was tall and dark with giant muscles, even those gnarly neck ones that make you look like you have a pin head – think Gaston from Beauty and the Beast. His profile read as if he was deeply intellectual and sensitive, but he also implied he was self-made and displayed himself next to shiny cars. Cue eye-roll. It wouldn't have been surprising to see him posing next to a drugged-out tiger in Thailand or proudly holding up a freshly caught fish because nothing says sexy like aquatic animal murder, right, gals? Nothing about him was what I would usually be attracted to, but since my usual instincts weren't working out so well, I decided to shift gears.

I drove for nearly an hour to get to his place. He hadn't given me his specific address; rather, he directed me to an abandoned RSL at the end of his street. He told me this was due to limited parking availability, which, upon arrival, didn't appear to be a problem. He came to meet me and took me back to his place to continue getting ready. From the moment I arrived, I was uneasy. My body was telling me in no uncertain terms to get the fuck out, but I ignored it because I couldn't stand the thought of being alone for one more second.

He called a taxi to take us to dinner. As we waited, he asked about my nutrition studies. I mentioned that we could tell a lot about the state of someone's health by looking at them. 'Alright then, do me,' he demanded.

I looked into his eyes, and they confirmed my suspicions from watching him flit erratically around as he got ready: he was clearly on some kind of stimulant. He was also paranoid, and the whites of his eyes were a dirty yellow colour from years of liver abuse. I already presumed from looking at him that he took steroids, so jaundice didn't surprise me. How much of that can you tell someone on a first date? I wondered. *Fuck it.*

'Do you take a lot of drugs?' I asked.

'Err ... I used to. Not anymore. Why?' I could tell he was taken aback by my bluntness.

'Your eyes are pretty yellow, which could mean your liver isn't working efficiently.' I decided against telling him that I could tell he was high as we spoke.

'Nah, I take liver herbs every day. My liver is fucking pristine.' He spat the words at me.

'Pristine, eh? Wowee,' I said, smirking.

'You don't understand. My liver used to be fucked, but I take these supplements now and it's strong as fuck. I'm literally the healthiest, fittest person you've ever met. Have you ever seen anyone like this before?' He motioned to his physique as I choked back a laugh. *What is happening? This can't be real.* 'I make these green juices every day with spinach, kale, apple, celery, ginger and protein powder. I'm fully paleo, too. Do you even know what that is? It's the caveman diet. I work out every day for two hours and my job is very physical. I take great care of myself. Look at me! Fuck! Don't say my liver is shit again.' He then went on to explain how much more he knew about nutrition than me, to which I responded with repetitious 'okay's and 'you're right's because I was already bored of him and his mansplaining competitive bullshit. *Well, this is going to be a fun night!*

In the taxi, he was belligerent and racist to the driver while simultaneously rude and sexist toward me. He tried grabbing and groping at me in the back of the cab, and when I told him to stop, he said, 'You know we could never work out.' Leaving me to wonder why we were bothering with the date at all, but please, go on ... 'You're too loud and obnoxious. I like quiet, submissive girls who agree with me.'

I laughed because I genuinely thought he was joking.

'What's funny about that?' he asked, offended.

'Oh, no, nothing. Sorry.' The whole scene perplexed me. It was impossible to tell when he was joking and when he was on the verge of losing it. I decided it was best to err on the side of losing it and just play along. I was already regretting getting in the taxi, but, despite his rudeness, I decided to stay through dinner and be a polite young lady. *Idiot!*

At the restaurant, he looked me up and down as if getting his first good look. Now that there were people around, it really mattered who he had on his arm. 'You know, you looked a lot thinner on your dating profile.' *Oh, good, this is what we're doing.* For reference, my biggest fear is that someone turns up to a date and is disappointed by my appearance; therefore, I never use filters on dating apps and try to remain current. I don't want to mention my specific weight at the time because I know how unhelpful that can be, but suffice it to say I was small. I had gained maybe five kilos since leaving rehab because my body was remembering what hunger was, but objectively I looked great. As I was processing how to respond, he leaned over and patted me on the stomach, saying, 'What's this?' Then he laughed. He took a long pause before adding, 'I 'spose your face is quite beautiful, though. Do you always wear your hair curly?'

'Ah ... yeah,' I replied, in shock. *Did he just pat me on the stomach? This motherfucker just patted me on the stomach!*

Rather than call him out, I laughed it off because I truly couldn't tell if he was joking. He had perfected the backhanded compliment into an art form. His negging was cruel and constant but always given with tiny little crumbs of flattery that made you feel validated. He was masterful at bringing you down and then building you up *just* enough. It was confusing, and that was the point.

Lucky for me, Amir was blatant as fuck with his own insecurities. He was around six-foot-three and steroid-ed to the gills, but as he ordered our food and I attempted polite conversation, he kept getting distracted and looking around the restaurant.

'Hey, hey,' he said, tapping me repeatedly on the arm like a toddler pulling at their mum's pant leg.

'Yes?' I replied, almost choking on a piece of lettuce.

'You see that guy over there?' I turned to look at a young man enjoying his meal with friends and wished I could *I-Dream-of-Genie* blink myself over there.

'Yeah, what about him?'

'Am I bigger than him?'

I smiled, once again about to break into laughter, before I realised he was serious.

'What?' I ask, desperate for him to say he's fucking with me.

'That guy over there, the one sitting down in the white t-shirt. Do I have bigger muscles than him?'

Oh my god. Realising that this dude was completely off his rocker, I decided to placate him and replied with a simple 'Yes', which didn't appease him, so he then went around the restaurant picking out men to compare himself to. I understood I was required to reply with adequate enthusiasm as to how much *harder, better, faster, stronger* he was than all of the lovely men I would much rather be sitting with. *HELP ME.*

For the record, he was massive. He was easily double the size of the biggest guy in there, and not an ounce of it was fat. He was huge, and it was terrifying, but his body dysmorphia ruled every second of his thinking. I started to realise why he was so concerned about my appearance. It had nothing to do with me and everything to do with how he thought he would be perceived. Women were not human beings to talk to and get to know. Women were just like those shiny cars on his dating profile – an object to flash about to the world that said, 'look how successful I am!'

I felt sorry for him. He was somewhat handsome, but that was literally all he had. His physical insecurities were incredibly boring and took over the entire night. I prayed that I was not as bad as him during my anorexia and was grateful I had gotten to a place where some loser frat boy could pat me on the belly and not spiral me into old patterns. He wasn't even charming. At least Alessandro pretended to be a decent guy in public, but even that was too hard for Amir. He was rude to me, to the waitstaff, and even to passers-by in the street – puffing out his chest like a rooster asserting his dominance. If he spent a tenth of the time he did working on his internal world rather than his outer presentation, well, he'd still be an arsehole but slightly less so.

Throughout the night, he kept getting up and going to the toilet. When he returned, he would be more erratic than when he went in. At one stage, he even flashed the little baggie of white powder right under my nose, telling me he'd 'be right back.' Stupidly, I had told him the reason I wasn't drinking was because I was in recovery. He used this as leverage to trigger me and watch me squirm under the weight of my cravings. He was sadistic in how he enjoyed watching me become more and more uncomfortable.

'It's so easy to get girls. I get girls six nights a week. You just get 'em drunk and flap a baggie in their face. Sluts'll do anything for some coke.'

'Okay, that's enough. I'm out of here! You and your misogynistic, racist, insecure, fat-phobic bullshit can fuck right off! You are a pig, a loser and will die alone. Have a terrible life!' ... Is what I should have said before running as far away from him as humanly possible.

But I didn't. I'm not sure why. Despite him being a giant jackass, I felt like I was in control of the situation. I thought I could stick it out, and it would just become another shitty dating story to add to the archives. Before meeting Simon, Ben had launched a podcast with a recurring segment called *The Kirsty Experiment,* where I would recount that week's most disastrous dates. There was the time I went out with a guy I met on the train, who dressed like an old-timey magic man and wore a feather in his cap. He was late to our date because he got 'distracted photographing blades of grass dancing in the wind'. In a bid to make me his dream pixie girl, he decided we should scale a fence and go frolicking through a park. It ended when I ripped my pants. *DO I SEEM LIKE SOMEONE WHO FROLICS?*

Another time, I went out with a guy who spent all his time talking on the phone. I got bored on the walk home from dinner, so I followed a stray cat with the goal of feeding it my leftover pizza. When it finally let me close enough to pat it, I recoiled as I realised it was covered in tiny bumpy pustules all over its skin, and its eyes bugged out of its head like, again, one of those side-eyed goldfish. The date ended then and there because I was contaminated and needed to go home and take 13 boiling hot showers.

Or who could forget 'the sweaty man'? He was so named because he rode a bike to meet me on a 40-degree day and turned up drenched in sweat and smelling like garbage. He then refused to take me to the pub for a cool refreshing drink because he had given up alcohol a week earlier. Rather, he bought a giant bottle of unrefrigerated water from the corner shop, and we drank it together in the unshaded park. He continued to sweat profusely while I contemplated running away with the Grecian god that was running laps, shirtless, around us. *Take me with you!* I'd plead with my eyes as he jogged past me, smiling.

They were quirky, silly stories of socially inept people trying to date. I should have realised this was more sinister than that.

I became increasingly concerned by Amir's volatility, and in my anxiety, I began to talk. During this period, I would talk to anyone who would listen about the state of my tragic life. I would start talking and, like word vomit, spew my life story into their scared little laps. Even as I watched people's faces change from sympathetically engaged to 'where is the off button?', I could not stop revealing my deepest turmoil. It was a compulsion that I couldn't control. Perhaps it was an attempt to make sense of what seemed senseless, or maybe I just wanted as many people as possible to know how much pain I was in. Either way, that night, I started talking about my dad's disappearance in intimate detail.

As I talked, his face changed, but it wasn't the usual glazed-over look of someone wondering how to escape a conversation; this was different.

'I've heard this story before,' he said as if I were recounting a movie plot, not my own life.

'You couldn't have.'

'No, I've heard this story. It happened in the UAE, didn't it?'

'What the fuck? Yes.'

He sat back in his chair, eyeing me suspiciously. It made me uneasy how he stared me down like I had committed a crime. Then it clicked.

'Oh my god, it's you. You're *her*.' More terrifying words have never been spoken to an ex-addict recovering from a severe mental breakdown.

I was trying to work out what terrible crime I had committed and obviously repressed.

He continued, 'You know Jay. You're *that* Kirsty.' I looked into his face, now red with rage.

'Yeah, he's my friend. He was good friends with my bestie Sam before she...'

'You fucked him. He told me everything about your fucked up life.' His words were like venom.

'Um, okay, well I wish he hadn't done that, but it doesn't really...'

'Fucking hell, I can't believe it's you. How can you be on a date with me when you've fucked someone like that?'

'What? He's my friend... my closest friend these days.'

'You're disgusting. I can't believe... Fuck! He's a fucking skinny, broke, fucking ugly cunt. Look at me! I'm fucking three times his size! How the fuck could you even be attracted to someone like that?'

Wowzers.

'Because he's my friend, and I like his personality.' I made sure to enunciate per-son-al-i-ty, so as to really relay the importance of not being a total fucking wanker, but he couldn't hear me. He was in his own dick-measuring contest in his head, and it was a battle he was seemingly losing.

It was astounding to watch. It was as though he was a malfunctioning robot. His eye was twitching, his chest puffed up, and he was clenching his fists, ready to fight. For the life of him, he could not mathematically work out why anyone might like to spend time, sexually or otherwise, with someone who didn't look like him. *Does not compute. Does not compute. Does not com- *head spins in circles and explodes*.*

This news sent him into a tailspin, and he could not let it go. If he was an arsehole before, now he was downright scary. Jay was all he could talk about for the rest of the night as he became increasingly agitated. I froze, unable to get up and storm out or fake an emergency phone call. I just sat and listened to him call me a whore and a slut for the next hour as he imbibed drink after drink. The only reprieve was his intermittent bathroom breaks. During one, I quickly got out my phone and messaged Jay. I got the impression that had he caught me with the phone, Amir's paranoia would reach new heights, so I kept it stealth.

Me: 'I'm on a date with Amir. He's just found out I know u & gone mental. WTF?'

Jay: 'He's an arsehole. We used to party together for a hot minute until I realised he was a total fuckwit. Leave n come here. I'd pick u up but I got the kids 2night & can't leave.'

Me: 'It's OK, I think we'll be done soon anyway. Am I safe? He's not dangerous is he?'

Jay: 'Nah he's not dangerous, just a dickhead.'

Me: 'Ha! OK I'll text u when I can get outta here.'

Jay: 'Cool, catch ya soon.'

After suffering through the longest dinner in history, we were finally leaving. As he paid the bill, Amir looked at me and scoffed. 'Pfft. A hundred bucks? You're not even worth a 12-dollar sub!'

By now, I was silent. I hadn't eaten a thing; I could barely sip my water. I felt nauseous and tense. Despite what Jay had said, I did not feel safe.

While waiting for a taxi outside the restaurant, Amir yelled at passers-by in the street. 'What the fuck are you looking at? You wanna fucking go me? I'd fucking destroy you, cunt!' he would yell at unassuming men enjoying a warm summer's night with their girlfriends. The whole time, he kept one hand firmly around the back of my neck or a fistful of my hair in his hand to keep me from moving.

I watched myself shrink down into myself for safety. I felt myself become smaller – just as I had when receiving my cancer diagnosis. I found myself hiding behind the layers of flesh and muscle. *I am not here. I am deep down inside and I am safe.* I must have looked as shell-shocked as I felt because a wonderful man came up to me, looking very concerned, and asked me if I was okay. I wanted to cry as I felt the hand tighten around my neck and replied with the weakest 'yes' you had ever heard. The kind man knew I was lying. He also knew there was nothing more he could do.

I directed the taxi driver to my car and was already searching for my keys as we pulled up. As the car pulled away, I thanked Amir for the worst date in history and started toward my car.

'Where do you think you're going?' he snarled.

'I'm leaving. This is over.'

He grabbed me and slammed me into my car, looked me dead in the eyes, and said the words that ring in my head every night as I try to sleep: 'I'm going to take it out on you.'

The elusive 'it' being whatever you want to make it. Jay. His jealousy. His anger. His pathetic existence. The fucked-up childhood I can only assume he had. All of it.

Suddenly he was dragging me down the alley behind his house by my hair. I thought of the horrific story Li had told me over contraband cookies and how scared she must have been. I wondered why I didn't feel scared, not in any way I recognised, anyway. It was as though my body decided the best way to survive whatever came next was to remain completely calm and clear-headed. Whenever I performed on stage, I would be petrified. My stomach would be doing backflips, hands shaking and teeth chattering. There were times I was sure I would get on stage and be so frightened I would forget how to sing. But I would walk out on stage smiling serenely through the stage lights, into the black well of faceless chairs, and pretend. In those moments, I dreamed of a calm like this.

With one elbow wrapped around my throat and a giant hand gripping my hair, I felt my toes skimming the pavement below, trying to find purchase. *How did Li's story end again?* I hoped remembering would help me prepare myself. *Beating or rape? Which would be the preferable option?*

'You idiot,' my inner voice helpfully chimed in. *'All the red flags you ignored, and for what? A story on a podcast? Because a text message said you were safe? Because you desperately wanted someone who disgusted you to tell you you're enough? You knew better. This is your fault.'*

Amir pinned me to the truck he kept parked at the back of the house and towered over me with hatred in his hollow eyes. *How can a man be so physically huge yet so pathetically small inside?* I wondered. I wanted to voice my nastiness but decided against it. His large hands tore at my body in all directions. It was as though he was trying not only to rip off my clothes but claw at my flesh. I felt my skin pinch painfully between his fingers like clay. Now he could feel those disgusting extra kilos squelching between his hands. *Good, be repulsed by me, you fuck.*

He held me face down against the bonnet, its coldness against my cheek. His forearm dug into the back of my neck. *'I didn't know you could choke someone from behind. It's quite effective,'* I thought, as the blood pulsated behind my eyes. He reached into the side door, still holding me down with his other arm, and pulled out a box of condoms the size of a cereal box. *Rape it is, then.* He took one out and put it on one-handed so as to not lose his grip on me. Seeing this enormous box of condoms emerge from his car also told me this was not a one-time slip-up for him. This was what he did, and he did it a lot. I felt a deep well of sadness for the women who had come before me while at the same time feeling less alone. Connected by sisterhood and vulnerability: two wonderful things of which he had absolutely no grasp. How pathetic that he had to take intimacy by force, love by possession and attention by fear.

He did all the things a rapist does to a person. It was brutal, degrading and violent, but this isn't a story of destruction. This is a story of mother-fucking resurrection! Everything I had learned in rehab taught me that this was all his shit and had nothing to do with me, and personally, I don't give a flying fuck about his shit. I care about *my* shit. If I could survive a spinal tumour, anorexia, drug addiction, every mental illness under the Sun and heartbreak upon mother-fucking heartbreak – all before my 30th birthday – there was nothing some juiced-up, insecure bloke could do that could destroy me. The thought was laughable! All I had to do was stay alive, and I'd been perfecting that skill for years.

My senses were on high alert, bringing intense clarity to what was happening. I had full awareness that this was a life-threatening situation, but I was able to assess my safety from one moment to the next. I processed which decisions could end up potentially fatal and which would empower me to save my life. Could I fight him off? Absolutely not. Instead, I alternated between relaxing as much as possible to preserve the air I had in my lungs and timing gulps of air during his momentary releases of pressure to my neck. I struggled with force when I could, but my strength was useless against his fury unless I could get a knee to his groin.

I considered running, but to look pretty for my big date, I'd worn the old boots that looked great but had zero tread left on the soles. If I ran, I would slip. If I slipped, he would catch me, now angrier and more panicked than before. If a coked-up, enraged giant finds you on the ground of a dark alleyway with hate in his eyes, there is a good chance he will kill you. Neither running nor fighting were viable options. All I could do was wait.

Over the next 30 minutes, I worked hard to distract myself in my head, whether it be praying to Sam to save me or hoping my dad wasn't seeing this. I looked at the darkness of the night sky above, wishing I'd listened when Dad tried to teach me the names of the constellations and lamented the light pollution ruining my fantasy. I thought about losing my virginity to my boyfriend on year 11 camp and looking out of the tiny tent window up at the stars. It was warm like tonight, dark like tonight, but nothing like tonight. He had been tender and romantic. I felt loved and cared for – nothing like tonight.

In middle school, some of the kids would talk flippantly about rape and consent. Somewhere along the line of Chinese whispers, it became shared as fact that if a girl says 'No' three times, she *really* means it and you must stop, or it becomes illegal. As an adult, this sounded both idiotic and terrifying, but at that moment, it just kept circling my mind like a dark comedy. In a way, it was useful because it gave me the courage to boldly say, 'No.' Because of that problematic high school rumour, I know I said those important words as many times as possible. At one point, looking him dead in the eye, I said, 'You know what this is,' and for a moment, I saw him flinch. *What's that? You're not afraid of a little woman, are you?*

I tried singing in my head, but that was a mess. I could only think of two songs. One was Adele's *Rollin' in the Deep,* of which I knew only the chorus. The other was Tori Amos's *Me and a Gun,* which, if you are unfamiliar, is a brilliantly artistic a cappella piece about a woman fleeing a rape. Unfortunately for me, that was the one I knew most of the words to, so I sang it on repeat until such time as I, too, could flee this rape.

As grim as that sounds, it helped me. I felt connected to Tori as she sang about the unusual places your mind goes to in times like these. For her, it was having never seen Barbados 'so [she] must get out of this'. I remembered seeing her play two pianos at once to thousands of adoring fans while painted into skin-tight gold leggings, and I thought if she can take her pain and twist it into something incredible, why can't I?

Tori Amos – my idol, my musical inspiration and now my strength – stood beside me, holding my hand and reminding me of my own immense power. She helped me feel dignified in a moment where humiliation was the goal. If a man needs to take a woman's body to feel powerful, they must be petrified of being seen for what they really are: a desperately sad, ugly, lonely little boy.

At times, I felt as if I was coming back to myself. The me who had been hiding deep inside for years, shrouded in misery. This man's rage and self-loathing outshone even mine, and I could see just how lucky I was. I thought about being five years old, curled up tight in my mum's arms. Giggling, I would pretend I was trying to wriggle free as she held me tighter and tighter, teasing, 'I'll never let you go, I'll never let you go!' I thought about how incredibly loved I was and how unloved he must have been to grow into such a monster.

In other moments, I was livid. I wanted to scream at God for letting this happen. But then I would remember there is no God. I was alone. No one was watching, no one was listening, and no one was coming to save me. It was up to me and only me to get out of this alive.

Some things only God can forgive

Soundtrack: *Kesha – 'Praying'*

In the movies, these scenes last mere seconds. We understand what is being alluded to by the close-up images of clothes being torn, bodies being grabbed, and the huffing and puffing of an angry man leaping atop a distressed woman, but a lot goes unsaid between those cuts in film.

I didn't black anything out. I remember every second in explicit detail. At about the 20-minute mark, he got bored with his surroundings and dragged me inside. He forced me into his lounge room, where all his sofa cushions were laid on the floor like a makeshift mattress. That, to me, was the saddest sight of all. He told me he hadn't been able to sleep the night before and slept there instead so he could watch TV. But this was a grand set-up meant for two. He had either pre-planned tonight, or another unsuspecting young woman was in my position just last night. I thought about what kind of girl would come here willingly before remembering myself only a few hours earlier, broken and alone, looking for comfort.

I already felt different. Stronger. It was as though my pained inner child had been in charge of the ship for too long, and adult Kirsty had finally come out of hiding to take the reins again. *Nice of you to show your face. Where the fuck have you been hiding?* Adult Kirsty put sweet little baby K away in a safe place and took over. *About fucking time.*

Half an hour in, and I needed a new tactic. He didn't seem to be slowing down or getting tired, and I was running out of songs to sing and people to pray to. It was then that I looked him dead in the eyes and said, 'You *know* what this is.'

This motherfucker looked back at me and said, 'Oh, sorry, do you want me to go gentler?'

Do I want you to rape me more gently? As opposed to what? Violently and degradingly? Um, if those were my only two options, then, 'Yes...' I replied. Because I didn't know what else to say or do. He had successfully gaslighted me into thinking I had a choice all along. Well played.

It made my head spin. I did say 'no' and 'stop', didn't I? Yes. I said it over and over again. I was clear, right? There was no way he thought this was some kind of fucked-up kinky game, was there? No, of course not. He said he wanted to 'take it out on me'. But the seed of doubt had been planted, and I worried that perhaps I hadn't been clear enough. Maybe he was just confused. I certainly was.

I wanted it to all be over. My skin was starting to crawl like I needed to take a burning hot shower and melt off the top layer. So, I faked an orgasm, hoping this would signal him to do the same. This worked, but I hated myself for it. I still have very complicated feelings about that moment because it just confused things more. Could he use that as a defence to prove I enjoyed it? I thought back to an episode of *Oprah* I had seen as an adolescent. She was talking about being molested as a child and how her predator would manipulate her into believing she had wanted his abuse because her body would 'respond'. At the time, I had no idea what that meant because I was just a sweet, innocent child.

As soon as the physical abuse was over, the verbal attacks began. 'You fucking whore, I can't believe you just did that, and on a first date, too! You better not have any fucking diseases. Do you? Fucking answer me! You probably do if you're doing shit like that with every guy you meet. I fucking swear if you gave me an STD, I'll fucking...' I hadn't even had time to process what had just happened, and now he was blaming me for potentially hurting him? What world am I in? His berating continued for several minutes as I responded only to appease him.

While my head still rattled with confusion, he took out his phone and started filming me. 'Did we just have good sex?' he asked with a sadistic smirk.

'Um …'

'Well, did we? Did we just have good sex?' He made sure to emphasise the good. As if it cleared his name.

Realising I wasn't going to get out of this without a response, I replied, 'We had sex.'

'Good sex?' he pushed.

I sighed, 'We had sex.'

He smirked and then, realising he wouldn't be able to get anything else out of me without force, which would defeat the entire purpose of his happy little video, stopped and put down the phone. I was proud of myself for this small act of defiance, and I was relieved when he didn't murder me for it.

I stayed the night because I didn't know how to leave safely. Not that I felt safe there next to him. I lay in bed all night next to the man who violently raped me because I was afraid and seriously confused. I thought that if he held me as we slept or kissed my forehead goodnight, maybe I could tell myself I had been wrong about it all. Maybe I could go on with my life fooling myself into believing this was just bad sex. But he didn't do that. He lay next to me, cold and distant like I was a bad smell he couldn't wait to get rid of. I wanted to leave, but I froze. So, I stayed.

I stayed while he boasted about the guns he kept in his closet only metres from where I lay. I stayed as he called me a whore and a slut because of what he did to me. I stayed, lying awake in fear and trying not to breathe too loudly in case it woke him and he started all over again.

In the morning, he sneered at me and croaked, 'What the fuck are you still doing here?' As if I wanted to be there. As if I had a choice. I collected myself and walked briskly toward my car without looking back, heart racing. He'd used a fake name, a discreet location, and a faux-friendly online persona. This had been his plan all along. I could have been anyone. How many dozens of girls had come before me was unclear, but one thing I knew for certain was this time, he screwed up.

He had made the fatal error of seeing my past trauma as a weakness. What he didn't see is that my audacity means I am not afraid to speak out. My emotional turmoil has taught me to withstand tremendous amounts of pressure, and my crippling anxieties have birthed bravery unchallenged by any man. He thought he had plucked out a vulnerable girl who would be too frightened to tell a soul, but what he actually did was awaken a voracity in me that will not be satiated until I bring him to his knees. I am not burdened by crushing shame – that is his cross to bear – and I shall be the one to make sure he bears it. *Mic drop!*

I drove away, feeling an alarming amount of nothing. I suspected this was what shock felt like and waited for the moment when my knees buckled and I couldn't stand under the weight of the abuse. But it never came. This event slid perfectly into the wounds that many men had left before. This abuse may have been more severe, but it certainly wasn't new. To be mistreated, humiliated, hurt and left for dead had become a staple of what I expected from men. Besides, compared to Simon's abandonment, which left me begging for mercy and praying for death, this was nothing. That was the nothing I felt.

Now let me demonstrate, in three simple recreations, why people might be hesitant to tell anyone about their sexual assault:

- *Exhibit A*

Unable to contact Simon to either draw comfort from his murder by thine own hand or warmth from his familiarity, I called Alessandro and told him what had happened.

'Hmm, what did you do?' he asked nonchalantly.

'What do you mean? It was just meant to be a date.'

'Yeah, but you must have done something to provoke it. Were you wasted?'

'What are you talking about? I just got out of rehab.' Of all the ways I thought this conversation was going to go, this had not crossed my mind. 'Do you think I caused this?'

'I mean, do I think you're perfectly innocent? No. You know what you're like.'

'What I'm like? You're an arsehole.' I hung up. It was clear I wasn't going to find any support here. He didn't believe me and insinuated I was asking for it. This was the first time he really showed his age with this fucked up, antiquated, victim-blaming bullshit. *Okay, Boomer!*

I went to the bottle-o to buy a six-pack and a bottle of wine. Rehab be damned.

- ***Exhibit B***

I then drove to Jay's, unable to bring myself to go home and face Mum. I hoped that with Jay, I would find the comfort I hadn't in Alessandro. Knowing how intensely volatile Amir could be, Jay believed me right away. I stayed with him all day, smoking cigarette after cigarette and downing a bottle of wine. After five weeks of sobriety, it went down far too easily, and I was drunk in no time. I crawled into Jay's bed and we continued talking. He was pacing around his bedroom.

'I bet he did this to get to me. I bet he knew who you were before you agreed to go out with him.'

'Err, no. He had no idea. In fact, finding out I knew you is when he flipped.' *Is he seriously making my rape about him right now?*

'Hmm. Nah, he could find a way.' *Okay, so that's a yes. Yes, he is.* 'I thought it was weird that he matched with you. You're not really his usual type.'

'What?' *Please tell me this isn't going where I think it's about to go.*

'It's just that he always dates size six, supermodel-type girls.' *Oh good. He went there.*

Seeing the horror on my face, he continued. 'No! I mean, you know that I think you're gorgeous. You're sexy and I personally love your body. You know that! It's just that he always dates these really tiny, traditionally striking girls. You know what I'm saying?' *I think I'm getting it!*

'No, yeah, I hear you. I'm not hot enough to be raped by your mate.' That is some Trump v. Hillary circa 2016 toxic, idiotic shit right there. News flash: Us fat, ugly, normal-looking gals can get raped, too. Happens a lot, actually. Why? Because rape has NOTHING to do with appearance and EVERYTHING to do with POWER. WHY DO I HAVE TO SPELL THIS OUT? WHAT EVEN ARE MEN?

I fell asleep a little while later with Jay next to me. This wasn't unusual; I slept over a couple of nights a week. What I wasn't expecting was to wake up to him caressing my body after everything I had just been through. Jay had been a dear friend to me, and perhaps more importantly, Sam loved him, but what he did changed me and broke my heart.

I could barely stand the sensation of my own clothes against my skin, let alone another's hands. He began exploring my body and kissing my neck. I felt my body tense, my heart drop and my mouth become dry. I felt the need to cry, but I couldn't. I felt a well of sadness collect in my belly and just stay there, churning up the dregs of the previous night.

'I want you to remember what sex is meant to be like. I don't want your last memory to be what he did to you,' Jay whispered, pulling down my pants.

Stop him, Sam, please, I prayed. I didn't say a word. I froze in disbelief. It was an extremely misguided attempt at comforting me, and he didn't read the signs that it was the last thing in the world I needed.

I thought about a story I had heard about a woman in India. She had been dragged to a field where she was attacked and raped by a group of 'men'. When she finally got away, she went to the police to report the crime, only to be raped once more by the attending officer. The one person who had vowed to protect her at all costs failed her. How could you ever trust anyone again? I'll let you know if I discover the answer.

This event didn't feel like nothing. This felt like something so huge I needed to tuck it away in the place where all the discarded screams go and lock it away. It felt like grief. Like a death was occurring in my solar plexus, and here I was, planting some daisies over it and pretending there wasn't a rotting green corpse stinking up my garden with its death juice. He had been my friend and my closest connection to Sam, and now I couldn't stand to be near him. What an idiot.

- *Exhibit C*

After staying the night at Jay's, I finally went home. As soon as I got in, I went straight to bed, trying to avoid the awkward conversation with Mum. I knew she would be able to tell something was up just by looking at me. But, by evening, she came into my room to check on me and I decided to bite the bullet and just tell her. The thing is, whether it's rape or consensual, it's still super cringeworthy talking to your parents about S E X. They don't want to hear it, and you don't want to talk about it, but, in some circumstances, it has to be done. For instance, I'll never understand why couples announce they are 'trying for a baby'. Ew, Sharron! I don't want to hear about your balding sweaty husband astride you! Keep your sex life and your babies to yourselves, please and thank you.

I explained to Mum in very limited detail what had happened. I don't know what I expected – maybe for her to cry or throw her arms around me and tell me *everything would be alright*. But she didn't.

'Are you certain it was rape?' she asked. *Okaaay, not quite what I was expecting.*

'What?' Am I the girl that screams rape or something? I have never said anything like this to anyone before, and suddenly I'm making this shit up?

'I heard a story a few months ago about a news anchor who has been accused by several women of sexual abuse. The women alleged that he had choked them, but he was under the impression that it was consensual. I think they call it BDSM.'

'Oh my god, Mum, gross! Firstly, don't say BDSM ever again. That's literally traumatising, and secondly, I am not confused. I know the difference between bad sex and rape. I know what this was.'

'Okay, then you need to go to the police.' I watched as it finally sank in and her face shifted from questioning to angry. That's more like it. What is it that the woke influencers preach? *If you're not mad, you're not paying attention.* Get mad, mamma; we got work to do!

A police officer would later inform me that this is quite a common reaction from parents and loved ones. The reality of what they are hearing is too awful to fathom, so their mind searches for any alternative, which, in Mum's case, looked a lot like doubt. I don't blame her – my brain was searching for an out, too.

These were the first three people I told – three people who were extremely important to me, but all of whom responded in a less-than-ideal way. I had nothing left to lose, so, for me, it wasn't such a big deal to then discuss what had happened with my family doctor, my psychologist and the police. But imagine if your job relied on you staying quiet, or it could tear your family apart, or it took all of your bravery to tell someone, and they responded like any of the people above?

I reported the crime, not expecting justice but to hopefully scare someone who I believe has done this many times before and whose violent behaviour could continue to escalate. I have no doubt he could and would beat someone to death. I reported it because I could, but there are so many women who can't for entirely justifiable reasons. I do not care what happens to me if it means bringing a person like this to their knees. I reported it because if I didn't, I would take justice into my own hands, and I deserve more than being locked up for life. He doesn't.

I must go on standing

Soundtrack: *Regina Spektor – 'Apres Moi'*

When I was around 12 years old, I asked Dad what he was most afraid of. I expected a generic answer like heights, snakes or spiders. But instead of creepy crawlies or things that go bump in the night, he said, 'I just want my family to be safe.'

I remember processing that for a long time afterwards. I was scared of the dark. Petrified actually. To this day, I am still not a fan, but he was right – there are much scarier things lurking among us, and they often come in the form of other people. An act borne of hate, as ugly as rape, that's the act of a monster. But something as deep as love carries the danger of hurt too; the risk that it may become damaged, broken or even die. So what can we do? I had no idea. So I ran away.

Everywhere I went in Melbourne, I was re-traumatised. So, I decided if I'm depressed anyway, I may as well be depressed in my favourite place in the world. I packed a suitcase and flew to Italy to get as far away from the crime scene Melbourne had become as humanly possible. I wasn't at all fearful about travelling alone in a foreign land. In the past, it would have seemed impossible to travel without a man by my side protecting me (LOL!), but the last few years had been a storm of confronting my greatest fears, and somehow, I was still standing. Somehow, I was still here. With that realisation came a bravery, or perhaps boldness, I hadn't had before. In fact, what scared me to death was staying in Melbourne. This not only felt like the best option but the only option. *Run.*

I spent eight months living and working as an au pair to a ten-year-old girl named Amara (Ama) in a tiny provincial town called Savignano. It was located in Italy's Emilia Romagna region, one of the greatest food provinces in the world. I lived next door to Grace, Federico and his parents, who became my family. I would love to tell you that being surrounded by flourishing peach orchards, travelling into the 'Red City' of Bologna for Italian lessons, and being responsible for a child's well-being, kept me out of trouble – but that wouldn't be entirely true. Because wherever I went, there I was.

My Italian sojourn provided me with enough of a pause to catch my breath and begin processing my heartache while surrounded by beauty, friendship and the best food and wine you've ever tasted. I wasn't using oxy, but I wasn't sober from alcohol (drugs of any variety, alcohol included, are frowned upon in 12-step circles). Booze had never been my drug of choice, so I wasn't too worried about a little Lambrusco here or Prosecco there. It's easy to fool yourself into thinking your level of self-medication is nothing more than an appreciation of the culture when you are in a foreign land.

As picturesque as life was, it wasn't perfect. The family I lived with fought a lot. Two weeks into my six-month stint, I noticed tension between the parents, Andrea and Teresa. After dinner on a warm summer's evening, I was drying dishes by the sink as Andrea handed me the wet ones he had just washed. I was gazing out of the window, enchanted by the lengthy twilight, a sight lacking in the southern hemisphere. We chatted in broken English and Italian, respectively, often stopping to look up words on Google translate before laughing at our own incompetence. It was nice. For the first time, I was connecting with a member of the household in a natural, friendly way and not in the stunted formalities we danced around as we all got to know each other. All of a sudden, we heard a door slam on the level above and angry footsteps stomping down the stairs. Teresa barged into the kitchen, now spotless, and whispered something to Andrea. She then turned on her heels and stormed back upstairs without looking at me. Andrea put down the washcloth he had been using to wipe the benches, drooped his head to his toes and hunched his shoulders. His entire demeanour had changed. He, too, avoided my eyes as he followed his wife upstairs. Living under the same roof, he wouldn't speak to me or look me in the eye for another month, and even then, only when Teresa was out. This felt all too familiar.

Oftentimes, the arguments between Ama and her mother reached uncontrollable heights. Teresa's screaming and Ama's crying could be heard from down the street. I never witnessed any violence, but Teresa's rage regularly veered into verbal abuse – or so I assumed, being unable to understand what they were saying. I pulled Andrea – the peacemaker – aside a couple of times to let him know of my concerns, but he brushed it off, saying, 'Oh, that's just the way they are together. Tomorrow will be better.' He had grown used to a life spent walking on eggshells. It was fine for him, he was a carabinieri (Italian policeman) and an ex-army man, but for Ama, it was causing irreparable damage. I watched the poor girl live in a constant state of anxiety that was reminiscent of my own childhood; only, in my case, my family had been my safety. I feared what would happen to a child that had no safe place to land.

One day, Ama excitedly rushed home from school and proudly presented her artwork to her mother, who worked as an art teacher at another school. Ama looked up at her mum in anticipation of an enthusiastic response. From my room upstairs, I heard wailing and sobbing from below, then a door slammed, and small footsteps ran away. I chased after Ama, realising these screams were more authentic than her usual dramatics (she had learned that while tears pushed her mother away, they elicited much-needed affection from her father).

'Ama, aspetta! Wait!' I caught up to her and pulled her into my arms, feeling her tiny body heaving with sobs. I thought of all the times my mum had held me through my tears. I was furious on behalf of this poor child that her mother was the one causing such heartache. We found a park bench and took a seat.

'What happened?'

'She said my picture era brutta (was ugly),' she said between sniffs and sobs.

'Oh, amore, I'm so sorry. She shouldn't have said that. Do you want to show me? Sono sicura che sia bella, come me (I'm sure it's beautiful like me),' I attempted in slow, stumbling Italian. Trying to make myself look silly.

'Come te? (Like you?) Do you mean like me? Or you think you are so beautiful?' Ama smirked at my ineptitude before correcting me.

'I do, actually, yes,' I joked back. She gave me a look only a 10-going-on-15-year-old could master. 'Dai, show me.'

'No, è brutta. I hate it!'

And, just like that, a child who had spent the day experimenting creatively, and had found pride in her artistic endeavours, learned that she was not good enough. FUCK! I wanted to scoop her up, run away and get her out of that house. But there was no doubt I would have found new and terrifying ways to fuck her up all on my lonesome. We hung out away from the house for a while, and when I was happy with the amount of laughter I had squeezed out of her, we ventured back.

Later, I would go to put something in the rubbish bin and find her art crumpled at the top. I took the paper, smoothed it out, and hung it proudly on my bedroom wall. Her mother never apologised.

I tried my best to be Ama's safe place, but it was a tricky line to tread. I was there for Ama, but ultimately, I was employed by Teresa. If I didn't stay on her good side, there was a very real chance that she could kick me out or, at the very least, make my living situation unbearable. I had seen what it was like to be on her bad side, and I wasn't feeling strong enough to withstand that wrath. To avoid conflict, I found myself retreating to Grace's place more often, staying longer in the city after language school and generally avoiding going home. I'd often go to the cafe near the train station on my way home and stop for *un cafe*. I'd talk in broken Italian to the man behind the bar about his pet gecko. A very difficult conversation to have between two people who do not speak the same language. There were many amusing hand gestures.

I also confirmed what I had always suspected: I am not cut out for children. The monotony of it began to wear me down and take a toll on my physical health. I don't have to tell parents this, but it just never stops. I lived with my host family, so even if I was technically clocked-off for the day, it's not like I could just switch off. When I was depressed, I still had to be polite. When I was exhausted, I still had to be fun and entertaining. Having fibromyalgia means I require a lot of rest and peace. I basically need to be wrapped up like a burrito, placed in a quiet room, and given gentle pats on the head several times a day. I *am* the child. When I am in an over-stimulating environment or under a lot of stress, my body retaliates by shutting down like a scared sea turtle. I get extraordinarily fatigued to the point where walking up a short flight of stairs requires a rest halfway through, and my body creates pain that resembles a full-body migraine. It's awful. The condition requires a lot of work just to maintain a remission phase, but when it flares up, I'm essentially out of action until I can hibernate for several months and return to the world gently and slowly. *Chronic illness sufferers, AKA Spoonies, I see you. You are important. Now take some vitamin D and go back to bed.*

By the time my work as an au pair was drawing to a close, I was ready to leave. But in that time, I had grown so much. I had never travelled alone, and now I knew how to navigate railway systems in a non-English-speaking country. I could speak Italian at the level of a (pretty thick) three-year-old, and although still depressed, I was no longer suicidal, which I had never believed was possible. *Can I get a woop woop?* I could see progress, and progress meant hope. Hope that there will come a time when I can laugh with friends over dinner and not have a bowling ball of dread in my gut reminding me of everything I have lost. One day, I would throw my head back in pure, unadulterated joy and just laugh. No strings attached.

I came home for a few months after Italy to test the waters and soon realised I wasn't ready to be back. This time, I fled to the country of my birth, England. More specifically, the county of my birth, Surrey. I stayed with Grace's sister and brother-in-law, Emily and Andrew, between pet-sitting jobs, which took me to far-flung regions of Greater London. It was wonderful. I felt truly free. Despite travelling and living alone (for the most part), I never felt lonely because wherever I stayed, I had an array of furry friends. I took care of cats, dogs and even some tropical fish – which I thought would be simple, but, in fact, I almost destroyed, despite the meticulous instructions from the homeowner. That was the level of responsibility I needed. Care for small animals and care for self. That was more than enough.

At one point, I found myself living in a charming market town two hours north of London called Market Harborough. I was there for six weeks caring for two dogs: one an oodle of some variety and the other an old, fat Shiba Inu. They were immediately affectionate and would sleep in bed with me every night. Together we would explore the countryside for hours each day. I was there in the spring, meaning I was around for the births of various farm animals. I saw paddocks of tiny grazing lambs that looked like waddling clouds, playful calves with wide eyes and enviable eyelashes, and clumsy ducklings desperate to keep up with the rest of the paddling (yes, that's what a group of ducks is called – isn't that just divine). There were acres of wild Gypsy horses that were so used to humans that they would come and greet me, expecting snacks, which I quickly learned to supply.

The small horses frolicked and played with the dogs as I threw a ball for them. There were a couple of chubby ones waddling around who I figured must have had access to the premium grassy knolls, but one day, on my walk, there were two brand new foals attempting to stand on wobbly Bambi legs and feed on their mothers' milk. I was so moved, I turned off *The Bloodhound Gang* playing *Bad Touch* in my ears and just stood watching the beauty of nature in the crisp air. I don't know if I had ever done that before that moment. Life had always been about rushing around, fearful I was missing out. Suddenly, I was met with this moment of stillness, watching the pure, natural connection between mother and baby, and I never wanted the moment to end. After years of wondering if I had been unwittingly flung into purgatory, I was viewing a scene that made me wonder if, even just for a moment, I was in heaven.

Between bouts of tranquillity, my grief and rage would occasionally bubble over, and I would need to let it out like a pot boiling over. My distress could simmer beneath the surface for weeks, suppressed by cute animals, new scenery and loving friends, but whenever I stayed in one place too long, the grief would churn and twist inside me. It often occurred when I was living far from Emily and Andrew and had been left to my own devices for some time. I would get lonely, angry, sad or all three, and find myself drowning my sorrows at the local pub with whoever would put up with the obnoxious Aussie brat I became when drunk. I learned quickly that my recovery story was not going to be smooth sailing. Not having easy access to oxy in London, I leaned heavily on alcohol and took the opportunity to participate in any little white baggie I happened to find myself in front of. It's easy to get away with being an alcoholic in England, 1. because seemingly everyone is, and 2. there is a pub every two metres, so if you get kicked out of one, it's as simple as 'On to the next!'

By now, I was an expert at spotting the town drug dealer. Without fail, he would be loitering in the corner chain-smoking cigarettes while regularly answering calls on one of the phones in his pockets, thinking he was stealth with subtle handshakes and money exchanges. I felt like Sherlock bloody Holmes, only I wasn't solving crimes for the sake of the greater good – I wanted to join in said criminal activities. Some would call these nights of debauchery relapses; I prefer to think of them as learning curves.

It was easier to act out in the UK. I didn't have the eyes of my family watching my every move, and there seemed to be more broken souls wandering around than in Italy. Or perhaps I was attracting them. This served me well on my nights of 'volatile healing'. See, there is 'tranquil healing', which is all kumbaya, meditation, a healthy lifestyle and a fuck tonne of therapy – all essential for a better life. And then there is what I have labelled 'volatile healing', used for blowing off steam and thus avoiding becoming a mass murderer. This includes copious amounts of alcohol, coke binges and fuck boiz. Some may argue this is less helpful. I'm on the fence.

One long night, while trying to forget, I found myself at the pub for last drinks with three lost boys. There was no fear around being the only girl in the group, simply because I no longer lived with fear. All my greatest fears had been realised, and I had nothing left to lose. But what I could gain was a night free from fighting the war inside me, and for that, I would do anything.

Rackie was the talk of the town for all the wrong reasons. Aptly named, he was aggressive, violent and a hardcore party boy, out from Friday to Sunday every weekend. Even more worrying was how charming and attractive he was in a *Peaky Blinders* type of way. He was blonde, blue-eyed and had a nice physique, but he was weathered. For someone in his early 30s, he looked a lot older from a lifetime of smoking and drinking. He was a self-proclaimed geezer and the only person left in Greater London who still regularly used Cockney slang. The local police had their eye on him. I once saw him explain away why he was carrying three mobile phones on his person at the local pub. He spun bullshit like it was going out of style, but instead of it feeling sneaky and manipulative, a la Alessandro, it was exciting.

Although a truly harmful person, he came across as more mischievous than anything else. We had a couple of dates that never went anywhere, predominantly because he kept skipping out on them halfway through. On our first date, he got a call from a mate who I could hear yelling through the phone. He was gathering his things and flying out the door as he called out, 'My mate's in a domestic with his girl. She's gone mental, throwing shit and threatening to stab him. I gotta get over there. Later babe.' It would make modern-day Kirsty's skin crawl to be referred to as 'babe' by a relative stranger, but when he said it, I found his assumed familiarity amusing. Likewise, the sense of responsibility he held for his boys, beyond all sense and fear of consequence, was intriguing. It made you feel that if you belonged to him in some way, you were safe. Life was a game to him, and he preferred it when he was right on the cusp of getting caught. I tried to imagine Simon actively running toward a knife fight in defence of his friend's honour. The thought was so far-fetched that all my mind could produce was an image of him clomping onto the scene wearing empty tissue boxes on his feet, toilet rolls on his wrists as armour, and slowly sweeping his cap backwards to duelling music from an old Western.

Joining us at the pub that night was an older guy, about 60, attractive but aged, with long hair and sad eyes. He was kind, but a little handsy as the night wore on. The third and final guest was tall and good-looking but too socially awkward to be attractive. He was funny without meaning to be, with his blunt and often brutal honesty throughout the night.

The four of us, not wanting the night to end, found ourselves hobbling back to Rackie's house at two in the morning. At his basic but surprisingly nice apartment, we drank cold beer until it ran out, then warm beer that had been resting on the floor next to the fridge. It was disgusting, but it didn't matter. Anything goes down a treat with a line or ten of coke. Rackie was both the town's debt collector and coke dealer. He was fascinating to watch. As we would finish one little pile of coke between us, thinking that was it for the night, he would start rummaging around behind TV cables, under candles on the mantle, even behind photographs of his young son, to produce yet another package of happiness wrapped in foil.

Between us, we'd alternate who was seated on his third-storey window ledge as we chain-smoked the night away. As the Sun started to rise, he pinned sheets over the window to prevent the shame from creeping in. Truth be told, this was a fun night. But then we did it again. And again. And very quickly, the appeal began to fade, shame and regret coming in earlier each time. It became harder to maintain the illusion that we were just mad kids having a wild night. Clarity slowly crept in that we were all deeply damaged and torturously sad individuals, using each other for some quick relief. Eventually, it becomes like trying to clean your dishes with grease. The harder you try, the more hopeless it becomes.

Everyone in that room had a heartbreaking story that had brought them there. Socially awkward, Ash had recently been left by his wife, who had been having an on-off affair with a gorgeous Brazilian. She had up and moved to Brazil to be with her new man, taking Ash's baby boy with her. His heart was broken in so many directions that he didn't know where to place his grief. I could relate.

The older man had sad eyes for a reason. He'd had a wife once and loved her deeply, but she had died of a heroin overdose two decades prior. He had been the one to find her body and blamed himself for her death. He'd never been able to love again. They had a daughter, and his eyes lit up when he spoke about her. He said she was my age and kept insisting I meet her. She, too, was a musician. I smiled and agreed, knowing he would re-think his invitation by morning. I imagined, solemnly, what would have had to happen in my own father's life to bring him to a place like this; A man who had one story about getting drunk on tequila when he was in his early 20s, and it terrified him so much he never touched the stuff or got drunk, ever again.

Rackie's story was the most upsetting. He told me how he'd seen his father shoot himself in the head when he was just two years old. He recounted the story like it was nothing, then shrugged and said, 'I don't give a shit. He was a prick.' I leaned in a little and examined his face for any micro-movements that might indicate he was disguising his incredible trauma, but there was nothing in his cool blue eyes. He was obsessed with power and notoriety. That was his drug of choice over anything else. Zero points to the shrink who can work out why the little boy who couldn't save his daddy might want to rule the fucking world. If I were him, I could imagine doing everything in my power to avoid ever feeling that scared and helpless ever again, even if it meant closing my heart so tightly that I would become a raging narcissist, incapable of love.

As someone who has been in therapy since I was a teenager and is medicated for my mental illnesses, I was shocked to learn how taboo this still is in England. The guys laughed at me for being so forthright about the fact that I took anti-depressants. Horrified, Rackie claimed he'd never put that shit in his body ... as he held a credit card in one hand, primed to rack a fresh line, and a cigarette in the other. He was about 18 beers down when he mocked me for going to rehab, 'That's a pussy's way out,' he called it. I laughed at the absurdity. I knew I wasn't perfect. I knew as an addict, I was in the worst scenario I could possibly put myself in, but I also knew that I was growing and I hadn't given up. I could see how much work I still had to do, but for the first time, I was also seeing how far I had come. I felt proud. I felt hopeful.

Rackie didn't scare me – quite the opposite, in fact. I found his anger and volatility comforting. Perhaps because it mirrored my own, or maybe because I had been living in a perpetual guessing game with Simon, always trying to make sense of his eternally calm façade. He was 'fine' even in the most distressing circumstances; therefore, I could only assume he was never actually fine. Rackie let you know what he was okay with and what wasn't going to fly. I didn't always agree with him, but at least there were parameters to work with. At least there was information exchange, which was reassuring after years of floundering in my internal guessing game. He did some unspeakable things. He hurt people in ways that destroyed their lives. He beat people half to death over something as trivial as money – ultimately, that lack of empathy is what pushed me away – but he made choices with conviction, which was attractive to me.

Simon would never actively hurt anyone, but his lack of action created waves of unimaginable pain. The only difference is that you can't see inaction, so you end up feeling more and more alone. Give me conflict, give me arguments, give me anger if it means we can grow. I'm not here for passive-aggression or burying emotions in the hope the 'bad thing' will go away. Has that ever worked for anyone? I'm not saying Rackie is in the right, but there has got to be a middle-ground between stagnancy and impulsive combat. Perhaps healthy communication. *Hmm, just a wild thought.*

Because of the wild trajectory my own life had taken, I tried not to judge those who might otherwise be labelled as dangerous or 'bad'. I could only assume they believed, as I did, that they were good people who had been wronged by life in some way: burdened by pain to the point of breaking and thus becoming people they were never meant to be. *'Who we are and who we need to become to survive are two different things'* – Kass Morgan. I was not someone who found growth or compassion easily. I was miserable for years, and then I got mad. Enraged by the lack of justice and callous randomness of life. I had been promised that if I worked hard and behaved, life would reward me. But it's a lie. Sometimes life just takes and doesn't give back.

There are people who never catch a break. Those of us with a fair spattering of good days to our bad ones find it hard to comprehend that. But I have met these people and spent hours, if not days, drinking with them, getting high with them and hearing their stories. Objectively, these are 'bad' people, but objectively, so was I. I would partake in illegal activity. I would go out looking for a fight. I would use drugs. I would drive drunk and generally just be a real shit to be around. I could be mean, rude, diabolically vengeful and clinically insane, but I never thought of myself as a bad person. I thought of myself as deserving of my badness. I felt that any kindness would be a gift back to the world that had taken everything from me, and of that, it was undeserving. I had nothing left to give, and what I did have, I was holding onto with both hands. That was mine. *My rage. My grief. My despair.*

It's always darkest before the dawn

Soundtrack: *Florence + The Machine – 'Shake It Out'*

Life looks very different these days. I have two rescue cats who are simultaneously cleaning themselves in various intimate areas as I write this from my bedroom in Melbourne. One has no teeth, but I'm trying to teach him manners, so I pretend it hurts when he 'bites' me with his gummy mouth. The other has just been shaved top to tail and, rather than showing off his gloriously luscious locks, now resembles a naked mole rat. They are *purr*fection.

I have been off opioids and other drugs for the majority of the past seven years with the occasional stumble; however, life has not been without challenges. Living alone, Melbourne's extensive lockdown was lonely and isolating. I'd be lying if I said I didn't think of knocking myself out to get through it at times. Instead, I got a perm. That's right; I took myself to the hair salon and wedged myself between two women in their 80s. Together, the three of us donned our black aprons and curlers. A week later, I would be found in my bathroom, hunched over the sink, hacking my hair off with children's scissors because I hated it so much. Did I end up looking like the Johnny Depp version of Willy Wonka? I did. Did I relapse? I did not. I call that a success!

Temptation was made harder still when, in 2021, I underwent three surgeries, the worst of which was for gangrenous appendicitis – the single most excruciating pain I have ever felt. As such, I was given a truckload of opioids to aid my recovery, which served to trigger me in every direction. My saving grace was my new GP, who told me in no uncertain terms that she would supply me with painkillers for two weeks and then I would have to make do with Paracetamol and bed rest. I was equal parts furious and grateful.

I got married to the love of my life, and we have three beautiful children named Ashwagandha, Amaranth Sun and Malachite Peony Rein. I can hear them practising in the other room, preparing for family band night, where we perform operatic covers of Peaches tracks. I couldn't be prouder. *Psych!* I am still way too emotionally and physically traumatised by love and sex to consider marriage or children for a very long time. I am, however, working with a therapist who specialises in sexual assault trauma, and she is gently guiding me back to myself.

There is no quick fix. My heart was broken to the point where I thought I would never love again, and my body followed suit. I'll be blunt (because why stop now?); the idea of having sex or opening my heart to love is repulsive to me right now, but I don't want that to always be the case. I do not always want to hate or distrust men to the degree I currently do, so I am doing 'the work' to better myself. It is not lost on me that, once again, I, the woman, have to pick up the pieces for the mess men have left behind. But this time I am doing it for me. I am worth more than having to carry the burden of someone else's shitty choices.

Amir was finally arrested and questioned in November 2023. From here, the case gets handed over to the bureaucrats to decide if there is enough evidence to take it to court. With a defeated sigh, every police officer I have spoken to has made a point of reminding me that the law favours the accused, not to intimidate or discourage me but rather to prepare me. To prepare me for disappointment if it doesn't get through, to be interrogated within an inch of my life on the most intimate issues if it does, and for all of my deepest wounds to be plucked from the depths of my psyche and used against me.

I know how depressingly low the rates of conviction are in these cases. After all this time spent anxiously waiting for an answer that seems farther away with each passing day, I understand why women in my position don't bother. But for me, I absolutely must take this as far as I can. As long as there is even a glimmer of hope that justice will be served, then I will pursue it. Men like this – angry, misogynistic, violent, sad little boys – need to know they are not safe and immune to justice. And they need to know that if they fuck with us, there will be consequences.

I don't want to live in fear the way I do now. It finds me in all kinds of places. To this day, I have chronic pain following my spinal surgery, so much so that I was sent to the Melbourne pain clinic to attend physiotherapy rehabilitation. During one of my gym sessions, my physio placed me in a suspended neck sling hanging from the doorframe. Straps wrapped around my neck and head as my spine lengthened under my own weight. I instantly began to panic as I remembered those big hands around my throat and my breath getting weaker as I started to see stars. Tears streamed from my eyes as I called out to be released. 'Ah yes, that can sometimes happen,' the white-haired physio assured me as he handed me a tissue box.

I no longer wish to live solely for external validation. I don't crave world domination or success that jeopardises my happiness; rather, I pursue creative activities that give me purpose. If people happen to like them, it's a wonderful bonus.

Everything I do these days is part of building a beautiful life for myself, which seems to look a lot like balance. After spending my life at the extreme ends of every spectrum, I'm finally learning that the middle isn't boring and mundane – it's peaceful. A note to all my addict buddies out there who hear the words 'peace', 'middle', 'balance' or, god forbid, 'moderation' and cringe. I promise you peace isn't boring. It makes space to let in all the wonderful things we never had room for because we were always running from something or chasing another. I never again want to live in perpetual fear nor be so closed off that I fear nothing at all. I am slowly learning what a healthy level of fear looks like and how it can be valuable.

I have found that the things I enjoy are very simple: providing love and protection to animals, pottering in my tiny balcony garden, going to the farmers market for a coffee and Nutella crepe, getting pedicures and cooking soul-nourishing food. Yes, I still stay in bed for hours at a time watching *The Real Housewives* – I haven't had a lobotomy! I'm still in here, but my focus has changed. My goal is peace. This is my life, and if I have to be here on this fiery rock hurtling through space, this devastating mortal coil, this simmering pile of terror and beauty, then I'm going to do it my way. I am going to live a gentle life, and maybe, in doing that, it will rub off on others. Maybe it won't, and that's fine too because at least I will have had a good time while I'm here and, after all, isn't that the whole point? Honestly, I have no idea what the meaning of life is. These days when something shakes my world, is radically absurd or hideously embarrassing, I heed my mother's advice and take notes because it may just be 'another chapter for the book'!

Acknowledgements

I have so many people to thank for helping me bring my vision of a book to reality.

To my mother, Tiina, thank you for reading my early drafts more times than I can count, for offering useful advice and barely ever flinching at some of the more challenging content. Mum was a superstar and just as integral to this book getting done as I was.

My late great father, Philip Moore, for always reminding me to 'take one step at a time' and that it doesn't matter how slow you go, as long as you keep going. I know there is a 'Starman waiting in the sky' for me.

My brother Ben, an editor for Cambridge University Press, podcaster and graphic designer. Thank you for being a reliably quick message away to answer my myriad of tedious questions. Everything from grammar, spelling and design to guiding me through the creation of my audiobook podcast.

A heartfelt thanks to my grandfather, Ken, the cheekiest of the Moore clan. Having written several books himself, I always took his kind words about my writing to heart. He was particularly enthralled by the more, shall we say, 'colourful' chapters.

Jenni, the baddest angel around. I wish you were here. If you were, I would tell you how grateful I am to have met you and how the bravery of your writing and sheer tenacity inspired me to keep writing on my toughest days. Thank you for always trusting I could be bigger and better than I ever believed. Every word of this book has a little sprinkle of your confidence, stubborn determination and the humour you brought to each moment of your life. One day we will laugh until we cry together again. Until then, I will live this life to the fullest in your honour.

Vanessa O'Connor, there aren't enough words to thank you. You're more than just a friend; you're my family. You brought me laughter when I never thought I would smile again, and you saw the good in me when the rest of the world condemned me.

To my dear friend, Yaz Erdodu, and the team from We Love It Productions, who knew that when we met to create my very first music video over a decade ago, our friendship would still stand strong today? The book cover would not have been possible without your photography all those years ago, as well as your recent feedback. It is so rewarding to have come full circle from that early project together to where we are today. Thank you for being there for me this last decade, and here's to the next!

Blake Ternacz, you have always been the biggest cheerleader of my writing. Our artistic collaborations have been some of the most exciting creations of my life to date. Thank you for always relating to my most unrelatable qualities and celebrating my smallest wins. We are forever perfectly imperfect.

Sarah Hammond, thank you for believing enough in my manuscript to bestow me with the *Nillumbik Artists in Own Residence* grant.

Cathy and Ed Green, thanks for bringing music back into my life and performing with me during my book launch.

Writing can be a lonely and daunting process. I would like to thank Hannie Rayson and Michael Cathcart for taking me under their wings and connecting me with so many talented writers via their Life Writing workshop. Melbourne's extensive lockdown would have been unbearable without our weekly discussions.

I am forever indebted to the talented team who transformed the inner workings of my mind into a reality on the page. My mentor, Kate Ryan, and initial editor, Myf Jones. These brilliant women never ceased to build up my confidence when the inevitable ebbs and flows of the creative process would get me down. A heartfelt thank you to the dedicated editing and design team from A Way With Words: Phaedra Pym and Thymen Hoek, and to Eric Hoek from Exlibris for production. Working with such a close-knit group of people has been a privilege. You took my work and gave it the precision it needed to be taken to the next level.

Hannah Nichols, what can I say? You have been an absolute delight to work with on my cover design. In my wildest dreams, I never thought I would end up with something that so perfectly encapsulates the essence of my book. Your hard work shines as brightly as you do.

Finally, I would like to thank all the gifted medical professionals who have kept me going over the years. I would not be here without you.

Kirsten spent her early adult life as a classical singer, songwriter, yoga teacher and nutritionist. She recorded two studio albums, *Bare* (2014) and *Breathe & Repeat* (2016) and performed her soulful work regularly in Melbourne clubs while studying music and health sciences.

In 2018, Kirsten travelled to Italy to work as an au pair and English tutor. While there, she began writing a blog about her experiences living with mental and physical illnesses. Readers connected with her unique voice and candour. Her raw honesty was always sprinkled with wry humour, making even the darkest topics accessible.

In 2021, Kirsten won the *Nillumbik Artists in Own Residence* grant for her writing. The funds allowed her to workshop her manuscript for *Gutter Glitter* with several notable Melbourne mentors. She was later encouraged to assemble a community performance of her music and readings from her newly completed memoir. Kirsten's first-hand experiences, as depicted in her memoir, make it an important body of work in a time of increased anxiety and mental illness.

www.ingramcontent.com/pod-product-compliance
Lightning Source LLC
Chambersburg PA
CBHW051535010526
44107CB00064B/2731